Acclaim for

MANUELA HOELTERHOFF's

Cinderella & Company

"Marvelous . . . delightful . . . there are few more entertaining writers on the music scene."

—*Dallas Morning News*

"Gracefully dishy. . . . An opera lover's 'Canterbury Tales.'"

—*Buffalo News*

"Hoelterhoff has a delicious way with a put-down—as she demonstrates time and again. . . . And when the book ends—before the fat lady sings, by the way—you'll be sorry."

—*The Grand Rapids Press*

"No one is safe from the sly sword wielded by Manuela Hoelterhoff."

—*USA Today*

"Reading Manuela Hoelterhoff's *Cinderella & Company* is a little like purchasing a ticket for 'Cosi fan tutte' and winding up with Little Richard singing 'Tutti Frutti.' It's just not what you expected. . . . Her uncensored look backstage is a wonder. Classic dishing."

—*Minneapolis Star Tribune*

MANUELA HOELTERHOFF

Cinderella & Company

Manuela Hoelterhoff received a Pulitzer Prize for cultural criticism at *The Wall Street Journal*, where she has served as arts and books editor and is now a member of the editorial board; she is also senior consulting editor for *SmartMoney* and a contributing editor to *Condé Nast Traveler*. In addition, Ms. Hoelterhoff is the author of the libretto for *Modern Painters*, an opera by David Lang based on the life of John Ruskin, which had its world premiere at the Santa Fe Opera in 1995. She lives in New York City.

Cinderella
& Company

Cinderella & Company

BACKSTAGE AT THE OPERA
WITH CECILIA BARTOLI

MANUELA
HOELTERHOFF

VINTAGE BOOKS

A Division of Random House, Inc.

New York

FIRST VINTAGE BOOKS EDITION, OCTOBER 1999

Grateful acknowledgment is made to Gene Ink for permission to
reprint an excerpt from "Another New Voice Teacher," lyric by Gene Scheer,
music by Andrew Thomas. Copyright © 1998 by Gene Scheer.
Published by Gene Ink. Reprinted by permission.

The Library of Congress has cataloged the Knopf edition as follows:
Hoelterhoff, Manuela.
Cinderella & company : backstage at the opera with Cecilia Bartoli / Manuela
Hoelterhoff.
1st ed.
p.   cm
ISBN 0-679-44479-3
1. Bartoli, Cecilia. 2. Mezzo-sopranos—Biography. 3. Opera—20th century.
I. Title.
ML420.B1353H64   1998
782'.1092—dc21   98-87037
CIP

Vintage ISBN: 0-375-70712-3

Book design by Virginia Tan

www.vintagebooks.com

Printed in the United States of America
10   9   8   7   6   5   4   3   2   1

Contents

Contents

Cinderella
& Company

Rags to Riches

"ONCE UPON A TIME," the story begins. Once upon a time, long ago and far away, there was a poor cinders girl who went to a ball and enchanted a prince. We heard it first when we were young, and travelled nightly in pumpkin coaches drawn by mice to sparkling palaces where we really belonged. Courtiers bowed as we waved to adoring crowds.

The story has the magic of the moon at midnight. It's cast a spell over the centuries, touching German burgs, the Sun King's court of Versailles, Disneyland. The French call the cinders girl Cendrillon; the Germans, Aschenputtel; and the Italians always call her Cenerentola.

"Not exactly fresh," Gioacchino Rossini was thinking as he lay in bed trying to keep warm in the underheated house of his impresario on a winter day just before Christmas in 1816. He was twenty-four years old and the rising star in the opera world, though just then he would have preferred to forget the disastrous opening night of *The Barber of Seville* earlier in the year. He'd been laughed at for the quaint conducting suit he wore, the one with the big buttons that was part of his fee, and booed at the end.

Rome's Teatro Valle was expecting a new show from him in a few weeks' time, and he still didn't have a story, even after a long afternoon spent sipping tea with Jacopo Ferretti.

Ferretti was the librettist. It was he who had just whispered, "Cenerentola?"

Rossini sat up to think. Well, it was a story.

"When can I have the outline?" he asked.

"By tomorrow," Ferretti replied grandly. "If I skip sleeping."

Rossini said good night and promptly fell asleep—very soundly, according to Ferretti, who left a detailed report of the great creativity that then befell him as he had another cup of tea before rushing downstairs to extract a contract from the impresario. Then he ran home, switched to mocha, and sketched the outline of *La Cenerentola*, finishing on schedule as promised. He sat down and fleshed it out, often helping himself to an existing libretto already set by another Italian a few years earlier, which was itself based on yet another opera by a Frenchman. He failed to remember this for his memoirs, but the practice was hardly unusual.

Opera stories in those days were often based on other opera stories in the way that, say, a Hollywood producer in our own time will brilliantly decide to remake *Sabrina* about a garage dweller dreaming of the big house, or enliven the old German doctor's lab with the familiar lunkhead. Ferretti's plagiaristic impulse was perfectly acceptable, though we'd all be thankful if he'd pilfered the *Mother Goose Tales* of Charles Perrault instead. Perrault was the seventeenth-century French courtier best known for his rags-to-riches story of the kitchen drudge lifted up by mysterious fate to become queen of the land. The fairy godmother and her magic wand, the coach dipped in gold, the lizards transformed into coachmen, the ball gown of silver and gold cloth, and the tiny glass slipper are all part of Cendrillon's glistening world.

Maybe Ferretti wasn't drinking mocha. By the time he got done with *La Cenerentola: ossia La bontà in trionfo* (meaning "goodness triumphs"), he'd exchanged the fairy godmother with a tutor named Alidoro (Golden Wings) and dropped the pumpkin, the coach, even the slipper. A naked foot displayed on the stage might have been rejected as subversively erotic by Rome's ever-present moral monitors, the equivalent of today's thought police. Cinderella arrives at the prince's castle outfitted with a pair of decorous bracelets.

But Rossini was easy to please and, besides, he was in no position to complain. To save a little time, he stole an overture he'd written for a comedy about a newspaper and sat down with the diva, Geltrude Righetti-Giorgi, to work up a suitably fabulous finale. She had sung in the premiere of *Barber* and become fond of one of the tenor's tunes. Could he adapt it? He would be happy to! In a little more than three weeks, Rossini looked up from a score with music that dances, whispers, charms, and dazzles from beginning to end. He might as well have been writing with a wand.

"Once upon a time there was a king," Cenerentola sings as the curtain rises on her tumbledown mansion. Her mother has died, leaving her with a violent stepfather and his two screechy daughters. "Una volta c'era un re"—a lonely, sad king who searched far and wide for a suitable bride. Wealth and looks are unimportant, he declared. "But not a good heart."

Taking the simple song as her guide, she gives breakfast to a beggar who knocks at the door. Strangers keep appearing, always in disguise. The valet is the prince, the prince is the valet, and the beggar turns out to be Golden Wings, the tutor. But nothing can disguise true human nature, and with Golden Wings leading the way ("Your life will change," he announces) Cenerentola moves ever closer toward the shiny castle of her dreams—and one of the great display pieces ever written: "Nacqui all'affanno."

"I was born to sorrow and tears," Cenerentola sings. "I suffered with a silent heart; but by some sweet enchantment, in the flower of my youth, swift as a flash of lightning, my fortune changed." Minutes of cascading coloratura reflect the silvery splendor of her new life. "Non più mesta accanto al fuoco," she sings. "I'm no longer sitting sadly by the fire." Placed thrillingly at the end, when Cenerentola has married her prince and forgiven her beastly family, it should bring the audience to its feet.

But as Righetti-Giorgi herself reported, the opening on January 25,

1817 did not go well at all. While a few tunes met with approval, the night still ended in a feast of booing and whistling—a bad thing in Italy.

Librettist and composer stumbled into the night, Ferretti close to tears. "Fools!" Rossini exclaimed. "Before Carnival ends, everyone will be enchanted. . . . One day it will be fought over by impresarios and prima donnas throughout the land."

He was right. There was a time when *Cenerentola* eclipsed even *Barber* and the nineteen other operas he went on to write. Then, after composing his most magnificent and ambitious opera, *William Tell*, in 1829, Rossini quit, taking the most mysterious early retirement in the history of music. Nobody knows exactly why he did so. But he was rich and sickly, musical tastes were changing, and he probably didn't anticipate living another four decades as the beloved, ill-wigged, and increasingly immense fixture of Parisian music life. Rossini was what the Italians call a *buon forchettone*, who always cleaned his plate. Occasionally, he would still compose—charming piano pieces and the lovely Stabat Mater—but he was mostly renowned for his Parmesan cheese, his kindness and wit, and the soirées at his Paris apartment.

"Have him come in, but tell him to leave his C-sharp on the coat-rack. He can pick it up on his way out," he once said, as a top-note strutting tenor was about to visit.

Friends in the Rothschild family took care of his fortune, which had been boosted early by a funding concept we might reconsider in our own era: the impresario of the Naples opera house gave him a percentage of the gambling tables set up in the foyer. Think of how much livelier our nights at the opera would be with roulette tables next to the bar and people betting on whether Fathilde will hit her C in the next act!

By the time Rossini's cortège trundled through Paris in 1868, twilight had set on bel canto—or "beautiful singing"—when embellishments, fluid scales, interpolations, and good taste were expected even of tenors. *Cenerentola* slowly disappeared into history's memory hole along with so many of his other dust catchers, serious works like *Tancredi* and *Semiramide*, and those clever comedies *L'italiana in Algeri* and *Il turco in Italia*. The world of opera was changing.

Full-bellied Wagnerians, lusty singers of clowns, baby-killers, and

Moors slowly pushed aside the delicately trilling, octave-jumping heroes and heroines who inhabit the flowery realm of Rossini and his two major contemporaries, Vincenzo Bellini and Gaetano Donizetti. Bellini's Norma and Donizetti's Lucia stayed around, but most of their friends disappeared, replaced by Aida, Violetta, Otello, Tristan and Isolde, Carmen, Tosca, Mimì, Elektra, and the Marschallin. High-minded conductors hammered a few more nails into Rossini's coffin. They found (and many still do) the lightly orchestrated scores too insignificant for their important orchestras. Rossini sounds perfectly splendid played with a small orchestra of forty, less than half the forces the gods require for their stately entrance into Wagner's Valhalla.

By the time I started going to the opera in the mid-1960s, taste had started changing once more, thanks to Maria Callas—La Divina to her worshipful followers. Born in New York in 1923, trained in Athens, and soon the queen of whatever opera company she wasn't feuding with, Callas stoked the embers of bel canto with her searing voice and high theatricality. Her soprano was not conventionally beautiful and was often reviled by fastidious puritans, but she was excitement incarnate on the stage and off, a fabulous actress with huge, black—if very myopic—eyes, a bad temper, and a flair for fashion.

I once saw half of her at a *Norma* concert performance at Carnegie Hall in the late 1960s. Elena Suliotis, a young singer with a short career, had just run off stage followed by boos and the rest of the cast. The audience kept hooting. Suddenly Callas, who once owned Norma's sandals, leaned down from her box and thundered, "Silenzio!" The goddess had spoken! People piped down; the performance continued. Right about that time, Callas had almost stopped singing and had suffered the humiliation of being dropped by Ari Onassis so he could marry the widow Kennedy, though Callas got a good line out of it: "Girls with glasses don't marry Onassis," is what she reportedly said. I'm told she once clasped radishes to her bosom flung at her during a curtain call thinking they were roses. The opera world is animated by passionate fans with expressive needs, and great aim.

Fortunately, the bel canto revival continued with the Australian Joan Sutherland, who made opera history when she sang *Lucia di Lammermoor* in 1959 and then began a tour of moldy libraries and basements the world over with her mentor, husband, and favorite conductor, Richard Bonynge, rescuing long-forgotten heroines from oblivion. The cause was joined by the jolly Catalán soprano Montserrat Caballé and the high-flying, late-blooming Beverly Sills, who supplemented the Sutherland queens, priestesses, and sonnambulists with portraits of their own. Sills's thrilling assumption of Donizetti's royal "hat trick" of *Roberto Devereux, Maria Stuarda,* and *Anna Bolena* was a high point of New York cultural life in the early 1970s.

Luckily, many of these operas provided equally virtuosic opportunities for a second lady of sterling vocal qualities, which were now assumed by mezzo-sopranos. (The nineteenth century did not make such neat vocal divisions.) Marilyn Horne was waiting in the wings with a voice of incredible flexibility and warmth. The Sutherland-Horne duo became the stuff of legend, one of the glories of the bel canto revival.

As for *Cenerentola,* already in the 1930s the bewitching Conchita Supervia made a hit of "Non più mesta" and even set up a little touring company that played all of the piece. And slowly the opera began reappearing whenever a mezzo with enough high notes and clout arrived on the scene. Giulietta Simionato, then Teresa Berganza, Lucia Valentini Terrani, Agnes Baltsa, and Frederica von Stade all made *Cenerentola* glitter again. (Von Stade also stepped out as Cendrillon in the gossamer French setting of the fairy tale by Jules Massenet.)

Today it is easier to cast operas by Rossini, Donizetti, and Bellini than Verdi or Wagner, which require muscle and volume instead of fleetness and light. Especially, mezzo-sopranos who can sing high and low while performing the vocal equivalent of high-wire acts without a net are sprouting like mushrooms in the forest. You'd need a jumbo coach to fit them all: Jennifer Larmore, Anne Sofie von Otter, Lorraine Hunt, Susan Graham, Susanne Mentzer, Sonia Ganassi—with a little red cart attached for the young kids on the block, singers like Vesselina Kasarova or Angelika Kirchschlager.

But in October 1995, when this story begins, the mezzo who sparkles most brightly in all the land is Cecilia Bartoli, born in 1966 in

Rome. An influential record producer for the Decca recording company discovered her at a talent audition in Milan. Decca (called London in the United States because of trademark restrictions), was just then planning to record *The Barber of Seville* and somewhat incredibly still casting about for a Rosina. Bartoli got the job. She was just twenty-two years old—mature by pop standards, but startlingly young in an opera world where thirty-five-year-olds still fill out grant applications.

The set came out in 1989 and I remember looking at it with dread—another *Barber* recording and I already had eight—but I also had a Christmas column to write and so I put the CDs into the machine, skipping directly to Rosina's entrance. A wily orphan living with an old buffoon who's scheming to marry her, Rosina has other plans involving a comely lad who has just pleased her with a serenade. Her lines in this scene are nothing much, but in the next she gets her chance.

"Una voce poco fa," she sings: The voice I heard just now has thrilled me to the core.

And so it was with me. In our era of trained-to-death singers, there are professionals by the dozen who can hit the tricky notes Rossini wrote; the ones who can play with them, caress them, color them are as rare as hen's teeth. Here was a special voice—a smooth, glimmering truffle of a voice, astonishing in its virtuosity and range. She had something few singers have today: personality, and a timbre that was all her own.

The rate of her climb since then has been astonishing. Bartoli immediately followed up *Barber* with a disc of showy Rossini arias and her first Mozart album, which sold two hundred thousand copies in one year. At one point she had three albums on the classical charts, pushing aside Luciano Pavarotti and Kathleen Battle. And though her voice is modest in volume, the singer who comes with it—a dark-haired, vivacious bundle invariably topped off by a large black bow—is so radiantly, appealingly communicative, she lights up the stage.

La Cenerentola is her role. She sang it first at Bologna's Teatro Comunale in 1992, and the closing bravura aria has become Bartoli's

Greatest Hit, revisited in concert programs and frequently trotted out as an encore in recitals.

The stylishly downtrodden outfit of the cinders girl is one she would like to wear again, and the Houston Grand Opera has imported the Bologna production just for her. The company's general director, David Gockley, can make his stomach turn humming the overture. He's more interested in unusual directors and cutting-edge shows like John Adams's *Nixon in China*. But Bartoli sells tickets and he's a savvy businessman. There was not a ticket to be had for the opening on October 27, 1995.

Now he was waiting for her train to arrive from Ann Arbor, where she was giving a recital.

Bartoli flies only under duress and once pondered the logistics of driving to Japan—from Rome. Earlier in the year, Decca arranged for a private rail car to be attached to the Amtrak train leaving New York for California. She learned some new songs and enjoyed the scenery. "I need to feel the ground under my feet," is how she explains it, and while this creates advanced logistical nightmares for her manager, it might extend her singing days. Singers invariably step off airplanes with their vocal cords dried up and incubating their sniffling seatmate's germs. But basically, it's just that she's scared to fly.

It does no good to point out that remarkably few singers have failed to arrive at their destination. The last opera star to crash was Grace Moore in 1947, though I suppose a plane could also be implicated in the death of Lina Cavalieri, another beautiful if excessively materialistic singer. On her way to the safety of an air shelter during a World War II bombing attack, Cavalieri remembered her jewels, turned around, and traipsed back to her villa.

At least flying phobia (which I also suffer) has saved us both a lot of money. "I can't possibly leave you," I would say to my dogs, feeling my back go out as I stared in dismay at a steerage ticket marked Tokyo or São Paulo. Fortunately refundable. An epigastric hernia kept Bartoli out of Japan in January of 1995; chicken pox deflected her from South America in the summer of that year.

Even so, Bartoli and I saw quite a bit of the world together and separately during the two seasons that passed between *Cenerentola* in

Houston in 1995 and *Cenerentola* at the Metropolitan Opera in 1997. We had no formal arrangement. I wanted to write about the life of an opera singer in the fast-moving, high-pressure opera world of today, and she consented to make herself available when she felt like it, once asking her manager with alarm if I was planning to spend my vacation with her. In return, she got to read what I wrote with no pressure on either of us. I'd describe our relationship as cordial.

As we rolled along, Bartoli's story became intertwined with others, most inescapably that of Pavarotti, the crumbling monument on this *tour d'horizon*. The sight of the great tenor, the embodiment of opera for millions, drifting reluctantly toward the last curtain call everyone eventually must take was painful to witness. The panicky search for a star successor, however, was pretty amusing. Opera's ancient heart needs new voices to keep thumping. Many step forth to take their curtain calls; few are called back again and again. The singers who become adored, and ultimately the stuff of legend, are those who project more than the correct notes (though often we're grateful just for that). I saw a soprano I first encountered in Omaha, Nebraska, finally step center stage; I followed an ex-waiter to Paris and a dieting diva into cyberspace. Another detour took me backstage to the Metropolitan Opera for one of the strangest galas in music history.

In opera, we see writ large the extremes of human emotion and the workings of fate carried to the greatest heights of absurdity and soul-stirring tragedy. Some of the people who live in this world travel pretty close to the rim. Is there another art form that attracts so many sublime sufferers and so many nuts? Just before starting *Cinderella & Company*, I quit writing criticism for the *Wall Street Journal* after sitting in aisle seats for nearly twenty years, and I worried that backstage might not be as diverting as the shows I saw onstage. What could I have been thinking?

CHAPTER ONE

Golden Wings

ATING BACK TO the first decades of the oil boom and probably rivalling Beverly Hills in its per-capita density of leaf blowers, lawn mowers, and four-wheel drives, River Oaks is the poshest of the residential areas closest to downtown Houston. Circling past Tudoresque castles and mansions large enough to house all the kings of France, on a sticky October morning in 1995, I wondered whether there was an ongoing local contest to see who could fit the most styles into one house. A new French chateau out of Dutch brick with colonial pillars looked like it might have an edge on the competition.

Cecilia Bartoli was tucked away in the vine-covered pool house (remodelled sufficiently to thrill Marie Antoinette) set behind a large yellow, pleasantly style-free house belonging to a throat specialist she met when she sang *Barber of Seville* here two years earlier. As my beagle, Sugar, began to howl, a window opened and Bartoli poked her head through the leaves on the first floor. "Ciao!" she yelled, requesting ten minutes to get herself ready. Her mother had made coffee and would be out in a minute. I sat down underneath a green-and-white umbrella by the pool.

Bartoli's parents have been separated since the start of her career. Both are singers who once hoped for solo careers; they met in Spoleto, where Silvana was singing Puccini's *Manon Lescaut*. But the kids started to arrive, money was tight, and finally they took chorus jobs at the Rome Opera. Silvana later joined the chorus of the Accademia di Santa Cecilia, but Pietro Bartoli was onstage for his daughter's debut in *Barber of Seville* in 1986—his last season. These days, Silvana often uses her maiden name, Bazzoni, and Pietro lives by himself in his hometown of Rimini, a modestly pleasant spot on the Adriatic. He doesn't seem eager to keep in touch and doesn't have a telephone. Cecilia once got him a cell phone, which he found mysteriously wonderful until the batteries ran out. He didn't buy new ones. She sometimes visits him, but big engagements proceed without him— perhaps he can't enjoy them without regretful self-scrutiny. If she minds, she doesn't say. An effusive performer, Bartoli is quiet and reserved offstage. It was a friend at the opera who told me that Bartoli's thirty-three-year-old brother, Gabriele, a talented violist, had had emergency surgery to remove a melanoma in his shoulder at Houston's M. D. Anderson Hospital. He had just returned home with his fiancée, Antonella, and a good prognosis. A third and youngest sibling, Federica, was studying scenery design in Rome.

The door opened and Silvana appeared, beaming over a little tray with two espressos, a bowl of sugar, and two spoons. She sat down with a big poof, patted Sugar, and swatted a mosquito. They have a dog back home, she said, named Figaro, and she invited us both to visit. Now in her late fifties, of average height and pleasant features, with dark hair, and unassuming of manner, Silvana still gave the impression of being not entirely secure in the glamorous new world her daughter had opened up for her. A floral top brightened her care-worn brown eyes. Her sentences often ended with a small shrug accompanied by "forse" or "ma," meaning "maybe" and "but."

She knew why I was there and helpfully offered a little family history.

"It was like this," she said. "When she was small, she liked to sing as much as talk. Always humming around the house imitating us. I thought she was musical and she had some piano lessons. When she was fifteen, I said: 'Cecilia, let's see if you have a voice.' We tried. There was a voice.

"She didn't want to go to the conservatory. She was dancing flamenco. I finally convinced a teacher there to get her admitted so she could study piano. I kept teaching her voice at home."

I asked her when Bartoli finally gave up flamenco.

"After a talent show called *Fantastico*, hosted by Pippo Baudo," her mother said. Italy's Johnny Carson, Baudo is a popular talk-show host who married Katia Ricciarelli, a briefly fabulous soprano bombshell and ex-girlfriend of José Carreras. Bartoli sang the Barcarolle from *The Tales of Hoffmann* with Ricciarelli and a scene from *Barber* with Leo Nucci, then the favorite Italian baritone of the Decca recording company.

(I've seen a tape of it. "Well," chuckled Ricciarelli to her husband while the studio audience kept cheering the scrawny nobody with the long black tresses, "I'm so glad she's a mezzo-soprano.")

"She was nineteen," Silvana continued. "There were two other important things that happened. Christopher Raeburn, who was then a record producer at Decca, heard her in a big audition in Milan. Then she sang in a tribute to Maria Callas on French television, the *Cenerentola* aria. It was plain good luck—someone cancelled. A lot of people saw it, because it was the great Callas—conductors like Daniel Barenboim."

The occasion was the tenth anniversary of the diva's death in Paris in 1977 after a tumultuous career of spine-tingling performances and equally lavishly documented fights with a long list of general managers, colleagues, and her mother. Callas saw as little of her mother as possible. "I would not give her the lice from my hair," is one famous quote.

Bartoli, however, seems to love her mother and gave her the Rolex watch Silvana was wearing. Like Plácido Domingo and Kiri Te Kanawa before her, Bartoli had just become a Rolex model. Select magazines would soon see a full-page glossy photo of her posing on a gilded settee in Rome's Villa Medici with a gold Rolex Oyster Perpetual, which she got to keep. It's the kind Houstonians during the go-go years used to call a "get-out-of-town" watch: If your business went bust, you could hock it for a plane ticket and disappear.

"Did we ever think she would make such a *carriera*? I suppose not, but we did name her after Santa Cecilia, so maybe there was something," Silvana mused. The patron saint of music was also Roman-born and precocious, singing with angels when she was just six and a real pro on the ur-organ. She achieved sainthood after a short life of chastity, good works, and hymn writing, and a dreadfully long martyrdom that included being steamed, boiled, and decapitated.

Her twenty-nine-year-old namesake arrived with a coffee mug, dressed in her usual outfit of stretch pants, sweatshirt, and sneakers, topped off by the familiar large black bow that has come to be grafted to her person the way Hermès scarves cling to Luciano Pavarotti. For her first albums and publicity shots, Bartoli dutifully put on slinky clothes and a lot of lipstick, taking them off the minute she could afford to say no, which wasn't long into her career. The recital of Rossini arias she recorded with Giuseppe Patanè shows her wearing trollop-red gloves and rhinestone clumps dangling from her ears. That was in 1989. This year, the cover was digitally transformed to give the mezzo black gloves and tiny earrings. The masses of terrific black hair tumbling down her shoulders stayed the same.

You figure she would look exactly like this even if she weren't a famous opera singer who got up a little late that morning and had just yawned at her mother, showing off her perfect white teeth.

"Can we please go inside?" she said after a few minutes of swatting. Bartoli isn't much for swimming, and the pool was lost on her, though the mosquitoes seemed to like it just fine. Silvana stayed outside with a crossword puzzle.

Boxes of Habitrol were stacked on the coffee table, extracted from her doctor host as a present for Bruno Campanella, the show's chain-smoking conductor. "Bruno," she said, gesturing. "It's really terrible. Always the cigarette." Bartoli doesn't smoke. Few singers do. The only smoker I ever met was the Wagner tenor Siegfried Jerusalem, who puffs like Fafner the dragon and sounds like it too. Smoking dries out the vocal cords. New compact discs constituted another pile. She'd been listening, with enthusiasm, to the first recital of the new tenor sensation, Roberto Alagna, the son of a Sicilian bricklayer who moved to Paris. Born in 1964, Alagna was still singing songs in a Parisian pizza joint five years before when one night his fortune changed. An elderly gent, Gabriel Dussurget, founder of the summer festival in the enchanting town of Aix-en-Provence, walked in for a slice and was so enchanted he called a friend, Jean-Marie Poilvé, a powerful French agent. After a practice run with the Glyndebourne Touring Company, Poilvé put him on the pumpkin coach to Milan's La Scala, the Vienna Staatsoper, and London's Covent Garden. This season Alagna, like Bartoli, would finally stop off at the Metropolitan Opera for his debut.

"Have you heard him?" Bartoli asked, picking up a cracker and leaning back on the sofa with a sigh that turned into a squeal as my beagle jumped into her lap. Sugar was permitted to eat the cracker and curl up between us.

I had, two summers before at the arena in Orange in the south of France, when a friend of mine directed him as Alfredo in Verdi's *La traviata*. His young wife was dying at the time from a brain tumor, leaving him with a toddler, and he could barely sing his way through the last act's death scene without crying.

"What a fate," said Bartoli, shaking her head.

The following night would be the dress rehearsal of *Cenerentola*. It had not been the easiest rehearsal period. The Bologna opera house had absentmindedly shipped parts of a touring version of *Cenerentola* that didn't mix with the full-scale show and a lot of unanticipated carpentry had been required. Houston was still searching for a scene curtain; the costumes smelled of mildew. The cone-shaped wigs for the prince's courtiers looked like they'd been dropped down by the starship *Enterprise*.

Even so, she was happy to do the show again. This is a role, she said, that helped her define who she is, and she was pleased to sing it.

"I try to play her as not so meek. Forceful. Not like a suffering martyr," she pointed out. "But the show is quality too, I think, in terms of materials and colors, which are very earthy, very Italian.

And the cast is good." She got to pick most of them, and they were all accomplished bel canto singers, longtime colleagues—and Italian-speaking, except for the two sisters, Jill Grove and Laura Knopp, who have been getting language coaching from mother Silvana, also hired by Houston at the urging of her daughter. The comic baritone Enzo Dara will sing Don Magnifico, her stepfather; Raúl Giménez is cast as the prince. The Argentinian tenor is beyond the first blush of youth—Cecilia once dated his son—but he's a nimble actor and capable of fancy coloratura. I've been told Bartoli had a wild couple of years in her mid-twenties, linked most famously with the American tenor Frank Lopardo. But offstage she's not particularly flirtatious, at least not these days, and she seems to have settled into a form of quiet domesticity and intense musicology with her current companion, Claudio Osele, who had just come through the door. A dark-haired, slender man, low-keyed, thin, and pale, with black, slightly curly hair and an aristocratic nose on his wan face, he wasn't taking well to the Houston humidity and had a cooked look. Two years older than Bartoli, he often travels with her when he isn't required in the vineyard belonging to his mother and grandmother near Verona. He loves the obscurer corners of seventeenth-and-eighteenth-century music (he once studied music history) and is a man of little conversation, though I once heard him hum the first movement of one of the minor symphonies of Haydn. They met on her twenty-first birthday when she was performing with Nikolaus Harnoncourt, one of the driving forces behind the original-instruments boom of the seventies and eighties, and still fond of stirring up hornet nests with his iconoclastic investigations all over the music map. For several years, Osele followed her around as a fan, bringing her bottles of wine and olive oil from the vineyard. Finally, he got promoted.

Osele disappeared upstairs and Bartoli picked up a Met brochure that included sketches for the season's new productions. In a few months, she would make her Met debut as Despina in a new staging of *Così fan tutte*, Mozart's comedy about two sisters who are tricked by their boyfriends with the connivance of their maid. The Met's music chief, James Levine, would be conducting; the director would be Lesley Koenig, not yet forty and just given her own show after years spent assisting others. Bartoli, who gravitates to fatherly directors and conductors, wondered if she should be worried by the choice of Koenig. It would really have made her day if that phone call just then had been Franco Zeffirelli, whose youth coincided with Callas's, saying nothing would please him more than to stage the *Cenerentola* the Met was planning for her two seasons hence. But it was just her manager, Jack Mastroianni, calling from New York. He had a question about a short recital tour that would take her to three Florida towns once *Cenerentola* was finished.

Looking through the program, Bartoli seemed reassured by Michael Yeargan's designs. Despina would be serving chocolate in a very pretty, very period Rococo house with views out over the Bay of Naples. Her taste runs to traditional productions.

"No raincoat," she said, darkly, recalling a *Così* at the Salzburg summer festival a few years ago, a concept production whose point seemed to be that the precious world of Mozart's *Così* falls apart during the course of the opera's dangerous games of love. The idea is hard to refute, but the director showed it by littering the stage with junk. The rain jacket made Bartoli sweat under the lights. She ended up getting a cold and cancelling the first two performances.

A lot of people, I remarked, have been asking why she is singing Despina and not Dorabella, which she recorded with Daniel Barenboim at the start of her career. Dorabella is the mezzo sister of Fiordiligi, the soprano role; Despina is the maid. She doesn't have any big display arias like the sisters. A lot of people don't think it's much of a debut role.

She took a deep breath. "I need to feel a special rapport with Fiordiligi, and right now I can't think of anyone I would want to sing with. Well, maybe Renée," she added, referring to the American soprano Renée Fleming, whose slow-burning career was finally igniting.

"But I also have another reason. I want to have some pleasure out of my debut and maybe change perceptions of what is a debut at the Met. Everybody goes crazy thinking about it. Big place. Big event. I want to have a good time. Don't you think it is possible?" She looked up with a frown.

Bartoli is a nervous performer who hides it well, though not enough to go out and have tips put on her chewed fingernails. A friend who used to be on the Met's coaching staff remembers seeing her get sick to her stomach after she sang an audition on the big stage for Levine in February of 1991. Of course, this is mild compared to the performance anxiety that besets one of her occasional colleagues, Uwe Heilmann, a German tenor who virtually quit singing in public for the safety of the hermetic record studio, where anything can be fixed. In a rare outing the previous spring, he'd clutched halfway into the rehearsals of Haydn's *Orfeo ed Euridice* staged for Cecilia at Vienna's Theater an der Wien, and dropped out. He reappeared for the recording. Bartoli likes Heilmann and is important enough to Decca's bottom line to get the colleagues she wants.

"You see, Hvorostovsky, he didn't sing a big part either," she pointed out, looking at the program sketches for the Met's new *Queen of Spades*. The popular baritone had just made his debut singing the smallish, one-aria role of Prince Yeletsky, though he may not have had much of a choice: the Met wouldn't hire him for a large role without hearing him in a stage audition, which he found beneath him. Crowned "Singer of the World" over fellow baritone Bryn Terfel in the prestigious Cardiff sing-off in 1989, and one of the "fifty most beautiful people in the world" according to *People* magazine, Dmitri Hvorostovsky's rise to the top had been as quick as Bartoli's. His lyric voice was no larger, either, and after some premature attempts at Verdi, the silver-haired Siberian slowly began drifting back to earth from the starry heights. Still in his early thirties, he essentially re-invented himself as a serious person, singing a lot of Russian repertoire mixed in with Mozart and devoted recitations of a powerful song cycle, *Russia Cast Adrift,* by the contemporary composer Georgii Sviridov.

Nowadays, Terfel was the real audience pleaser, a guy with the body of Meat Loaf and an exuberant performing style similar to Bartoli's, though his huge, gut-wrenching bass-baritone has the kind of decibel punch usually reserved for tenors. Terfel, the son of sheep farmers in a Welsh hamlet, would probably delight Wagnerians one day with his Wotan, though—much like the top god—he was starting to be a bit casual with his commitments, of which he had too many. Still, Bartoli thought the two of them would probably be singing at the Met together in a new *Le nozze di Figaro* in three years' time.

Bartoli looked up from the program. "Anyway, I better get myself together." She had a last-minute costume fitting.

As I started to leave, the doctor in the house, Richard Stasney, poked his head into the living room, holding a small tray of tiny quiches and pigs-in-blankets. Director of the Texas Voice Center, which is affiliated with Methodist Hospital and the Baylor College of Medicine, Stasney is the Houston Opera's ear, nose, and throat consultant. After a few pleasantries, he left Cecilia with the tray and saw me to my car.

I asked him if there was anything special about her cords.

He beamed. "You know, I've looked down thousands of throats over these twenty-five years. By themselves, what we call the vocal folds may not seem special. It's the whole resonant apparatus: wonderful breath support, a splendid resonant cavity, subtle tongue movement."

Leaning against my car, he described with the enthusiasm of someone who had just glimpsed the Zabar's deli counter for the first time the view of the Bartoli larynx as it appeared through a rigid fiber laryngoscope. Then he put a flexible hose through her nose. That, he said, was truly fabulous.

"We could see on the screen the entire milieu into the sinus cavity opening as she sang bits from various arias," he reported cheerfully. "The oscillation of the folds themselves as she hit a high F was so exciting!"

He gave me directions to the opera house. Wortham Center, a brick behemoth the opera company calls home, is just a fifteen-minute car ride away in downtown, where the building boom in the eighties collapsed right outside the stage door. Weedy parking lots and billboards clutter up the horizon on one side of the building. Reflecting skyscrapers line the plaza side, clad in so much glass they could beam distress signals into outer space. A two-lane highway runs right through the opera house, as befits a town where only social outcasts prowl the streets, along with a few car-phobic visiting opera nuts who seek refuge in the clubby comforts of the Hotel Lancaster. The hotel is within walking distance.

Christopher Raeburn was waiting in the lobby, recognizably foreign in his air-conditioning-resistant tweed jacket, brown vest, and garden-gnome-green trousers cut out of the heaviest English wool.

After ordering some hot tea with biscuits, the avuncular elder statesman of the recording industry told me in his precise, emphatic British locutions about the first time he heard his greatest discovery.

"The Viennese Vladarski agency had sent out a notice to just about every manager and opera executive about this huge audition of young singers they were presenting at the Casa Verdi in Milan, a retirement home for needy singers Verdi set up with a bequest. A little tatty now. The year was 1986. She sang two arias, from *Italiana in Algeri* and *Tancredi*. I was so impressed I called my colleague Ray Minshull, who was then the head of Artists and Repertoire at Decca. I simply insisted that he listen to her, especially since we wanted to do a recording of *Barber* with Leo Nucci, who by luck had actually done that talent show with her. We did another audition in Bologna and we knew she was the Rosina we were looking for.

"What's interesting, looking back, is that a lot of other people just weren't that impressed. They thought the voice small. But while it's certainly not large, it had focus, and she was already such a complete musician. She phrased so beautifully."

"Is a small voice particularly hard to record?" I asked.

"The reverse," he said. "It's a perfect studio voice. Some voices just don't sound quite the same recorded as live. But not hers. That appealed to me right away when we were doing *Barber*. In fact, loud voices can be difficult to capture sometimes."

Raeburn illustrated with a story about tenor Mario del Monaco, who had a voice so big he could fit Domingo into a tooth cavity. But even so, he was determined to stand as close to the microphones as possible.

"Finally, we just gave up and let him sing right into his mike. But he didn't know we hadn't turned it on."

Raeburn is now retired from Decca, though he returns regularly to the studio to supervise Bartoli's recordings. That's why he was in Houston. Jack Mastroianni, Bartoli's New York–based manager, had recently formed a video company, whose first project was the Bologna/Houston *Cenerentola*.

In opera, midnight always comes too soon. Mastroianni wanted to stop time and preserve the moment forever. But making videos is increasingly hard to do in a world of larcenous unions who work hard at working as little as possible for as much as possible. Once upon a time, opera companies thought videos would capture new audiences and generate a little income. As it turned out, few American opera companies can afford telecasts, never mind videos, because every single stagehand, musician, chorister, dancer—even those not in the show—must be paid above their already excellent salaries. Making a video of *Cenerentola* would cost over $1 million. Though Rossini requires only a small orchestra, Mastroianni would have to pay each instrumentalist in the company. But he had managed to raise the funds from several sources in the corporate and nonprofit sectors. Decca, for instance, was providing the audio, and Raeburn, the expertise of a lifetime. Decca viewed its subsidy as a form of promotion.

I asked Raeburn if he'd been around for the free fall from the edge of great fame of Suliotis, the Callas-soundalike who recorded for Decca in the mid-1960s, only to blow out her voice in one-fifth the time it took the greater Greek. He had. He blamed a faulty technique and a happy-go-lucky lifestyle. But that was twenty-five years ago, and Raeburn had a more recent story of early burnout. He was absolutely sure that the unknown Leonora on the newish *Il trovatore* with Luciano Pavarotti was one of the greatest dramatic sopranos of the modern age. That's one reason she got to make the album. But unlike Bartoli, Antonella Banaudi dropped from sight as speedily as she arrived. "She seems to have suffered a crisis of confidence," Raeburn said sadly.

"What is required for immense success?" I asked, reminding him how Callas, in a conversation with Edward R. Murrow, once said that you absolutely had to believe that you were the best in the world. Is that it?

Raeburn smiled into his little beard. "Possibly. You must communicate. But it's invariably a combination of elements at a particular moment in time. And then there's always something that can't be explained. That's the magic."

. . .

THE NEXT EVENING was the dress rehearsal. As in most companies, it is really a performance in front of invited guests and company members, though parts of the auditorium are roped off for the director and designers, who cluster around work tables and computers, fine-tuning the lighting scheme.

Campanella, the chain smoker, stepped into the pit and the show started. His overture turned out to be the liveliest component of a long evening.

Cenerentola really could be funny, even though it could also be shorter. For proof, there's the enchanting 1981 video with Frederica von Stade as the slipperless ash sitter, in a much-fêted production by Jean-Pierre Ponnelle that continued to make the rounds even after the designer-director's untimely death in 1988, when he was just fifty-six. Rehearsing on the stage of the Tel Aviv Opera, he stepped backwards into the pit and never recovered from his injuries. Few directors had his humanistic depth, his cultivated references, his quirky wit. His clockwork ensembles and full-dimensional characters lifted away the heavy shtick and layers of cardboard so often suffocating the comedies of Mozart and Rossini. In the view of many buffs with long memories and an international perspective, his *Cenerentola* ranks even in its posthumous appearances as one of the greatest productions of anything, ever.

Von Stade, who was born to riches in real life, supplies the vulnerability and the sense of wonder that make the story worth telling. D. W. Griffith would have adored the mezzo, who has the fragile aura and the perfume of Lillian Gish. Despite the wittily baroque Italian settings, the video's sharply observed foibles and follies transport us straight to the golden age of film comedy. Musically, the two stepsisters may be two noisy peas in a pod, but one loves to dance and the other to dress up, and Ponnelle used this to create fizzy comic sketches. The Mexican tenor Francisco Araiza plays his part not as some bland Prince Charming, but as a sulky boy who really doesn't want to get married. Consequently, he is resentful, and resentment in others is always a great sport to watch. The choristers dance in and out of the wings; Alidoro seems to glide around on fairy dust. The show is heaven.

Maybe when the Houston production opened in Bologna it too had magic, which simply faded in the oceanic transit. In Houston, the curtain went up and the curtain went down on what was essentially the same graceless set: two staircases joined together at the top by a landing with a gloomy cavern underneath, where Bartoli was stuck much of the time wearing a brown potato sack with a little extra drapery. The atmosphere lifted whenever she sang, but this is an opera dominated by fast-paced ensembles and witty duets, and these had gone virtually unstaged. It looked like a candidate for the American Funeral Services Museum, also in Houston, where you can enjoy a special video, *The History of Embalming*.

The director, Roberto di Simone, had stayed home in Italy and left the show to an assistant whose idea of humor was to have the valet Dandini drop his handkerchief a few dozen times for the prince to pick up. Nothing at all happened during one of the opera's most famous moments: the *temporale*, or storm scene. As the orchestra mimicked the sound of pelting rain and thunder, the prince's carriage is meant to break down right in front of Cenerentola's house. Here in Houston there was no storm and no coach. The prince walked on as if a bus had dropped him off.

Hurrying home, I called Jack Mastroianni, thinking he might wish to feign a heart attack and get out of the video project.

"Oh, really? Not funny enough?" he asked. He seemed unconcerned.

"How's this for funny?" he said, reading me the opening of an interview with Bartoli that had just come out in the London *Times*. " 'Cecilia Bartoli, Diva of Divas. Famously, impossibly, ludicrously tetchy. Hot blooded? Undoubtedly. Temperamental? But of course.' "

Mastroianni refused to worry about the show. "Brian will fix it."

Brian is Brian Large, a video director who specializes in adapting stage performances for television. It is Large who adapted the legendary centennial Bayreuth *Ring* cycle by director Patrice Chéreau for video, not to mention several classic productions by Ponnelle. His style favors reaction shots and close-ups, a technique honed during long years of labor at the Met, where the sets often look like moldy dioramas of stuffed wildebeests at the Museum of Natural History. His greatest technical feat is the Met's *Götterdämmerung* video, featuring a soprano and tenor who never sang in the same performance. After a styrofoam-coated wood beam from the Gibichung home dropped on Hildegard Behrens, sending her to the hospital (and to her lawyer), Large cross-edited two performances in which either Behrens had sung with another tenor or the Siegfried had hugged another Brünnhilde, patching it together with footage from a dress rehearsal.

Maybe he could work similar miracles on *Cenerentola*. But that wouldn't help the show as it actually took place onstage.

The next morning, I stopped by to see David Gockley in his office that overlooked a few billboards. Pushing aside a pile of scores with his foot, he pulled over a leather club chair and sat down holding a sheaf of papers. A youthful fifty-two-year-old with tennis-pro looks and a funereal manner even when he's happy, he seemed barely capable of breathing unassisted. The awfulness of the dress rehearsal had hit him right between the eyes, and he was making lists of things that just might be in the realm of improvement: lighting, Cecilia's costume, the prince's wig. Down the list he went, stopping at the surtitles. There were some four hundred surtitles, of which he might have to adjust sixty.

Gockley managed a wan smile as he described one he might rewrite himself: Don Magnifico's description of his stepdaughter: "All her worries have made Cenerentola look like a bag of bones." Bartoli had put on a few pounds since the Bologna production.

"Any suggestions?" he asked. "The libretto says 'bag of bones,' but must we be literal?"

"How about 'a sad sack'?"

He managed a faint smile and then drifted back in time to remember a legendary telecast of *La Bohème* with Renata Scotto and Luciano Pavarotti, whose epic embraces one critic compared to two dumplings in love. Scotto was so unnerved with her appearance she went on a diet the day she saw the tape. "Maybe Cecilia will look at the tape and . . ."

Gockley stopped himself to look on the bright side. Importing the show was a lot cheaper than spending, say, $400,000 knocking together a new production. Bologna's rental fee is around $40,000, plus $35,000 in transport and another $115,000 in cosmetic improvements.

"The way opera is scheduled today, so far in advance," Gockley pointed out, "means we have to decide what will be interesting three and four years ahead. And thus you could say this is successful. All performances are sold out. Beyond that, I suppose I looked on it as an investment. What was going through my head when we committed to this is that Cecilia is a perfectionist and that she will ally herself with organizations that pursue her own goals. And to the extent that it is within the bounds of reason, I am willing to go along."

Not so long ago, Bartoli had indicated she might do a whole Mozart cycle in Houston. "So has she signed up for that?"

He paused for a minute.

"No," he said, frowning, as he returned to his surtitles. "Not so far."

And not ever, as it turned out. Earthbound performer that she is, Bartoli eventually concluded that she much preferred the orchestra and geographical proximity of the Zurich Opera, which had also invited her to sing Susanna in Mozart's *Le nozze di Figaro* in the spring of 1998.

CHAPTER TWO

Diva Dienst

How many divas does it take to screw in a light bulb?
Just one. She holds the bulb and the world revolves around her.

ANAGERS CALL IT "diva dienst," *diva* from the Italian for *goddess* and *dienst* from the German verb *dienen*, "to serve." Diva dienst is why they exist; scarcely a day goes by when managers are not reminded of this by their diva clients. (Extreme narcissism is not unknown in the male of the species, but they're rarely called divos. "Tenor" is sufficient.) Managers spend half their time answering four questions: "Why am I not opening La Scala/the Met/Covent Garden?" "Where's my contract?" "Why is my fee so low? I am insulted!" "Was I wonderful last night? . . . Really? I did feel a cold coming on and I was up all night with reflux." Reflux is a newly conceived singers' ailment. Often, when they've been up late eating after a performance, the juices flow toward their head and inflame their innards while they slumber. You and I call it indigestion.

Flower deliveries, visas, bank deposits, tax accountants, more flower deliveries, limos for the top earners, throat doctors, therapy— that's what managers are there to provide.

Their solicitude does not go entirely unrewarded. Typically, managers slice off around ten percent for opera bookings and twenty percent for recitals, though once singers start making a lot of money, they usually try whittling down the percentages. What is a lot of money? Top fees at the top companies of the world, places like London's Covent Garden, the Vienna Staatsoper, Munich's Bayerische Staatsoper, the Metropolitan, the Lyric of Chicago, and La Scala, Milan, range from around $13,000 to $20,000 a night, meaning a reflux-free frequent flyer could conceivably make a million dollars by singing around fifty performances a year. Sensible singers rarely sing more than twice a week. They don't use mikes, and honking away for hours on end swells the healthiest vocal cords. Besides, most shows have limited runs (say, ten performances), and rehearsals take up a lot of time for little pay. European houses typically require singers to rehearse free for two weeks, after which they get one-twelfth of their fee for every day on the job. That's why they don't always show up on time, especially for new productions that require four or five weeks of pacing around chilly rehearsal rooms with a director who will try to keep them from their favorite spot: center stage and close to the prompt box.

Until the fifties, nobody much bothered with this rehearsal business. Those were the golden days of song. Adelina Patti, the legendary nineteenth-century diva, sent her maid to rehearsals. In our own century, Kirsten Flagstad drew a circle on the stage within which she could be expected to roam as Brünnhilde. Those days are gone.

How many opera singers make a million or more these days? It's hard to say, because even houses with firm fee structures can loosen up a little extra by providing housing or travel perks like Concorde tickets, which singers invariably cash in. Even so, fewer than ten singers probably make the kind of money the sports agent Jerry Maguire in his humble phase might consider serious.

Three of them are, it will not amaze, the Three Tenors: Luciano Pavarotti, Plácido Domingo, José Carreras. Global media stars since their 1990 World Cup concert in the Baths of Caracalla, the trio's money-minting capacity was showing no signs of fading just yet, though they would be sixty years old (Pavarotti), fifty-four (Domingo's official age) and fifty (Carreras) by the time they started their third outing that summer. Each would bank around a million dollars per night. While no female singers commanded that kind of pay, recital fees as high as a hundred thousand had kept Jessye Norman, Kiri Te Kanawa, and Kathleen Battle in foie gras for some time. But all were heading into their fifties, and their money days—generally shorter for women, anyway—were dimming.

In 1995, Bartoli's were just beginning. When she sang one of her first public recitals in 1991 at the tiny Hertz Auditorium on the Berkeley campus, it was for the normal debutant's fee: around $6,500. Of the seven hundred seats, maybe half had people in them. Four years later, fees of $50,000 were common, to the amazement of the music world and the great satisfaction of Jack Mastroianni and his mezzo, who appeared as frequently—or infrequently—as she wished in a select number of prestigious theaters and concert series. Adam Smith, whose world economic theory was partly shaped by the effect of supply on demand, would give her manager a gold star. Limited appearances seemed agreeable to Bartoli, who showed no signs of turning herself into a workaholic like Domingo who warms up on airplanes, hastening to his next engagement. Bartoli usually signed up for only two opera productions a season and maybe thirty concerts a year.

Her reticence is unusual. Mezzo Jennifer Larmore, her hardworking sometime rival, once packed four new roles into one year, learning one while singing another and recording a third. Finding a balance is as hard for ambitious singers as it is for ambitious managers, who do not get paid unless their clients are onstage. A creative manager I know managed to book a client into two engagements the same night in London. The soprano was singing the love-saddened Marschallin in Richard Strauss's *Der Rosenkavalier*—an opera in which the princess sits around in her dressing room for the entire, very long second act. She tucked in the Brahms Requiem at Albert Hall and then hurried back to Covent Garden for the third act's tearful adieu.

One morning in November 1995, not long after the opening of the Houston *Cenerentola*, I paid a visit to the offices of Bartoli's manager, who works out of a white luxury high-rise a short walk from Lincoln Center. He would explain his career strategy along with a little history.

Mastroianni has desk space for four people, one fax machine, two word processors, and a large Xerox machine in his L-shaped office, which comes with a small balcony and a separate conference room. His assistant Hilary Merrill used to be in private banking; Marco Bisazza, a young Italian, is just leaving, for what he isn't quite sure, but it won't involve opera singers; and Henry Gronnier, who folded his own agency, is thinking of restarting his career as a violinist.

"How's Bartoli?" I asked.

"Sleeping in Houston," Mastroianni replied.

"How have the performances been going?"

"Just great," he answered, turning off his laptop, shoving it between a vase filled with roses and his address book, which comes in two frayed volumes. His windows overlook a quiet side street, though Central Park can be glimpsed by leaning sideways from the balcony. A tall, intense forty-six-year-old with a dark, carefully trimmed beard and sharp brown eyes, he was wearing a yellow sweater with a white shirt and a solemnly striped dark green tie. I've heard he's color blind and buys things in limited hues to preclude aesthetic offenses.

Brian Large, he said, was in Houston looking things over before taping the last two shows. "The singing is so good nobody will notice the rest, though I've got to say, the stage director, was he in a coma or something? That storm scene—what a disaster. To fill the time, Brian is going to have to add a coach electronically in the studio. Very expensive."

He frowned.

"That reminds me. When Bartoli wakes up, we must clarify her participation in the Levine gala, please," he said, turning his bird-of-prey profile towards the chicly tailored Merrill.

At the end of the 1995–96 Metropolitan Opera season, the company's artistic director and chief conductor, James Levine, would be throwing himself a huge party, to which he was inviting his favorite singers. Bartoli barely knew him, but had agreed to appear, even though it involved a live telecast. Few singers like instantaneous transmission; they prefer the so-called "live" telecasts that are live only in the sense that the singers in them are not dead. These days, live telecasts, especially from the Met, are usually the best scenes culled from a minimum of two tapings.

Mastroianni excused himself to take a call from soprano client Mirella Freni, with whom he speaks in the Italian he learned as the coddled only child of a first-generation Italian engineer and an American mother with a comfortable home in the leafy enclave of Scarsdale, near Manhattan. Though a music buff from puberty, he earned degrees in comparative literature at Brown University and then left to study Spanish literature at Oxford, where he became known as the first student to have a private telephone installed in his rooms at Trinity College.

"He was enormously popular at Oxford," Jane Glover, the English conductor, once told me. "He gave fabulous parties and had a sharing way with his phone. Never did a stitch of work as far as we could tell. When he wasn't on the phone, he was blasting opera on his excellent stereo or going to Covent Garden. It was the beginning of the Kiri era."

In his open briefcase was an early-model portable phone. In 1995, they were just getting popular with the marketmakers on Wall Street.

I reported Glover's recollections. "Never did a stitch of work?"

"What slander!" he groused. "While Glover was researching Cavalli, a rather dull composer, I was writing liner notes and doing musicological research for the Met's *Siege of Corinth* by Rossini, a fabulous composer."

Three phones were ringing. Merrill picked up one. "It's Sarah Billinghurst."

Billinghurst is the assistant manager at the Met whose large domain includes casting. Her hems are worn thin from the solicitous managers and singers who pass her way.

He took her call, which appeared to concern an upcoming production of *Carmen* in which his cerebral client Russian baritone Sergei Leiferkus would look like Elvis in his Nutty Buddy phase.

After Oxford, Mastroianni left for Houston during the oil-gush years (over by the mid-eighties), becoming associate director of the opera, where he perfected the talky art of significantly reducing the wealth of his dinner companions by the time the dessert tray rolled into view. He provided the financial safety net that allowed Gockley to experiment with cutting-edge, diva-free pieces like *Nixon in China* or Philip Glass's *The Making of the Representative for Planet 8*. Ambitious, Mastroianni finally left Houston in 1987, when he was thirty-eight. Gockley was only a few years older, and not about to retire; Mastroianni jumped the fence to Columbia Artists Management, the biggest artist-management company in America.

He became prince-in-waiting and principal water carrier to CAMI's secretive president, Ronald Wilford, a man who avoids interviews (I've tried) and personally controls the movements of most of the major conductors in the world, from Seiji Ozawa to James Levine. Ordered to expand a dismal diva roster, Mastroianni added Kiri Te Kanawa, June Anderson, Mirella Freni, Eva Marton, and finally Bartoli, the only mezzo in the lot. Generally, mezzos don't get to be divas, because sopranos sing the bigger roles with the bigger paychecks.

Mastroianni put down the phone. I asked him when he first heard Bartoli.

"Summer of 1988," he said. "Christopher Raeburn had kept at me to hear this young mezzo he had discovered at the Casa Verdi audition. I was reluctant, because what I did was manage singers already at their peak. A developing young singer needs different contacts. Finally, when I was in Pesaro for the Rossini festival, I agreed to set up an audition. Cecilia arrived around twenty minutes late with her mother. It was a hot, sultry day, and she was wearing something floral that hugged her in a very attractive way. She had long sensual hair and big, flashing eyes and a truly incompetent pianist. I think the original one hadn't shown up, which is why they were late, though Cecilia sometimes doesn't look at her watch.

"He played terribly. And then she did something that got me interested. Suddenly, she walked over to the bench, pushed him away, and played for herself. The aria was, appropriately enough, 'Cruda sorte,' and she sang it well—Marilyn Horne couldn't have done it much better. The use of words, the beauty of the voice, the secureness of the technique, and all in all, an intensity, a radiance that shot out at you. Few singers have it—that light," he said.

"Cruda sorte" means "cruel fate." The shipwrecked but very shrewd Isabella sings it as she washes up far away from home in Rossini's *L'italiana in Algeri*. Her luck will change: Like Cenerentola, Isabella knows what she wants and figures out a way to get it.

"You might say that the winds of fortune blew her my way," he continued, leaning back in his leather chair. "I remember asking, What is it you think I can do for you?

"Well, she wanted world management, but in talking to her I discovered she already had a clutch of agents, all pulling her in different directions in Italy and the rest of Europe, including Walter Vladarski and his mom, who work out of Vienna and arranged the audition that Raeburn attended. In addition, she already had a verbal agreement with another CAMI division, run by Bruce Zemsky and Alan Green, who scoop up dozens of very young singers every year hoping a few might rise to the top. She insisted that they had not contacted her since agreeing to represent her some three months earlier, but it created an unexpected problem when I got home. We all worked for the same company, albeit in different divisions. Zemsky-Green thought I was poaching on their territory, their artist. They threatened to leave CAMI, taking all their clients, though she wasn't earning them any money then. They caused such a ruckus, Wilford ordered me to drop all communication with her. 'I will not allow this little Italian mezzo to destroy my company!' he stormed. I was ordered to stay away and not to contact her. She and I did not speak again until she fired Zemsky-Green about a year later. At that point, I was allowed to represent her. That was in September of 1989."

He paused for a minute and frowned.

"Less than four years later, I got fired."

In a big way, too. His assistant claimed he punched her in the stomach after an argument about a fax number, and threatened a harassment suit. Nobody saw it; few believed it; everybody talked about it. Wilford by then had decided he didn't want to retire anyway, and probably found the incident useful to move his flamboyant junior out the door. Mastroianni had also aroused the enmity of Wilford's second chief slave, vice-president Matthew Epstein, who was pleased to see him pack.

By the fall of 1993, Mastroianni had set up his own boutique agency. Bartoli, loyal and shrewd, soon exercised the termination option on her CAMI contract. Freni and her husband, the veteran bass Nicolai Ghiaurov, also signed, followed by Leiferkus. Mastroianni has been quick to take advantage of the remarkable singers suddenly flooding westwards from the ex–Soviet Union. His roster soon included the lyric soprano Elena Prokina, the mezzo Larissa Diadkova, and for engagements in the United States, the overcommitted and sometimes double-booked Galina Gorchakova, who also has an active European manager and a powerful booster in the conductor Valery Gergiev, the globe-trotting supremo of the Kirov Opera in St. Petersburg. Mastroianni also took a chance on a very young Austrian mezzo who sings a lot of Mozart and Richard Strauss named Angelika Kirchschlager, and was just about to sign up his first nonsinging client, Jean-Yves Thibaudet, a French-German pianist with a treasured Decca recording contract, a big solo career, and a Versace wardrobe.

Henry Gronnier approached, his shy manner a contrast to his leather pants and blazing red shirt.

"Apparently Cecilia has said she might not be able to do the dinner after the Dallas concert because she has to be back in Houston early the next day. She has to be there by ten-thirty in the morning, because the train for New Orleans is leaving at eleven. I guess she is being driven to Houston from Dallas. Is that right?"

"A forty-five-minute flight. She won't fly?"

"No. I guess not. So should we explain something to Dallas, should we?" he continued, looking at Mastroianni.

"Can we handle this delicately, please?" Mastroianni ordered. "To the extent that trains, buses, and scooters are impacting on her engagements, we need to pay more attention to this."

Cecilia's Dallas concert was a fundraiser for the symphony. When an artist is being paid her kind of fee, dinner with the sponsors is obligatory.

"The thing is that the train situation from Houston to New Orleans is not so frequent." Henry's first language is French.

"We need to discuss this with Cecilia. I do not see leaving before dinner. By the way, have you responded to the Rolex people?"

Gronnier returned to his desk and dialed.

"Hello! This is the office of Jack Mastroianni," he announced, grinning. "I am returning your call about the change to the Rolex ad. Well, here it is. We spoke to Cecilia and this is the change we would like to make in the copy you sent to us. We would all prefer 'astonished by her own voice' instead of 'amazed by her own voice.' Thank you."

News about the Rolex ad was about to be added to the Bartoli home page that Decca had set up as a publicity tool on the World Wide Web. Mastroianni clicked on and a few commands later watched dots assemble themselves into a portrait of a sultry Bartoli sitting in a gondola.

There was another site, updated by a fan, which included reviews and other postings. Bartoli, who keeps her schedule in a small, dog-eared, Scotch-taped diary, is computer-phobic and as far as any of us know has never seen her Web site. Which is perhaps just as well. Some fans have noticed that the slender nymph of the first Decca releases has not always said no to second helpings. "To Stairmaster or not to Stairmaster," goes one conversational thread.

"Could I relate to you a problem I had on Friday?" Henry asked, getting up from his desk again. "We got this strange fax from the University of Florida about a concert they hoped Cecilia might do. 'It is no longer of interest to us at this time in receiving a reply to our fax. We have taken the $75,000 we were prepared to offer for her engagement and made offers to other artists. Maybe our fax machines can do lunch sometime in the future.' Is that strange or what?"

"Can you call Greg Barbero?" Merrill interrupted. "He's called you twice."

Barbero is a recording executive—specifically, the marketing manager for Decca's American company, London Records. (Like Deutsche Grammophon and Philips, two other classical labels that are more prestigious than profitable, Decca is owned by Poly-Gram, itself part of the Dutch Philips Electronics conglomerate).

Determining release dates for new albums and the allocation of advertising dollars fall into his bailiwick. It's a challenging job in dollar-stretching. Years ago, the record stores themselves would pick up the costs of advertising. Nowadays, record companies pay retail outlets like Tower or HMV substantial sums to feature their albums in newspaper ads and store windows and to display those popular stand-up portraits that can spook you in the aisles. Only the biggest stars are turned into cardboard effigies and, not surprisingly, Bartoli is one.

From the beginning of her five-year exclusive Decca contract until February 1995, when she signed a new contract, Bartoli had surpassed the one-million-record mark worldwide, which may not seem like a lot by, say, the lofty standards of Celine Dion, but is phenomenal in the classical realm. In the United States alone, Bartoli's *If You Love Me*, a 1992 album of arias by Scarlatti, Vivaldi, Caldara, and Paisiello, was already pushing past the 200,000 mark, about 180,000 more than the average classical CDs.

Artists typically take home maybe eighty cents per album, meaning Bartoli sees a sizable uptick in her royalty statement every quarter. Where does the rest of the money go? It varies; but overpaid, unionized orchestras, grotesque overhead, packaging, distribution, and advertising all take huge bites out of the shrinking pie. Decca records all of Bartoli's solo albums, but she's free to tape full-length operas with other companies if her own label doesn't choose to exercise first refusal rights. Exclusivity doesn't exist in the classical business anymore, the way it did a generation ago when labels immediately conjured up certain names and faces.

Mastroianni got off the phone. "The classical environment is changing," he said. "Years ago, you'd have to position someone as an opera singer first. In fact, opera stars really didn't sing lieder until later, if at all. Callas never sang a song recital in her career! But we both recognized that with Cecilia, the goal would be to establish her as a recitalist who does opera, not the other way around. From the first moment I heard her, I could sense she had the capability to create an atmosphere on the recital stage all by herself. Not many people can. They need a costume.

"The other goal was to be precious. Less is more. We didn't take any offer just because of income. We looked for certain strategic venues, houses, productions, and recital series. One way to build up a career is to get your artist to appear on what's called a Great Artists series, sold on subscription by, say, Lincoln Center. They'll take a chance on an emerging artist because they have a built-in public. To enhance Galina Gorchakova's reputation, for example, I am trying to get her on a prestigious series in Toronto's Roy Thomson Hall."

The phones kept ringing. Merrill interrupted to say she had someone on the line asking for a phone number for José Carreras's leukemia foundation. Carreras successfully battled the disease in the late 1980s, but sings little opera these days, preferring to concentrate on less strenuous (and also better-paying) concerts, especially in Europe, where he remains popular.

Mastroianni continued with his career philosophy. "We turn down a lot of things to emphasize rarity. Stadium concerts for sure. Cecilia hates them. Doesn't like singing with a mike. And stories. Part of what Edgar Vincent does is turn down article requests—an unusual situation, God knows, but we both realize that someone not yet thirty years old has only so many stories in them. The reservoir of experience is still small."

Edgar Vincent is Bartoli's press agent, a dapper gentleman who looks like Vincent Price's lost brother. He started out in the golden years of publicity when New York had half a dozen dailies, of which at least one was eager to print glossies of client Lily Pons making crème caramel while wearing a mink coat and a tiara. Nowadays, he's a classy legend in a dying business, though he keeps active enough tending to such clients as the hyper Plácido Domingo, the secretive Mikhail Baryshnikov, the single-minded Verdi mezzo Dolora Zajick, and the mysterious Teresa Stratas, who has never accepted an engagement she didn't wish to cancel. But with New York, still the North American capital of the classical music business, down to one newspaper with regular arts coverage, he's lately added management to his portfolio, guiding the careers of such promising younger singers as the mezzo Catherine Keen and the soprano Audrey Stottler.

"Just now Edgar turned down *Opera News*, which wanted to put

Bartoli on the cover when she makes her Met debut. But *Così* is an ensemble opera, and we thought it was inappropriate to have Despina on the cover."

"Jack," Hilary interrupted. "Judy Drucker wants to know what Cecilia would like for Thanksgiving. What does she want to eat?"

Drucker is a big-hearted Florida impresaria and a Pavarotti pal since the sixties, when he made his American debut at the Miami Opera with Joan Sutherland in *Lucia di Lammermoor* and Drucker as a solicitous chorus woman. Years later, when Pavarotti edged gingerly into the solitary world of the recital, he chose friendly Miami, where Drucker had built up a flourishing concert agency in the intervening years. She wrote out the words for "Granada" in big letters in Magic Markers in case he got lost—inadvertently starting his lifetime devotion to his music stand. In fact, Mr. P does not read music. When he is looking at a score on his music stand, he is looking at the words. This is rather unusual in this era of highly trained singers, but puts Mr. P in the company of the eighteenth century's *orecchianti*—literally "earers"—who memorized the music as it was played for them because they could not absorb it in the conventional way.

It is a learning method Pavarotti is keeping alive all by himself with the assistance of recordings and coaches. The other two tenors read music, though Domingo, a very good musician with a terrific memory, has sometimes been too busy to remember words. To help him get through his first performances of *Lohengrin*, the Vienna Staatsoper developed a special teleprompting machine that was hidden from the audience in the footlights. The system was sent to Rome for the first Three Tenors concert in 1990 and accounts for those lizardlike eye movements captured on the video.

Fortunately, while Mr. P's repertoire is small compared with Domingo's one-hundred-plus roles, Mr. P enjoys singing things he has sung many times, though even this can lead to disaster, as he was soon to discover.

Drucker would be presenting and feeding Bartoli in Miami during the Thanksgiving holiday after she finished *Cenerentola* in Houston. She was still holding the line.

"How about turkey with pasta?"

CHAPTER THREE

The Long Goodbye

THE MET'S STAGE DOOR is off a dingy passageway in an underground garage filled with carbon monoxide and moldy old posters. I am forever surprised that the stars who come here don't specify complimentary gas masks and blindfolds in their contracts. Once you're inside, there's the busy, undersized reception area with emergency-room furniture, a plastic tree that once had more branches, and a battered table on which messengers drop their packages and diva bouquets. Met employees pass by a guard on the right. Visitors are deflected to a trio of faintly smiling receptionists who sit behind a glass partition surrounded by heaps of mail, dog-eared phone books, forgotten packages.

I imagine them going home every night to huddle—like the three Norns in *Götterdämmerung*—over an ever-lengthening text they are secretly scribbling of the comings and goings they witness every day and night. "Sang flat the entire performance," they write. "Cried during rehearsals."

Unlike the folks of Valhalla, they all work in a place designed not by giants but the midgets of modernism. Along with the rest of

Lincoln Center, the Met started sprouting in the very early 1960s—the demon years of architecture, if not of opera—in what was then the working-class neighborhood popularized by Leonard Bernstein's *West Side Story*. It's largely gone, though if you walk the dark streets directly behind the Met toward the Hudson River, you can probably revisit tenser moments from that show and not live to sing and dance about them.

Even so, there isn't a singer who doesn't dream of stepping through this door at least once in his life. No career is considered complete without a Met debut. The place is tightly, tensely, temperamentally run by general manager Joseph Volpe, while the orchestra has been honed to perfection by James Levine.

Even better, chances of getting booed are almost nil. Unlike the easily apoplectic cognoscenti of La Scala in Milan or the Vienna Staatsoper, the friendly audience usually only yells at directors who have failed to provide the expected tonnage of old-fashioned sequins and elaborately realistic and outsized sets topped off by a chandelier. A singer who has records to sell really has to appear at the Met, because it is the centerpiece of the American opera world, in which the greatest number of compact-disc consumers happen to reside. You can bet Decca is looking forward to the day Cecilia Bartoli will finally make her debut here in February 1996.

But now it is only November of 1995, and the three Nornettes at the switchboard are eyeballing each other in disbelief. Luciano Pavarotti has just stepped out of his limousine for the opening night of Donizetti's *La Fille du régiment*. Why is he here?

Most people had assumed that the production, out of wistful cardboard, had disappeared forever in 1994 along with its then-current *fille*, Kathleen Battle, who had been fired by Volpe for unprofessional behavior during the rehearsals, which she had found inconvenient and unnecessary besides. Her sudden departure made the front page of the *New York Times*. Yet it was, at first, a mysterious eviction. What was to rehearse?

First heard in 1840, *Fille* is a wan comedy about a girl foundling who is adopted by a bunch of soldiers and serenaded by a Tyrolean oaf. It just needs two stars to putter along. Neither was there anything surprising about Battle's manners. Stories had circulated for years about her unblemished narcissism and strange remoteness. Once, feeling a trifle chilly in the stretch limo that was driving her through Los Angeles, she got on the car phone and called up CAMI in New York to have them call her driver and tell him to turn down the air conditioning. Everybody has a favorite Battle anecdote. The one I like best has her feeling the need for paper conservation: annoyed that correspondence from the CAMI office to her New York apartment ran up her thermal paper bills, she instructed the staff to shrink all communications so more could fit per page.

This one isn't bad, either: Determined to conserve her voice, which is pure but small, Battle would never, ever speak on the day of a performance. But she would still take phone calls from her CAMI office. How was one reconciled with the other? She would sit by the phone with a glass and a spoon. Callers knew to speak only in yes-or-no questions. One clink meant yes.

But Battle was invariably well prepared once she actually got onstage, where she sparkled like a Meissen figurine. If she couldn't easily talk to people, she could definitely sing to them, in an exquisitely schooled light soprano that made up in perfection for what it lacked in volume. Petite and very chic—and for all her antics, very private—Battle had come a long way from a very poor black family in Ohio to the highest perches the music world could offer.

Why am I defending her? Nobody else did publicly, not even Levine, her most ardent booster during the years when she was a Met ornament. The fact was that Battle, born in 1948, had become expendable, as most problematic singers usually do when they have reached middle age and no longer sound quite as clear and flexible, and need either to acquire new repertoire or to live off the goodwill they've accumulated like deposits in the bank. That there's always younger and less expensive talent waiting in the wings is a fact of opera life the younger ones often don't learn until it is too late.

Pavarotti was different. In November of 1995 the tenor was way past forty—he was sixty years old—but definitely not expendable. He had his moods and he didn't like to rehearse, yet when he got out onstage he could still light up the sets with his smile and reach the last seat with his perfectly focused, shiny tenor. He had been careful with his vocal capital and on a good night sounded better than most tenors half his age, provided the repertoire was right. Even more than that of Plácido Domingo, his only tenor rival, Mr. P's name on a poster instantly guaranteed a sold-out house. The Met has been utterly unimaginative about conceiving of a time when he could no longer sell the house's thirty-eight hundred seats.

That was why Joseph Volpe, the Met's general manager, did not drop his teeth when Mr. P turned to him during a visit to the Met and said: "Hey, Joe, I've got a crazy idea. Let's do *Fille* again. Are you as crazy as I am?"

Volpe and Pavarotti go back to 1968, when the tenor, who was not feeling well, made an underwhelming debut in *La Bohème* and Volpe was still wielding a hammer as chief carpenter. Volpe's rise to the top took him through several layers of Met bureaucracy and a snobbish board that turned to him only after one of their own— Hugh Southern—immediately drowned in the complexities of running a huge organization with a huge budget (now $150 million), around 850 full-time employees, and some 210 performances a year.

A blunt guy with an opera villain's chin beard and a healthy hunger for prestige, the fifty-five-year-old Volpe had now muscled his way past Levine on the totem pole, acquiring excellent suits and independent taste along the way. For a while there was tension between Levine and Volpe, but they seemed to have worked things out. Levine fussed over the shows he conducted and Volpe took care of the rest. Unlike Levine, who avoided confrontations, Volpe didn't mind controversy and he even occasionally invited unconventional directors and designers to do a show, though he often disinvited them once he saw their models and imagined the faces of his donors. A new production at the Met often costs a million dollars or more (the Met spent $1.7 million on a 1987 *Turandot* by the unstinting Franco Zeffirelli), and unlike subsidized European houses, the company relies almost entirely on private sponsorship. *Fille* was just a revival, but Volpe hated making mistakes, and now as the opening night of *Fille* drew ever closer, Volpe was probably very sorry he and Mr. P hadn't been inspired to sing *La Bohème* instead. ("Joe, I've got a crazy idea.

Let's do *La Bohème* and eat Big Macs with extra cheese at the Café Momus!") At least Mr. P could still sing Rodolfo. Now, a year and a half later, Mr. P and Mr. V were about to find out just how crazy they were, or at the very least had been at a moment they must have wished had never happened.

Fille had established Mr. P as a Met superstar in 1972, when he cavorted around the stage trading jokes and high notes with the amusingly awkward Joan Sutherland, who was really the one we had come to see. Tonio, the oaf, has a spectacular aria with nine very exposed high Cs. That is about as high as most tenors can sing. Hearing a cocky tenor belt out a bunch of them is like seeing Ken Griffey Jr. hit a beautiful home run on a sunny summer day with the bases loaded. Pavarotti stepped to the footlights and sang all nine as if he were flipping pancakes into his mouth. The crowd roared.

But twenty-three years had passed, and with it his youth. He started ducking high Cs in public years ago. And his health was not the best. With his weight gain, he sometimes brought to mind Cecil Fielder, hanging on for another payday. A few months before, at London's Covent Garden, Mr. P had quite a fretful time with Verdi's *Un ballo in maschera*, sipping from strategically placed glasses of water all over the stage.

Why was he singing Tonio? The prospect boggled the mind. Why destroy a great memory? There was no point in singing the part without the many high Cs. But Mr. P could not sing them.

Did he feel the need to prove he was still the vigorous guy he had been long ago? It was no secret that he had become romantically involved with his young secretary, Nicoletta Mantovani. And while it was hardly the first time that the tenor had shown an interest in a woman not his wife, Signora Adua Pavarotti was filing for divorce.

But after testing out his Cs at a rehearsal, he resigned himself, sadly surely, to taking the piece half a step down, though when the *New York Times* came calling for a pre-performance interview he toyed with the incredulous journalist, who ended up writing an article titled "Pavarotti Risking High C's Again."

Meanwhile, the glamorous oddball singing Marie was telling *New York* magazine that only her huge mortgage had convinced her to sing such a dumb role. June Anderson was another singer tethered to the ground by a fraying silk thread. After starting out at the New York City Opera singing the Beverly Sills repertoire of high-soprano roles, she'd decamped to France, where she became thin, chic, and hugely adored. A Yale graduate, Anderson was brighter than a lot of singers. She read books, knew a lot about art, and had interesting taste in clothes and antiques. In the coloratura roles she could be spectacular—Lucia, the Donizetti bride driven to murder on her wedding night, or Violetta, the consumptive courtesan of *La traviata*. And she had something only a few singers, like Pavarotti or Bartoli, have: an identifiable timbre that you are born with and can never acquire, even if her cool, glacial sound did not appeal to everyone. But if her success was everything a singer can dream of, Anderson seemed determined to be miserable even so. Something was always wrong, she would claim to anyone in listening distance: the set smelled, the tenor was an idiot, the composer a bore, the director crazy. It was an Anderson ritual, a strained, strange exercise in self-inflation that obscured an insecure, accomplished artist who seemed to find her talent more of a burden than a blessing. The shoe just never fit. Of all the artists I have met, she made me most aware of how hard it can be for shy singers to come to terms with a mysterious gift that requires them to face several thousand strangers who do not necessarily wish them well.

So that's who was in the show when it finally creaked to the stage in November of 1995. Anderson looked snappy in her pigtail and uniform and actually managed a few smiles as she paraded in with her regiment. She sang with spirit, but Marie isn't onstage for the dread aria of the nine high Cs. And when the moment of truth arrived, there was nothing to distract us. Pavarotti was all alone as he fell apart and cracked on the first note. He seemed to freeze with the rest of us. Then he attempted the other high Cs by shaking his torso and raising his hand. It was futile.

The King of the High Cs had missed his Bs.

He reappeared for the second act, but the show was essentially over. Nothing could erase the misery and memory of his squawks. Backstage, the mood was gloomy as his guests shuffled around waiting for him to open his dressing room door. When he finally did, he looked as if he'd just received a visit from the Grim Reaper. Ashen underneath his heavy makeup, he signed programs and slowly brightened as he listened to his fans telling him how much they had enjoyed the performance. The artists who transport us into the realm of fantasies also have a great need for myths. Anderson was in the green room, receiving emissaries from Omega, whose watch she was modelling in newspaper ads. I wondered if she was telling them she really hated their watch but needed to buy a car.

TWO DAYS LATER I went down to Philadelphia with the tenor's manager, Herbert Breslin, a motor-mouthed, bullet-headed, forever-tan egomaniac who is adored and loathed in about equal proportions among those who've had the joy of doing business with him. I used to go through the obituary section of the *Times* looking for his—a little squib tucked under the fold, somewhere beneath retired postmasters and minor-league ballplayers from the 1950s. That was after he'd thwarted a book I had planned on his most famous client. But we'd patched things up. His reasons probably had something to do with money. Breslin loves money as much as Mr. P, and since he's managed Mr. P since the late 1960s, he has a fair amount of it—which he holds on to very tightly. You can get old and gray waiting for him to pick up a dinner check, though sometimes he forgets himself. When the French opera star and then Breslin client Régine Crespin fell ill with cancer many years ago, he was on the phone in a state, saying he would help her pay for the absolute best treatment money could buy. She said the shock nearly killed her.

With his small and underpaid staff, Breslin does both management and publicity, and these days his client list includes Hildegard Behrens for management and Deborah Voigt for publicity. The day Mr. P stops singing, he will probably close shop, but right now there isn't an opera house that won't return Breslin's phone calls. Herbert is seventy-one, and though he's got the vigor and venom of a much younger man, he hates getting older, and spends twenty minutes on the treadmill every day so that his Armani jackets will close neatly over the little pot belly into which, just now, he was stuffing a doughnut.

We were en route to the Pavarotti Voice Competition in Philadelphia, which Mr. P judges every few years. He's always devoted a fair amount of time to a variety of good causes, whether it's giving young artists a needed boost or joining pop singers to raise money for traumatized children in Bosnia. Now, rather miraculously recovered from his self-imposed Met ordeal, the tenor was commuting down from New York in his white stretchmobile. One hundred singers were waiting.

Breslin had promised to give me his two cents on the state of today's opera world.

"Boy. I really didn't want to get up this morning," Breslin gasped. "Okay, give it to me. How bad is it? Let me see."

Normally, Breslin could care less about the press. As he liked to say: "Whatever you guys write isn't worth a thimble-full of rat's piss." Even so, he had not been looking forward to a *New York* magazine piece on Mr. P and his manager by Michael Walsh, moonlighting from his regular post as music critic for *Time* magazine. Walsh probably bore both a grudge. A few years before, Walsh had started work on a big PBS series on music hosted by Mr. P. Everybody was pretty excited about it. As a friend of mine at PBS once told me, the network's dream fundraiser looks like this: a musical about the survival of furry animals during the Holocaust starring Luciano Pavarotti. This music project came pretty close to that ideal. But then Pavarotti's attention drifted, and an annoyed Walsh was waved away.

Holding tightly to the magazine, Breslin sank deep into the Metroliner's plushness to read "Snake and the Fat Man."

One line caught his attention immediately: the one that stated quite firmly that he was the most hated man in the music business.

"You think that's true?" he asked, looking faintly disturbed. "I thought Matthew Epstein was the most hated man in opera," referring to the portly kinglet at CAMI who had helped shorten Mastroianni's tenure.

"It's probably a toss-up."

Breslin, who is unoffendable, shrugged and returned to the piece.

"This must be my lucky day," he muttered after a few minutes. "All it says is that I'm a vulgar son-of-a-bitch who makes money for Luciano. Big news. Big deal."

Breslin, in Walsh's description, was a crass hack who had turned a tasteful artist into a rich clown.

"Evil genius?" he snickered, staring at the cover. "Well, he's half right."

He stuck the magazine into his briefcase and looked out the window as we drifted past Princeton, picking up a clutch of bureaucrats heading for Washington, D.C. Two of them spread out in the rows in front of us, speaking loudly across the aisle about budgetary reform and the deficit. After five minutes, Breslin wanted to kill them. "Christ," he hissed, "no wonder this country is in a mess." Finally, he leaned over and tapped the smaller one on the shoulder. "Could you keep your voice down?" he suggested loudly. "We're having trouble with our own conversation." They stared at him, outraged, but stopped yelling about marginal tax rates for the rest of the trip.

Actually, conversations with Breslin tend to be one-sided. He continued with his monologue.

"Do you realize that there is not one soprano in the world today who has captured the public imagination?" he said, warming up. "Kiri is pretty much out of it. She plays golf. Jessye Norman? She's a caricature. You can't take her seriously now."

Actually, I thought, Te Kanawa sounded pretty splendid for someone just past fifty.

"Now your Ms. Bartoli. She has talent, she has a voice. I don't know her, but she is probably an ambitious piece; although represented by that dumbbell who also represents Mirella Freni, not a fascinating lady."

Jack Mastroianni and Herbert Breslin are barely on speaking terms. They were just then fighting over a proposed collaboration between the fabled tiny Spanish pianist Alicia de Larrocha and Bartoli. The issue was—is this a surprise?—money. Should each get her usual fee? If so, that would mean that Bartoli would get more than an artist more than twice her age. Should they be equally compensated?

"Italians, they are calculating, ambitious, and extremely greedy,"

Herbert continued. "They carry money around their necks and they sleep with it. They have pillows to put it in. Did you know that? They have the most incredible imagination when it comes to money. Luciano showed everyone how it could be done. That's an achievement. He changed the face of opera today and hasn't given up the art in the process. He wants his money, but he hasn't lost the artistry, the voice. At the start, I said to him: If I can make you independent of everything and you can decide what you want to do and when and how, then that is the greatest achievement I could make.

"He showed Domingo how it could be done. He showed everyone. He opened up a whole new area of entertainment. Nobody in the tenor world has Luciano's sound, that Italian sound. In a fat body, but it doesn't matter. Domingo would have to go pray in seventeen churches in Guadalajara to find that sound.

"What is the future of the world of opera? I don't know. But today Mary Curtis-Verna would be worshipped as a goddess." The underappreciated Curtis-Verna was the soprano the Met pushed out onstage in the fifties and early sixties when someone more glamorous couldn't make it.

Herbert's institutional memory goes way back. He got into the music business after a miserable life as a speech writer in Detroit working for the automotive industry. His first major client was Elisabeth Schwarzkopf, the Prussian perfectionist whose artistry remains for many the touchstone, while detractors revile her as insufferably mannered and the politically conscious deplore her Nazi connections. His second was Joan Sutherland, the statuesque, down-home Aussie whose queen-size voice and awesome facility in coloratura earned her the nickname La Stupenda. Not much later, he did publicity for Sutherland's American mezzo counterpart and frequent partner, Marilyn Horne. She made him seventy-five dollars a month. That was in the early 1960s. Three years later he signed de Larrocha, who, in the days when it was still possible to say this, was said to play "like a man."

And as Breslin tells it himself: "In my thirty-five years in music, there have been few great singers I've had nothing to do with. Leontyne Price was one, and that was, I think, her mistake. And Maria

Callas, whose record company has succeeded in making people think she is still alive.

"The marketing is incredible," Herbert continued dreamily. "EMI merchandizes this stuff in their vaults as if it's new. It's a little bit like conversations with the other world. But no one at EMI sells as well as she does. She has an absolutely devoted following. She is the one single name in opera which is the standard by which others are measured. She is the quintessential opera singer and name. She was exciting. She was the Luciano Pavarotti of another time.

"Who is the Pavarotti of this generation? There is none. No, not Bartoli, because she doesn't sing the standard repertoire. She can't sing Mimì, she can't sing Tosca or *La traviata*, and she can't sing Aida, Manon Lescaut, or Desdemona. There is not one major role she can sing. . . . What did you say? Rosina? Are you crazy or something? She is a speciality singer.

"She has made a career out of singing two operas and twenty-four songs. Unbelievable! You can't build an opera house around someone who sings *The Barber of Seville*, Cenerentola, Despina. You can't be a major opera singer without singing the bread-and-butter repertoire. Big, big, big things don't happen to little Despina. Horne in her heyday could sing coloratura, but she also sang Carmen, Eboli, *Le Prophète*. And she sang Amneris—whether she did it fantastically well is something else. You can't even suggest Eboli to Cecilia Bartoli."

He laughed at the thought of it and looked out the window at a barren wintry landscape that spoke to his mood.

"You and I are a generation apart," he continued. "You name a protagonist of an opera and I'll tell you who I heard sing it. Aida: Madame Nilsson, Tebaldi, Milanov, Price—that's just four off the top. You cannot find anyone who is even in the shadow of these people. And Radames? Richard Tucker, Corelli, Mario del Monaco, Carlo Bergonzi. And I am just talking about artists who made opera tick. Today directors make opera tick, or they think they do. I think it's just marking time.

"I'm not only talking voice, I mean personality. Mariella Devia is a very good singer. She has the personality of a dead fish.

"And you must totally want your career. Luciano wanted it. He loves attention. He wanted it from the very beginning. You can't make big stars out of nobodies. Take Alessandra Marc. I got her her first concert. She rewarded me by going to another manager."

Herbert's client list has quite a high turnover, in both management and publicity. Not long ago, the soprano Carol Vaness flew off the management list in a rage, claiming she had lost gobs of money because the Breslin office had not properly handled tax payments on her overseas engagements. The settlement reached by lawyers forbids either party to discuss any details.

He was already having fits about something else anyway.

"Without voices in opera we are really screwed. How many times have you walked out of an opera house in a state of exaltation? Today there is too much opera. Too many houses that put on performances without a sufficiently high quality."

He launched into a favorite topic: the cluelessness of the potentially important singer, at sea without anyone to trust. In no time such a person will fall off the pedestal and nobody will care. He was talking about the talented Aprile Millo, pushed by the Met until her technique proved faulty. After a quavering encounter with Verdi's *I lombardi alla prima crociata*, a piece about confused crusaders, her career there began faltering badly.

"Long ago," Breslin insisted, "the Met had a serious coaching staff. At some point, Levine should have said: 'Aprile, get in here, honey. We have to talk.' But there's no money there. What's she gonna do, pay him fifty bucks an hour? Yet they have, what? over a thousand people who work in the Metropolitan. Where's the music department? The artistic department of the Met? I call it the autistic department of the Metropolitan." Herbert laughed so uproariously, he began choking and gasping for air.

People on the train craned their necks, staring at us. Breslin ignored them.

"They didn't give a shit, that's why. If you succeed, it's us; if you fail, it's because you're a talentless twit. C'mon. The art of singing opera is a very involved and complicated thing."

He began talking about Schwarzkopf. "She had more than voice and looks. She had preparation, and she wanted the best and surrounded herself with the best conductors. She made Strauss's Four Last Songs the most popular they have ever become. Her Elvira and Marschallin set standards. Was she a nice person? She was an extremely guarded lady, greatly intelligent, very careful. Now when I go to Germany, to Berlin, and look at all the people attentively attending concerts and being very civilized and polite, I say to myself: What happened? How could a country like this have bought into a philosophy of destruction and become marketers of poison?"

Breslin was having a *Weltanschauung* moment and not enjoying it. He picked at the remains of his doughnut with the defeated air of an aging Roman emperor.

"I worry about the world. You worry about Cecilia Bartoli and the world is going to hell. She can't even sing a Mozart song in German." True enough. Like most Italian singers, Bartoli has a block about learning German and was probably the first singer who had managed to combine a serious recital career with an avoidance of Mahler, Brahms, and Hugo Wolf—composers most closely identified with the more profound reaches of the song-literature repertoire.

"Maybe someday she will be remarkable. Luciano never wanted to be the most distinguished tenor in the world. He wanted to be the most successful. But there would be no Luciano without Luciano, and what that means is, boy, he's got it upstairs. Now, you talk about Cecilia Bartoli. It will be hard for her to be the future of opera without singing *La traviata*."

I struggled to demur. It was useless.

"Shut up and listen to me. Even *Cenerentola* is a minor piece, a dreary piece. I'm sure the public will love it. But let's see. Part of it is her charm. I'm not talking about her talent. She's doing very well. But I wouldn't want to put on her shoulders being the next Pavarotti.

"Talent is everything. . . . Are you awake? There is today a very serious threat to talent. That is the nature of the situation today. You have to assume that opera is a great, great art or you have to assume it is just tricks. What's in between is mediocrity, and I really . . ."

I must have passed out around then. Screeching brakes and a seismic jolt woke me up and announced our arrival in Philadelphia.

The ballroom of a luxury hotel blighting the lovely scale of

Rittenhouse Square was just filling up for the media event preceding the Pavarotti Competition. Right on time, the star attraction ambled up to the dais accompanied by Tibor Rudas, the Hungarian promoter of Pavarotti's mega-events (including this one). Breslin followed with Jane Nemeth, the competition's organizer, and various local politicos. Rudas expected to get his money back by videotaping an opera that will feature Mr. P singing with prizewinners. The press, mostly local-color writers, tossed him a few easy softballs ("What's your advice to young singers?" etc.).

Nobody brought up the C-free *Fille* or the "evil genius" seated by his side. "What I am looking for," Mr. P said before leaving for the auditions, "is someone to take your attention. Not perfect, not boring. So you don't turn to someone seated next to you and ask, 'How's your wife?' " (Otherwise, Adua Pavarotti and the divorce suit went unmentioned.)

Two days later, Mr. P was back in New York for the second *Fille du Régiment*. He wasn't feeling well, but got himself onstage anyway, only to stumble badly in the aria. "Pavarotti Chokes Up Mid-Opera, and Leaves," reported the headline in the *Times* the next day. He missed his Bs, took the rest of the aria down an octave, and did not reappear for the second act, leaving Anderson, who wasn't well herself, to soldier on with an understudy.

The farce continued. On Friday, November 10, 1995, the day before the *Fille* matinee, the *Times* ran another story, "Pavarotti Plans to Sing the Remaining *Fille*s."

But Pavarotti must not have read the *Times*. The next day he cancelled.

"What's to be learned from this story?" I asked Joe Volpe. The Met's general manager was sitting at his pristine desk framed by two towering palm trees. His shiny black shoes shone like spotlights under his desk, which was completely empty except for a pocket-sized date book and a small white pad on which he doodled incessantly, filling up page after page with straight lines which he would then tear off and fold neatly in half. The sleek dark suit, tightly cropped beard, and faintly sardonic air radiated the Machiavellian image he enjoyed cultivating.

"Get him here early," he said, somewhat mysteriously. "He was in Pesaro singing one of his pop concerts, and because this show got slotted in late, he didn't have the right time to prepare. Not that I really care if he sings Cs or Bs."

"What about the last Fille, Ms. Battle? Is she ever coming back to the Met?"

He beamed. He loved this question. "You know what I've said: Bing will be remembered for firing Maria Callas; I'll be remembered for firing Battle. Mine will be the bigger funeral."

Rudolf Bing, a legendary Met tyrant with an exaggerated sense of his own altitude, punished Callas when she thwarted his scheduling plans by refusing to alternate performances of Lady Macbeth and Violetta—roles requiring different attitudes and techniques. Before drifting into senescence, he muttered something about maybe feeling some regret, but Volpe seemed free of second thoughts.

"Wilford, Battle's manager, he really didn't care. CAMI is interested in the money. Their cut. Rarely have I heard anyone say to an artist: 'No, turn that down. It's not right for you.' "

I guessed Battle wasn't coming back.

"What about Bartoli?" I asked. "I hear you're doing *Cenerentola* for her?"

Cenerentola had never been staged at the Met in its entire history, which went back to 1883. Never mind the ever-present *Barber* and a very occasional special treat like *Semiramide* or *L'italiana in Algeri*, the bel canto operas are largely ignored in this house, because Levine, having buffed his orchestra, wants to show it off in Wagner, Puccini, and Verdi. A regular visitor to the Met would never know a major bel canto revival has been under way in the rest of the opera world.

"Yup," Volpe said. "It's on. Right now, the director is a question. First she wanted Zeffirelli. But that won't work. Then Giorgio Strehler, who takes four weeks to return a phone call. I guess he's old. It's probably not going to happen."

Volpe smiled and drew another set of prison bars. "These young people have such definite ideas," he continued. "Bryn Terfel, he's also telling me who we should get for the new *Nozze di Figaro*. He says to me: 'I know this opera better than any director. There's nothing I don't know about it.' But that's not what we're hiring. We're not hiring an expert. We're hiring a *director* to take a new look at it."

The Bartoli *Cenerentola* wasn't premiering until fall 1997. He had other things to worry about, he said.

"Like what?"

He ran down a long list that included the new production that spring of *Andrea Chénier* with Mr. P and Millo. Had she repaired her voice? He was going to Chicago soon to hear her do the same part, but he wasn't going to tell her so she wouldn't get nervous. "And then—" he took a deep breath and laughed his wheezy laugh—"then there's Teresa." Kurt Weill's *Mahagonny* was about to open with Teresa Stratas, meaning her understudy was on red alert. The general manager clearly had fond feelings for the Canadian soprano, a gut-wrenching little dynamo who had once escaped to India, where she joined Mother Teresa at her Calcutta hospital. But the sojourn had not increased her resistance to any number of germs, accidents, and afflictions, and nowadays she made Cecilia Bartoli with her occasional cancellations seem like the Health Department's poster child. Stratas had called him the other day, he said, moaning that her pipes hurt after she accidentally drank coffee left over from the day before.

"Well," Volpe said, leaning back in his leather chair and looking pleased. "We shall see. Sometimes this place is like an asylum for the insane."

CHAPTER FOUR

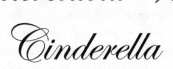

Cenerentola Visits Cinderella

ALL THAT REMAINS of the days when Orlando wasn't just the gateway to a jillion-dollar kingdom presided over by a courtly mouse are a few morsels of ornate architecture, including a defunct rail station. We'd now seen it several times twinkling in the dark. Energetic highway planners have been very active here these last few decades.

A few spooky wrong turns later, we finally arrived at the right shopping mall and the area's only starred Italian restaurant. The cozy place, possibly overdecorated with old bottles and fake bouquets, was full up when I reserved, but there's always room for a celebrity. A huge round table set for five was waiting for us smack in the center, surrounded by happy eaters. "Why doesn't Ms. Bartoli want the best table? . . . What did you say? It's too noisy?" Cupping his ear, the owner was visibly distressed. He glided away to see what could be done.

It was just after Thanksgiving, 1995, and Bartoli had finished a short, sold-out recital tour through Florida. She had two free days before driving to Fort Lauderdale to board the *Queen Elizabeth II* for the trip back home with her mother, sister, and boyfriend. I'd come down to join them on a visit to nearby Disney World, where the other Cinderella lives. She was expecting us at the castle tomorrow. Bartoli had been to Disneyland in California and liked it so much she didn't mind another visit to the Magic Kingdom. "Besides," as she said on the telephone, "what else is there to do in Orlando?" She doesn't play golf and had already explored some of the area's 148 outlet stores looking for a bargain camcorder by the time I arrived.

The owner reappeared. He had worked a miracle! he exclaimed, leading us excitedly to a table next to a small partition that was promisingly adorned with a photograph of a smiling, well-fed Pavarotti. It also seemed protected from the wandering accordion player.

Large menus arrived. Federica Bartoli, a disturbingly thin girl in her mid-twenties, giggly and sweet, couldn't find anything she liked. "Oh, come on, eat something," begged her mother. A risotto? A salad? No? Please, how about a brodo? She was persuaded. She would join her mother in a brodo and maybe pick at some pasta. Federica's eating habits are different from her sister's, who always finds something to eat. Rossini would have adored Cecilia. He said he cried twice in his life: once when he heard Paganini play his fabled violin and then again when he saw a lovely truffle-stuffed turkey fall off a wobbly table on a yacht. His healthy appetite is commemorated in tournedos Rossini—thick slices of beef filet browned in butter, resting on toast and topped off by a slice of foie gras or truffle slivers. Unfortunately not on the menu here in Orlando.

My Italian goes beyond menu and libretto reading, but not by much; Silvana and Federica don't speak English, Osele speaks a little but is taciturn even in Italian: a polite, pleasant fellow in a blue blazer, he's forthcoming to a point. "What wine do you prefer?" was his question for the night. We left that to him, with his vintner's knowledge, and the Bardolino was well chosen. Bartoli, fortunately, was becoming quite fluent in the colloquial English she started picking up on her first visit to the United States in 1990, and had taught herself a surprisingly good French. Though not a big talker in any language, she's a good listener and inquisitive when the topic is music. I'd just started V. S. Pritchett's biography of Turgenev, the Russian playwright who became obsessed with the Spanish-French celebrity Pauline Viardot-Garcia. Bartoli happened to be recording the songs of the diva, who was also a composer, writer, and Slavophilic eccentric.

When Pauline visited St. Petersburg in the 1850s, Turgenev attended all her performances. So overcome was he, yelling after every song and making such a spectacle of himself, she finally became curious. "Bring me that large young madman," she decreed. The dream of every opera fan! He was brought backstage and allowed to sit at her feet on her bear rug. Three years later—Viardot returned regularly to Russia—he followed her back to Courtavenel, where she lived with her husband, Louis. There he enjoyed for many years an opaque ménage à trois with Pauline and her husband that inspired his great play *A Month in the Country*—and several librettos the restless Pauline set to music. They're totally forgotten, but perhaps Osele with his musicological interests could dig them up.

"The songs are delicious," Bartoli said. I'd heard a few at a recital she once gave in Munich with Myung-Whun Chung at the piano, and they are indeed enchanting. Songs like "Havanaise" suggest Viardot wrote easily, seductively for the mezzo voice while inspiring others to even greater creative flights. Brahms wrote his Alto Rhapsody for her, and Meyerbeer one of the great mother roles in opera history: Fidès in his scary opera about religious dementia, *Le Prophète*.

"A role for you?"

She thought probably not. "It's heavy for right now. A Horne role, correct?" Yes. Horne sang Fidès in a rare staging at the Met years ago.

We talked about Viardot's more celebrated sister, Maria Malibran, who made her debut at age seventeen in *Barber* in London and died when she was only twenty-eight. Injured in a riding accident while pregnant, Malibran succumbed to septicemia accelerated by exhaustion. So possessed was Malibran of a need to sing and triumph, so devoted was she to her audience and art, she engaged in a vocal duel with a rival diva at a concert that took place only days before her death. By then she could barely stand up.

Her story seems like material for an opera or a movie.

Bartoli liked the idea.

"But who would you duel with?" Osele asked. "Jennifer Larmore?"

She raised an eyebrow. For a while, things had seemed to be heating up between Bartoli and the American mezzo with the ruby-rich voice. Larmore sang many of the same roles and had already made her debut at the Met, in *Barber*, but her way to the top was considerably longer and more difficult. Several inches taller and a few decibels louder, Larmore was also older and went through a phase in which she liked to wonder aloud whether Bartoli was in fact the age she claimed to be. "She looks forty! at least!" she liked to say. Which led Bartoli to flash her passport at whoever wished to see it. Teldec, Larmore's record company, even issued a *Cenerentola* album with their mezzo on the cover in the same costume from the same production as Bartoli wears on hers. But neither really has the personality for a good old-fashioned war of the divas in the Callas-Tebaldi mode that so entertained another generation.

"It's . . . it's, well, it's like comparing champagne to Coca-Cola," was how the Greek deity assessed their differences to a delighted reporter long ago.

"I actually like a lot of my colleagues," Bartoli insisted, "but real friendship is a little hard now that I travel so much and life is so different. I don't even see the people I went to school with."

She paused as her steak was presented with great flourish. "But I must mention Fiamma. She made the connection to Karajan."

Fiamma Izzo d'Amico was three years ahead of her at the music conservatory in Rome, a dark-haired, lavender-eyed beauty who was already making a name for herself. She took a tape of Bartoli to Herbert von Karajan; he quickly invited her to Salzburg, which he ran like a private fiefdom, presiding over both the Easter and the summer festival until his death in 1990. The charismatic *über*-maestro and rooster-haired tyrant had a reputation, entirely deserved, as a voice killer. He fancied, for instance, lyric sopranos singing Wagner.

Karajan asked Bartoli to sing Bach's B-minor Mass, including the part for contralto. "I told him that I can sing the first aria but I cannot sing the Agnus Dei. It is too low for me. He said: 'Oh, don't worry, I'll keep the orchestra low for you.' But I still wouldn't do it. So finally he got Florence Quivar to do the contralto part, and fortunately still let me sing the rest."

I was impressed. Someone not yet twenty standing up to Karajan—not an experience many survived without punishment. Thomas Allen, perhaps the most elegant Mozart baritone of his generation, who would sing Don Alfonso to her Despina at the Met when she made her debut there in February, once told me how Karajan tried bullying him into singing heavy Verdi roles during an audience (that would be the right word) at Salzburg. Allen was just into his early thirties and eager to appear in the summer festival. But he decided to say no. While the offer could be a passport to the greatest success, it could also be a death warrant. More than a decade passed before he—one of the world's acclaimed Don Giovannis—was invited back to Mozart's hometown.

Bartoli's friend Fiamma was not so strong. Karajan cajoled her into singing the mature role of Elisabetta in Verdi's *Don Carlo* while still in her twenties, and she soon ran into vocal trouble that prematurely derailed her promising career. But Bartoli must have charmed the maestro, and he was planning future projects with her at the time of his death. All that remains of their brief encounter is a video showing bits of the B-minor rehearsals. Utterly unknown then, she was listed by Deutsche Grammophon as Cecilia Bardi.

"What's the worst part about getting famous?"

She reflected. "At home in Rome actually, it is not a problem. People don't know me really. I can go anywhere. But elsewhere, I guess it's the strangers who come up to you after a performance. Sometimes, it's too much."

Opera singers invariably attract strange people. June Anderson used to be shadowed by a man she called Dracula for his glistening hair, cape, and teeth that sparkled out at her from the dark. I've seen men sitting in the first row with field glasses at Bartoli concerts. In Munich, even that was not close enough for one admirer, who leapt to the stage holding a bunch of flowers. He was just a love-besotted boy. But Cecilia told a story of a woman in Miami who recently shook her up.

" 'Please, please, you must help us,' she said in a mixture of Spanish and English. 'My husband, he is dying. Please, you must help us.' I was signing autographs. What could I do? So I asked: 'What do you want?' And she goes on about how he is dying and I am the only person in the world who can help him. 'But how?' I keep asking. 'What do you want?' So she says: 'He is a pianist and he wants to play for you before he dies.' Mamma mia! 'What is his malady?' I asked her. Anyway, I can't quite figure out what she is saying, but finally she gives me a video. Well, a while later we play the tape and it's a thing very peculiar. You see the woman, the husband, a daughter, and her fiancé. The daughter starts with this strange, rehearsed little speech, saying, 'Cecilia, you are a wonderful human being and we know you will help us.' So on. Like that. Then finally, the husband begins playing the piano. He's not very good, but his health is obviously not bad. Certainly he's not dying. Or sick. The wife is sick. In the head. It's all some weird thing to get me to what? I don't even know. Hire him? It was bizarre."

"It's true," said Silvana, shaking her head. "We meet so many peculiar persons. They have great fantasies, and we sometimes worry what they are."

WE REGROUPED the next morning in the lobby of our hotel for our trip to Disney World. Bartoli was looking a little confused standing by the counter talking to our guides, two girls dispatched by the VIP office. "What's Epcot?" she asked, adjusting the money belt she usually wears around her waist. She had somehow signed us up for a tour of Epcot, the futuristic part of Walt Disney World and a long monorail ride away from Cinderella's castle. This was not good, and I must have looked horrified.

"What is the thing with Cinderella's *castello* anyway?" she asked, a little suspiciously. I told her that's where little American girls go to dream dreams that probably won't come true while they look up and hear songs like "When You Wish Upon a Star" booming from the turrets. "Wouldn't it be interesting to hear what their dreams might be?" I asked her.

"In a way, even your dream didn't come true," I joked. "You got someone else's dream. You really wanted to be a flamenco dancer, right?"

She didn't seem to share my curiosity but shrugged amiably. "Okay," she said. "The *castello*. Later in the afternoon."

The parking lot was already half full by the time we arrived at eleven in the morning. A motherly talking monorail sped us along until we arrived at the gates, whereupon the disembodied voice reminded us to be very careful as we got off. An excruciating concern for our well-being (or litigious instincts) was the day's leitmotif. Here in Walt's World the infantilization of America has reached its purest, highest state.

"Have a wonderful day and watch your step," cautioned a young astronaut easing us into little cars called time machines. We entered the dark inner sanctum of a large, shiny geosphere called Spaceship Earth and now travelled smoothly on conveyer belts past huge dioramas with robotic, spookily lifelike pharaohs, Roman senators, and Michelangelo painting the Sistine ceiling. Just as we reached the space age, where "distances are immaterial," an old guy fell out of his space capsule, briefly bringing our infinite journey to a jolting halt.

Otherwise, everything functioned as beautifully as most of America does not, which is why this place is the most popular vacation spot on the planet.

For twenty-seven bucks a day you get a glimpse of the good life you might someday lead in a retirement community, perhaps in this very state, a place with fabulous garbage pickup, pleasant and omnipresent security guards disguised as ordinary folk, and surrounded by a moat.

"What do you think of this place?" I asked Cecilia's mother, as she stumbled out from Spaceship Earth blinking at the sun.

She is a polite woman, and she struggled for words as she looked around the geosphere with its many litter receptacles and little people attached to beaming adults in gym clothes.

"Very clean, *bello*," is what she said. They do live in Rome with all those old ruins.

Over the next two hours, we watched sea cows eating large cabbages at a very leisurely pace, and ate ice cream shaped like mouse heads, sold by a pod person who warned us they are "very frozen."

"What else would they be? It's ice cream? Isn't it?" Cecilia asked, turning to me in confusion. As the Bartolis stared in amazement, the pod person continued, "You bite on it hard and you can break a tooth! It's like a lethal weapon. Be careful!"

The mouse head's 330 calories seemed more of a threat, but we probably walked them off marching past replicas of Japan, Morocco, and the United Kingdom.

This is a small world only if you're Peter Pan.

Finally, we came to a slack-jawed stop on the shores of an artificial lagoon. Far away on the other side, the Piazza San Marco gleamed like a mirage in the humid haze. The scaled-down replica is part of Epcot's "immensely amazing" (in girl-guide speak) World Showcase, where visitors can make believe they are in Norway (why would anyone want to do that?) or China or Canada without having to go there and deal with funny people speaking funny languages like Italian.

Why any real Italians would want to see a fake Italy is really hard to figure.

Osele suddenly stirred to life. "I think they make a mistake, no?" he asked, staring across the waters toward Venice in the distance. Something wasn't quite right. He was trying to figure it out. Indeed, Epcot engineers had seen the need to improve on the real thing and shifted the piazza's cumbersome tower to the right of the Ducal Palace. It just looked better that way.

"L'Originale Alfredo di Roma" was the destination chosen by our guides and hardly resisted by the Bartolis. The restaurant shared a piazza with two shops: Delizie Italiane, featuring Perugina cookies and chocolates, and Il Bel Cristallo, a Capodimonte outlet.

"Ever go to the original Alfredo?" I asked my Roman companions, who had just been seated with gratingly extravagant courtesy at a huge table in a room ten times the size of any trattoria. "Never heard of it," said Silvana. Even so, I knew we were sunk. The Bartolis had spied the menu, and all interest in Cinderella's castle was receding by the nanosecond.

A brodo maybe? Followed by the antipasto plate? A little pasta? Maybe the ravioli? Gamberoni? Insalata? Steak? Two hours later, when dessert was contemplated, I gave up. My plane was leaving in three hours, and it looked like Delizie Italiane would require a visit.

Maybe they were worried about the cuisine aboard the QE2 and thought it wise to stock up.

WALKING ALONG Central Park West three days later, I just about collided with a pallid-looking couple. The weather had been so terrible, they'd decided to fly home, Osele said as Bartoli grabbed her stomach. A few hours before, when the QE2 pulled into New York to pick up more passengers, they'd dragged their bags off and headed for Mastroianni's apartment. "The winter seas," Bartoli explained. "I just hadn't realized. What a nightmare. My mother was up all night. She wants to go home and, well, we're all going. Tonight." They were off to see her accountant, having left Silvana and Federica to prepare lunch.

I continued up Central Park West to Mastroianni's office. He was in major diva dienst, dialing one number after another, while his assistant dealt with the business-class Alitalia bookings.

"What a mess," he said, as we walked from his office to the apartment behind Lincoln Center. Cunard Lines had expected Bartoli to give a recital in exchange for her passage. A limo needed to be arranged for the trip to the airport. Was there enough room for Christopher Raeburn and his luggage? Her sound guru had spent Thanksgiving with his daughter in California. Bartoli had bought him a ticket on the QE2 as a gift, but he obviously wasn't going to travel by himself.

"On top of that, there's Jeff Cohen," Mastroianni continued, referring to the pianist who'd flown to New York from his Paris home to work on new music with Cecilia during the crossing. He was leaving plaintive messages on the answering machine.

"Mamma! How's everything!" Mastroianni yelled, stepping over six pieces of luggage. I guessed Raeburn would need his own cab. Silvana waved with a ladle from the kitchen. She was cooking up a pot of spaghetti and slicing tomatoes. Federica was setting the table. Raeburn was sitting on the sofa looking through a new biography of Renata Tebaldi. The Italian superlegend was coming to New York next week for the first time since she quit singing. She was Decca's big recording star well into the 1960s, and was still a godsend to Poly-Gram's bottom line. Newly pressed onto CDs, her old recordings of *La Bohème*, *Tosca*, *Aida*, and *La Gioconda* sold better than most new releases.

Raeburn leafed through the book unperturbed, it would seem, by the sudden change in plans.

"Actually," he confided as I sat next to him, "I'm eager to get home. This is quite all right with me." He stared at a photograph of Tebaldi looking imperious on the cover of *Time* magazine in 1958. "What bearing. Lovely woman, very thoughtful. Always courteous to her colleagues. And really quite dismayed by Mario del Monaco's manners. He was a natural bully who just never considered anyone but himself."

Maybe he just couldn't help himself. Tenors are not highly regarded for their spiritual or brainy side.

Mastroianni peered over his shoulder and offered his favorite tenor joke, which went like this:

"How can you tell if a tenor is dead?

"The wine bottle is still full and the comics haven't been touched."

The door opened and Bartoli and Osele came in from their hour with the accountant, throwing their coats on the luggage. "You really must meet Tebaldi sometime," Raeburn said to her as she flopped down on the couch looking beat. Maybe she was overdrawn at the bank.

"Cecilia," said Mastroianni, stepping on his terrace and looking over the Hudson River. "Look what's leaving."

We both got up, Bartoli pulling her sweater up around her throat. The QE2 was slowly gliding out to sea without the promised entertainment. She looked more tired than guilty.

In Milan, Renata Tebaldi was dusting off her luggage, heading the other way.

CHAPTER FIVE

Queen of the Met

THOUGH SHE WASN'T EXPECTED for another half
hour, the crowd had already swelled from a handful of
early arrivals to several hundred huddling in the chilly
underground passageway outside the drafty entrance to what the
Metropolitan Opera calls Founders' Hall, though it is somewhat lacking in festive dimensions. Founders' Hall is where you catch pneumo-
nia standing on long lines waiting to check your coat or buy a
brownie during intermission.

Most were carrying shopping bags stuffed with old LPs and photographs. The age range seemed from around twelve to maybe one
hundred. Finally, the limo arrived, half an hour late, but she's Italian,
and cries of "Renata! Renata!" echoed through the corridor just like
in the old days when Renata Tebaldi was queen of the Met.

Policemen extracted the mink-draped divinity from her car and
led her into the hall, which has glass walls on the passageway. Worshippers pressed their noses to the cold glass to watch her maid of
many decades relieve the diva of her coat and pocketbook. Slowly,

she approached a table set up with flowers, Magic Markers, and copies of a new biography that had just been translated into English.

Tebaldi: The Voice of an Angel is somewhat lacking in investigative vigor, as the title might suggest. The connoisseurs standing on line passed the time pointing out mistakes in the captions ("That hairdo! Definitely from a later period!"). But the pictures are great, the book had brought the seventy-three-year-old diva back to New York after nearly twenty years, and who could object to its question-and-answer section, which includes this heavenly exchange between writer and singer:

Question: "What physical discipline did you impose on your body? Posture? Thorax? Neck? Position of head?"

Answer: "A cardinal rule of singing is an erect posture without rigidity for maximum use of the diaphragm. . . ."

Watching her sign away, happy memories were mine. In the mid-1960s, when I was very young and she was already legendary, Renata Tebaldi was opera incarnate. She was approachable yet mysterious, classy and charmingly corny. I first heard her name from a school friend's mother, who worshipped Ayn Rand and made me read *The Fountainhead* for its inspirational story of a master architect who refused to be bound by the pedestrian rules of little people. Mrs. Kubovsky, who came from the Old World like my parents, and who was possibly even more eccentric, knew a lot about classical music. One day she told me there was a singer at the Met who built empires out of sound. This soprano was so spellbinding she transformed the ordinary notes available to everybody into the stuff of memory. Her name was Renata Tebaldi and she came from Milan. My mother, already horrified that a thirteen-year-old was reading libertarian propaganda that seemed unpleasantly reminiscent of *Übermensch* theories she had barely survived, only slowly came around to the notion of taking me to the Met, and finally got us tickets to *Aida*. But when I looked at my program, Tebaldi was not listed. I was astonished and upset. I thought Tebaldi sang every night, like in a Broadway musical. I extracted from my mother a highlights album with a glamorously glowering Tebaldi in an off-the-shoulder green gown (and I had thought opera singers were tubs of lard!) and a promise to return. To this day I can remember the strange excitement that came over me as a tall, aristocratic woman with a radiant smile, a walking staff, and a long train swept into the church of Sant'Andrea della Valle looking for her painter boyfriend. "Mario, Mario!" she called, but it might as well have been my name. Nutty Mrs. K had been right. As *Tosca's* lush music swirled up from the darkly glistening immensity of the stage, I was swept away into a world of mystery and poetry so different from my everyday existence in blue-collar suburbia I could not bear to leave. And I suppose I never did.

None of us knew much about her private life and liked it that way, because we could dream she was still searching for the perfect person to carry her suitcase or more. Leafing through the book, I was even now dismayed at the suggestion that she may have had an affair with hack conductor Arturo Basile. I put it down and returned to the past, the "Merry Xmas" cards she sent, the dressing rooms filled with poodles and sables. She brought a personal charisma to every part she sang and knew us opera kids by name. Well, pretty much. "Emmanuella," she would smile. "Have you finally passed French?" Tebaldi weeping into Mimi's muff, Tebaldi coughing into Adriana's poisoned flowers, Tebaldi throwing cards into the air as Minnie, Puccini's Bible-quoting, gun-toting saloon mistress. We have all expunged from our memory, of course, the high Cs. High C was never a favorite Tebaldi note, and as the 1960s gave way to the early '70s, when she retired, high B could also be a problem, so we helped her out, yelling "Brava!" early. Never mind her cardinal rule of singing: as her career was ending and her technique failed her, Tebaldi spent a lot of anxious time staring at her shoes and clenching her hands so fiercely she could give blood immediately after an aria.

I saw her only once after her singing days were over, in London in 1993 in the lobby of the Savoy. Two days earlier, she had caused a traffic jam at a record store in the Strand signing CD releases of her old recordings. I had somehow found out she was leaving that morning and had run over with a friend to see her off. I'm not sure she recognized the kid who was always flunking French, but she was immensely polite, if apprehensive about returning to New York. "Do you think they remember me? So many years . . ." she asked pensively.

Here was her answer: hundreds waiting for their turn at the table, where Jane Poole, the managing editor of *Opera News*, was hovering attentively. For many years, Poole showed her deep devotion by wearing a teased flip à la Renata. Victor Callegari, the Met's makeup artist, himself in his thirtieth season, stopped by to stare in wonder and remember a diva who never gave him any trouble. "None of that 'make my eyelashes longer' stuff; she was so sweet," he said. CAMI's Matthew Epstein arrived to survey the scene, standing not far from the tunnel to the Met's parking garage where as a young man he often slept clutching the "snakes"—the weekly cast sheets printed up on cheap paper—and waiting for morning, when standing room tickets would go on sale for Ponchielli's *La Gioconda* (Happy Girl), a deluxe B opera about a suicidal singer of ballads that used to provoke great mirth in the late sixties when the corps de ballet arrived to dance to music that had been transmogrified into the song, "Hello muddah, hello faddah, here I am at Camp Granada."

"I just had to see this," he said, looking around at the growing crowd. He raised his eyebrows and looked satisfied.

Tebaldi hadn't been in this house since 1973, when she submitted to one last strangulation as Desdemona. A Carnegie Hall recital in January of 1976 marked her unofficial farewell to New York. For a while there was talk of a concert at Avery Fisher or a formal adieu from the Met, but it never happened, and finally she simply stopped.

A misty-eyed elderly man approached with the news that he had built a private Tebaldi museum in his house in Queens, and got to hold her hand for a minute. The line pressed forward at a glacial pace. Elegantly enshrined in a superbly tailored carmine suit with big gold buttons, gold earrings, and a gold choke, she signed away. Underneath the swept-back hair, a few shades down from the flamboyant Titian red of her younger years, the blue eyes and famous dimples that lit up the darkest stage still worked their magic. By two-thirty the line outside was so long it looped out of the Met into the plaza and toward Broadway. Met officials saw a problem in the making. Tonight the doors were to open early for Wagner's endless *Die Meistersinger*, an opera Renata once sang in Italian before she thoughtfully concentrated on pieces that finished in three hours. Disappoint her fans? Never. Gathering up her Magic Markers, Tebaldi moved across the corridor into the Met's gift shop and signed for another hour.

"How do you explain over a thousand people showing up to see a senior soprano who disappeared from town nearly twenty years ago?" I asked Epstein.

"People are starved for stars and for the generousness of her spirit. She gave so much love to us," he said. "And now she's getting some back." He himself had done his share, going through old Rolodexes, calling everyone he could remember from the standing-room days, looking for the old-timers who had seen all twenty-six Tebaldi *Giocondas*. They were invited to a champagne reception at eight p.m. at his apartment. Tebaldi was expected.

I'd only seen fifteen. But how was he to know? I invited myself to his party.

Epstein holds court at the Ansonia, a bulbously grand landmark on Manhattan's Upper West Side that has accumulated dust and eccentrics ever since it opened at the turn of the century as one of the largest apartment-hotels in the world. Caruso called it home for a while. Musicians love the Ansonia because the walls are three feet thick.

Long ago, when I'd just started working at the *Wall Street Journal*, I visited Teresa Stratas here, who told me one of the saddest stories I've ever heard about the lonely center so often at the heart of fame. A friend of hers had called on Maria Callas in her shuttered Paris flat not long before she died. The singer was sitting in her living room surrounded by clip books. "Why didn't they like me?" she asked softly, leafing through a large volume of reviews. One of the greatest singers of the century, pained by the squirrelly words of little people writing on deadline. The thought gave me quite a fright and writer's block for some time.

Either a lot of people had endured a lot of *Giocondas* or a lot of people had lied. By eight, a weepy, noisy crowd of aging singers and standees spilled out from Epstein's apartment and into the wide hall.

Mignon Dunn, the mezzo who sang La Cieca, Gioconda's blind old mother, in the premiere of Tebaldi's Met production, sat on the couch eating pastries with Marilyn Horne, who sang Laura, Gioconda's high-born rival for the unworthy tenor, in Tebaldi's recording. They were about to receive a visit from a legendary fan. Buttressed by two shopping bags stuffed with photographs, Lois Kirschenbaum, once the standee line's stern head mistress, had arrived.

None of today's stars would draw such a crowd at a record signing. "Not Luciano, not Cecilia," mused Hans Boon, and he should know. Once employed by Decca, the bony Boon now works with Herbert Breslin on the Pavarotti account. "No, not even Luciano has them standing for hours," he insisted. "She had the kind of mystique that is really gone from the opera world. She was larger than life. She was special."

Television had something to do with this. Though Tebaldi tapes exist, the cameras did not peer down this queen's gullet. Her upper lip never glistened with pearls of sweat. From the Golden Age of Fantasy we have plunged headlong into the Iron Age of Documentary and lost a good deal of mystery. In the Reign of Rivals, of Callas and Tebaldi, singers who did impossible feats onstage were not expected to deflate into normal-size next-door neighbors when the curtain fell.

Would Tebaldi never arrive? Finally, the elevator opened and she stepped out with her maid. Tired? "No, no! Thank you very much!" she chirped, nearly crushing a tiny woman, perhaps four feet tall and at least ninety. "You know who this is, don't you, Renata!" Epstein yelled, grabbing her arms. "Dio!" she exclaimed, bending down until she was within earshot of Nelly Walter, her manager at CAMI long ago, who came over as a child from Austria, where she had sat on Gustav Mahler's lap.

Their whispers were interrupted by a phone call from Bonn. *Bonn?* She obviously looked puzzled. The caller was Eugene Kohn, a standee who grew up to be a conductor. The phone rang again. "Renata," Epstein announced, "I've got Aprile on the phone!" Millo, who tends a shrine to the diva in her New York apartment and on a good day sounds eerily like her, was calling from her dressing room at the Lyric Opera of Chicago, where she was singing *Andrea Chénier*. After a few minutes, she put Bruno Bartoletti on the line for another long-distance embrace. He conducted Tebaldi in a 1970 recording of *Un ballo in maschera* with Pavarotti, her last complete opera recording and not her best, though the set sounds pretty golden by the standards of today.

As if to make that point, Tebaldi spent one of her evenings attending a performance of *Ballo* at the Met in an outsized, nonsensical production once staged for Pavarotti, but now offering only the pitch-free, pint-sized Francisco Araiza. When he stood next to the ample Amelia of the evening, Deborah Voigt, it looked as if she were ventriloquizing with a hand puppet. Not that it much mattered. Word had gone out that Tebaldi would attend, and many people bought tickets just to see her in the audience. As she slowly walked down the aisle (having refused Volpe's box so her audience could approach), people stood up and cheered.

Suddenly, a familiar plump presence leaned down from a box, yelling, "Renata, Renata!" It was Millo, dressed in black with a huge décolletage; she was half over the railing, waving with both hands. Her balance seemed precarious. "Aprile," gasped a friend, looking up. "Aren't you meant to be singing in Chicago? What are you doing here?"

"I just had to come!" she yelled back. "I had to see her!" She had flown home between performances. "It's like the second coming!"

"HOW HAS THE OPERA WORLD changed in the last thirty years?" I asked Matthew Epstein after Tebaldi had gone back to Milan and things had simmered down. We were sitting in the Ansonia apartment washing down macadamia nuts with seltzer.

One major change of course was that Matthew had gone from standing room to orchestra seats with a clear view of the select group of CAMI artists he managed, singers like Samuel Ramey, Catherine Malfitano, Frederica von Stade, and lately Renée Fleming, perhaps the most gorgeous lyric soprano to come along since Te Kanawa and maybe even Tebaldi, though without her pathos. That Epstein also advises the Lyric Opera of Chicago, the San Francisco Opera, the Santa Fe Opera, and Sony Classical records puts CAMI smartly right into the supply-and-demand side of things in ways that would provoke fascinated inquiries from the SEC in the investment world but are accepted in the music business. Young singers dream of auditioning for Epstein right here in this living room with its posters from La Scala, autographs of Rossini, and statue of Mickey Mouse peeking in from the veranda.

"First let me show you something," he said, mysteriously padding away on his thick white socks. He reappeared, holding a compact disc. "Look at the cover," he ordered.

I did as he told me. The cover said: "Queen of the Night: Cheryl Studer. Mozart Arias. Priced so low, you can't say no."

Epstein raised his eyebrows. "This is a lady who had it all. Everything happens so quickly nowadays. That's what is interesting and different. In the Bing years, he would send his talent scouts around and they would say to him in 1951: 'We hear there is a wonderful soprano coming along.' 'Oh,' he would say, 'who's that?' 'Her name is Callas,' they'd say.

"And he'd go: 'Ahaaaa. Mmmm.' And she'd turn up five years later at the Met.

"Everything is faster now, and what is really interesting is the lack of long-term vision, really long-term." Epstein's CAMI had been myopic with Bartoli, but that is not what he was getting at.

"What I'm afraid about is exactly this," he said, gesturing at the Studer CD. "This was made in 1990, and here it is in the close-out section of a record store. When I heard her as Micaëla in Chicago in about 1987–88, she had a real full-voiced lyric soprano of superb quality. Then she went into Wagner, Strauss, and insane *ottocento* stuff. Everything." He paused.

"No one is good at everything. The challenge of a career is finding a very small number of roles you're good at. I'm of the opinion there is something good about being a great Verdi tenor, a great bel canto soprano.

"I'm not in the Bartoli camp yet," he continued. "Will she go the distance? I don't know. I first encountered her accidentally. I was in Rome because Leonard Bernstein was recording *Bohème*, and there was a production of *Barber of Seville* at the Rome Opera. So I toddled over and I heard a charming young girl sing Rosina. An unknown pretty girl with a small, attractive voice. I called up some colleagues, Bruce Zemsky and Alan Green, and said, 'You should get her.' And they did.

"She was talented. I didn't think she was more talented than many young artists I'd heard, though I did make that call. So something obviously impressed me. I'm still not sure. She's got something in addition to great PR. But it's hard to say why it happened or how long it will last. We won't know for another five or six years."

I asked him why some singers last and others don't.

"It's not always voice," he answered. "It's emotional security, intelligence, chance. Careers are determined by so many factors. What I can contribute is keeping someone on the right trajectory. But I'm not a shrink or marriage counselor. I've seen people's careers harmed by emotional difficulties, wrong repertoire choices, and schedules that were too unchallenging and kept them from growing artistically."

"Ever make a mistake?"

He hesitated for a second. Is it conceivable? "Well, Thomas Hampson proved me wrong years ago when I told him he shouldn't do the Count in *Le nozze di Figaro* at the Met." Hampson's Count, sung on short notice, whirled his career into a higher orbit.

Epstein reached for a nut and leaned back on his beige sofa sectional. "What is not often recognized is that ninety percent of career self-destruction is done by the artists themselves. They are willful. They get lonely. Some have terrible parents.

"And then, let's be honest about it, they sing to be loved by a lot of people. That's already a peculiar interaction. A lot of people get to the top and think they don't deserve to be there. What does a little black girl, one of eight children from Ohio, who was brought up in poverty, think when she's making $15,000 a performance and more?" He meant Kathleen Battle.

"It's got to be somehow distressing. Can she believe she truly deserves that? Add adulation and of course it creates peculiar behavior sometimes."

Tebaldi was also famously stubborn and once insisted Bing give her a production of Cilea's brainless *Adriana Lecouvreur*.

"What's different now?" I wanted to know.

"Different expectations," he answered. " 'Diva' meant something in the old days—grand and unknowable. Today, we like divas, but then we also demand that they be easy and nice. Everybody's got to be nice. Cecilia Bartoli's got to be the girl next door or the best Italian thing since pasta. That's stupid, boring. If she wants to be difficult or impossible, she should jolly well do it. It's the job of people who work in the profession to be helpful and supportive of her. Opera managers don't seem to understand this anymore. They're quick to fire someone because they aren't singing well for six months or because they had a baby or are going through some bad patch.

"Things didn't move so fast in Tebaldi's day. There's a quick cruelty to the profession now."

"What's the worst that could happen to Bartoli?"

"One major disaster in an opera house and the career could disappear. Why? Because she has not established the kind of loyalty we saw with Tebaldi. For whatever reason—the excessively high fees charged by her manager or her own concepts—she hasn't sung enough opera."

He popped another macadamia into his mouth and smiled.

CHAPTER SIX

Where's the Maid?

*S*ARAH BILLINGHURST said goodbye to Despina and looked up from her cluttered desk at the Metropolitan Opera. Ideally, Despina should have been at the Met, rehearsing for her debut on February 8, 1996, which was just three weeks away. But Despina was in Rome, in bed. Just after Christmas, Bartoli had gone to London to record *Orfeo ed Euridice*, Haydn's little-known treatment of the most perennial of all operatic subjects. It rained; she caught a cold and flew home without completing her part.

"Well, she promised to get on the Concorde flight from Paris to New York next Thursday at the latest," Billinghurst announced, peering over a blooming orchid in her sunny office, a corridor and secret door away from the Met's lobby. Now it's Tuesday. "She better get here, don't you agree?" Her phone rang again and distracted her. She listened to the caller while staring blankly out the window.

Billinghurst, a New Zealander who spent long years at the San Francisco Opera, is number three at the Met, hired in 1995 by Joe Volpe, the general manager, as a soft buffer between himself and Levine. (In transit, Sally became Sarah, in keeping with the Met's greater formality and her expanding sphere of influence and sense of self.) Responsible for casting and artistic planning as well as the Met's video projects and telecasts, Billinghurst spends her days talking to singers and their managers, to directors and conductors, and her evenings watching and listening—wondering, just for example, if the evening's wan tenor is just going through a bad patch or losing his voice.

Years ago, the Met pioneered forward planning to an insane degree—signing up artists as far as five years in advance, which was then unheard of, but forced other companies to follow suit. That is why singers sometimes find themselves in inappropriate roles they hate or have outgrown, because when the offers came they were hungry and eager, and why programs can't be easily changed to insert new stars. Billinghurst's position is newly created and overlaps in degrees even insiders cannot fathom with the duties of Levine's loyal retainer Jonathan Friend, the man who turns the maestro's wishes into contracts. He's been at the Met since the 1980s, an apple-cheeked workaholic in his late thirties with a curly head stuffed with facts and numbers. Say "Rodolfo" to Friend and he can tell you who is singing Puccini's threadbare poet in every opera company in the world this season, and who among the current crop of youngsters might undertake the part a few years hence. He keeps an eye on the vast army of covers—the ever-hopeful bunch of understudies—and also has a grasp of the amount of expensive rehearsal time each opera requires and how it will likely fare at the box office.

By now union regulations are so complex that magic and contortion and truly generous donors are required to get instrumentalists, choristers, and soloists together in one place at one time. Cosseted by contracts that would be laughed at in the profit-making world, orchestra players, for instance, are usually protected from rehearsing for more than fifty minutes without pausing (difficult for Wagner), nor do their mandated breaks always coincide with those of the delicate flowers of the chorus, who also require constant resting.

Having to report to Billinghurst drained Friend's reservoir of charm for a while: "You're sorry you got my voice mail, and so am I. So why don't you do us both a favor and dial o. But if you insist, *insist* on leaving a message, oh, I suppose I check my voice mail once in a while. Don't bother having a nice day. I'm not." He was finally persuaded to change his message after the switchboard nearly broke down with insistent callers.

Friend is often the gray-suited bearer of bad news who steps in front of the curtain at performances featuring singers who are feeling the show will just have to proceed without them. These cancellation speeches have been known to provoke spontaneous applause for their polished variations on a theme, especially this one, delivered without notes during a 1995 performance of Mozart's *Idomeneo*:

"Ladies and gentlemen: As you will have noticed from the slips in your program, Anne Sofie von Otter is ill and was unable to perform today, and we are very grateful to Susanne Mentzer for coming in to sing the role of Idamante. However, as some of you may have noticed, her voice began leaving her during the course of the first act, and it is with great regret that she has said that she is unable to continue. We have prevailed upon Ms. von Otter to come in to continue the performance, which she has kindly agreed to do, although it will be immediately apparent that she is not at her best health—which is why she had cancelled in the first place. In order not to delay the evening's performance, and to give Ms. von Otter, who has just arrived through the stage door, time to get into costume, wig, and makeup, the first entrance of Idamante in this act, in which she does not sing, will be taken by Ms. Mentzer, but by the time we come to Idamante's second entrance, we hope that Ms. von Otter will be completely in costume, wig, and makeup. We are very grateful to both ladies for agreeing to this somewhat unusual circumstance, which I mention in some detail so as not to further confuse those of you who may be unfamiliar with the plot. Thank you."

Entertaining visiting singers fell into Billinghurst's bailiwick, and she regularly fed her favorites large meals in her book-lined apartment and then spent painful mornings with a personal trainer. Russians were particularly welcome at her table, especially the Kirov Opera's celebrity conductor, Valery Gergiev, whom she had cultivated during her years in San Francisco.

That morning, her fluffy plumpness was camouflaged by a flowing, dark-green ensemble with a scarf that set off her sea-blue eyes and short, dark, easy-to-comb hair. Billinghurst was always running a little late.

I noticed that the excitable person on the phone was not making much headway with whatever cause he was pleading. Unlike Volpe, Billinghurst rarely loses her temper, though her icy stare is no less unnerving, especially when combined with her habitual "don't you agree?" which cuts off annoying conversations very effectively.

This one was ending so she could address a really major problem that would deflect her from Bartoli's absence—James Levine's twenty-fifth-anniversary gala in April. The Cincinnati-born conductor made his debut in 1971 with a performance of *Tosca* starring Grace Bumbry and quickly turned himself into a smiling, immensely popular and hardworking podium hog. As the Met's artistic director and chief conductor, he often awarded himself as many as one-third of the Met's performances while still finding time for extensive recordings and frequent guest appearances, especially in Berlin, Bayreuth, and Salzburg.

That's why I was in her office. Billinghurst is in charge of the Met's media productions, and the gala would be telecast live. It would require a script—short introductions for the singers and something about the pieces they have chosen. Usually, the Met relies on the services of the avuncular, properly patriarchal announcer who hosts the radio broadcasts and telecasts. But Volpe had decreed that the Met do something "different" for the gala. Whatever that was, I had been invited to write it. The offer was irresistible and also mysterious. As Levine's years at the Met turned into decades, the number of people who thought he should be persuaded to at least take off his artistic director's hat had started to grow, and I was among them. Shy and private outside the pit, he really wasn't much of a company leader. The sophisticated productions of John Dexter and Jean-Pierre Ponnelle that once brightened his stage gradually gave way to the most traditional stagings money could buy. The twiggy *Ring* cycle he did with the director Otto Schenk and the designer Günther Schneider-Siemssen looked so old when it opened, you wondered if the composer might actually come out to take a bow. But it was popular with the audience and musically unassailable.

"Here's the list as of now," Billinghurst said, handing me two sheets of paper. "These are the singers who have accepted. There are rather a lot of them. And I have no idea at the moment of how to fit them all in. A bit of a logistical challenge, don't you agree?" She appeared to control an impulse to laugh.

So many singers, in fact, that I had condemned myself to writing a script for a show that would run about eight hours. Beginning with Anderson and ending with Zajick, the list included just about everyone except the dead and two sopranos closely associated with his career: Battle and Renata Scotto. Battle, of course, disappeared from the Met after *Fille*. Scotto wore out her welcome and her voice long ago.

An oversight?

"I have no idea," Billinghurst answered primly, as she walked me down the corridor and to the exit.

B ARTOLI WASN'T THE ONLY ONE out ill. As snowstorms and freezing temperatures battered New York, one singer went down after another. Even sturdy Jane Eaglen got the flu and stayed in bed with her laptop. Like so many singers who have found the Internet a boon to their often solitary travels, Eaglen was a web potato.

If she didn't get up soon, she would not make her Met debut as Donna Anna in *Don Giovanni*. There were only two performances left of the Mozart opera. Would Eaglen sing the Saturday matinee broadcast internationally by the Texaco–Metropolitan Opera Radio Network? For hardcore opera fanatics, this was one of the burning questions of the winter season. In concert, Eaglen's metallic soprano reminded old-timers of the redoubtable Swedish Valkyrie Birgit Nilsson, though Eaglen also had a real flair for florid music, and a big-voiced dramatic soprano who could sing coloratura was the sort of bird the opera world hadn't seen in a long time. That the talent came in a tart, jolly, jumbo-size package only made the Eaglen phenomenon even more delightful. She would be joining two other promising singers of size already at the Met, Deborah Voigt, increasingly recognized for her bountiful way with Strauss, and Sharon Sweet, who had unwisely consigned her ample voice to the inevitable horrors of a new *Forza del destino* with Plácido Domingo this season. Pavarotti had been originally scheduled, but had decided to leave learning a new role to another season. As opera buffs know, Verdi's opera is for singers what Shakespeare's *Macbeth* is for actors, a bad-luck piece whose name must never be mentioned. "That opera" or "that play" is enough. *Forza*'s reputation really sank after star baritone Leonard Warren died onstage at the Met in 1960 just as he finished the aria that starts with the words "Morir! Tremenda cosa!"—"Dying is a terrible thing."

But back to the Eaglen health watch. Encouraging signs of life periodically blipped across the screens of CompuServe subscribers. Every few days, someone signing on as Kathy Kent would leave informative postings about the singer's recovery process. If Kathy Kent seemed remarkably well informed about Jane Eaglen, it was not surprising. Kathy Kent was Jane Eaglen, who used an alias to defend fat people and to keep opera nuts (who did not know this) abreast of Jane Eaglen's many activities.

"She also sings the other song featured in *Sense and Sensibility*," Kathy Kent politely informed the cyberfan who had requested information about Jane Eaglen's contributions to the soundtrack.

After that, Kathy Kent fell silent for a few days, just like Jane. Jane did not sing Donna Anna in the *Don Giovanni* matinee, and many listening to their radios were bereft. "Dear Kathy," wrote one admirer. "Would you be kind enough to tell Ms. Eaglen that I missed her this afternoon? Will you also tell her that I hope her heart didn't hurt too much as she listened?"

The bedsprings must have creaked somewhere on the West Side of Manhattan as Eaglen chortled into her pillows. (Hurt? *Not quite!* Loved listening to that girl bumbling through my role. I felt better immediately!)

I started worrying about Bartoli and called her in Rome for a health update.

"It's not a strong bronchitis, but even so, I think I better stay here for a few more days. I have to be one hundred percent," she said. She was in her mother's apartment reading an excerpt from *Prima Donna*, a witty history of the breed by the British critic Rupert Christiansen.

But Bartoli had the new edition, which had a photograph of her on the cover and some advice on the inside which was not in my edition of the book.

"Listen to this!" she said, and started reading. " 'There's always talent coming up to warm the heart of even the most jaded opera queen—how can one follow opera in 1995 and not be impressed by the promise of Cecilia Bartoli, Elena Prokina, and Amanda Roocroft?— but equally it is impossible not to worry about the loss of the old system of apprenticeship whereby novices were weeded out early by a solid stint on contract to one provincial house, during which stamina and experience could be built up without all the extra pressures of travelling.' "

She took a deep breath and continued.

" 'Bartoli, for instance, fabulous talent that she has already proved herself on record and in recital . . .'—right, blah-blah, anyway, here's the good part—'. . . was launched on the international scene far too early and has since proved a disappointment in the major houses: she should be singing in a small and stable house like Glyndebourne, but the management reportedly refused to break their normal ceiling and pay the fee which her agent demanded. Instead she appears in the vast caverns of Salzburg and Houston, where the smallness of her voice disappoints audiences who expect to hear the full glory—"at once bright, warm, smooth, sparkling and ductile" as Max Loppert put it in *Opera* magazine—of the recordings.' "

Bartoli paused to cough.

"What's he mean, I sing in huge houses? Is Houston huge? The Theater an der Wien? Where has he heard me? And Glyndebourne after I auditioned years ago never invited me."

She got off the phone to save her voice and perhaps ponder the irony: on the cover, her photograph, sure to pump up sales; inside, an indictment of hype and management that had helped make her a hot commodity.

THE LONGER BARTOLI stayed in Rome, the grumpier the *Così* crew was getting across the ocean in the Met's subterranean rehearsal rooms, taking marching orders from Lesley Koenig, the increasingly frustrated director. A strange, sophisticated opera, at once disturbingly sad and overtly comic, *Così* is complicated to stage.

Apart from its musical riches, *Così fan tutte* boasts one of the more notoriously untranslatable titles in the repertoire. Literally it means "Thus Do All Women," though the title is sometimes mistranslated as "They All Do It"—i.e., fool around—though it is not, in fact, *Così fan tutti*.

Title and story have been branded as sexist, not without cause. Two officers in Naples are engaged to two sisters from Ferrara. The officers, besotted by the apparent devotion of their fiancées, brag that the ladies would never betray them. A cynical older friend, Don Alfonso, makes them a bet that they will, within a day. Under his direction, the officers say goodbye to the sisters, supposedly to go to war, leaving them suicidal with despair, whereupon the fellows instantly return in exotic disguise, each romancing the other's lady. Egged on by their maid, Despina, who is taking money from Don Alfonso, the sisters let the fellows stick around to entertain them in their misery. Lo and behold, within twenty-four hours they are summoning a notary and signing marriage contracts with their new beaux. (Despina, having masqueraded as a doctor at the end of act one, is back dressed up as the notary in act two.) Drumroll, the boys doff their fake mustachios, ablaze with righteous indignation, and the ladies, to the righteous indignation of the card-carrying feminist, actually express contrition.

But do the sisters return to their original partners? Mozart and his librettist, Lorenzo da Ponte, provided no absolute answer.

"What do you think happens at the end of the opera?" I figured Jonathan Miller might have an idea, since he'd staged the opera five times, once with Bartoli.

The British director and medical doctor (his specialty: the brain) looked darkly at a bagel and poured himself more coffee. Miller, who is best known in the United States for a witty restaging of *Rigoletto* among New York mafiosi, had just stomped into my apartment from his hotel on Manhattan's Upper West Side for breakfast on a snowy, icy morning. Wrapped into a bulky winter coat, he looked like he'd gone missing from a hunting scene by Breughel. Miller is a frequent guest at the Glimmerglass Opera in Cooperstown and he was at the Brooklyn Academy of Music to polish his production of Monteverdi's *The Coronation of Poppea.*

"The last time I staged the show at Covent Garden, everyone ended up hating everyone. There were no couples at the end. In my previous ones, I stuck to the eighteenth century."

"You mean, order must be restored?"

"They must go back. That's the whole point. Honor must be preserved and you must live with your mistakes. It seems to me you must actually make it painful in some way. It must be rather bitter and sad at the very end."

Who's in the show? he wanted to know. I told him Bartoli was making her debut.

He glowed. "Wonderful actress," he said. "Well, wonderful if encouraged by a good stage director. I worked with her and Frank Lopardo in Florence . . . while they were working on each other." Miller snorted cheerfully and patted Frieda. "What a beautiful dog," he said. "What is it?" It seemed inconceivable that a Brit would not know a beagle from a bagel, but the compliment was received with pleasure anyway.

He returned to the topic. "She sang Dorabella and it was really very good. So now she is singing it at the Met. Good."

I told him she was actually singing Despina.

"Really!" he said, raising both bushy eyebrows. "Now that seems rather odd—like using a sledgehammer to crack nuts. Anyway, in Florence, she wasn't a great star yet. She was just on the edge, with all these contracts coming her way. Very fresh. Blooming. Enormously attractive and like some wonderful, beautifully made piece of confectionery. And she was charming, easy to get along with, and everyone enjoyed it."

Miller was recovering from a very different experience, he said, a Bastille *Bohème* with Roberto Alagna as Rodolfo. Increasingly adored by audiences tiring of the same old faces, aggressively marketed as the Fourth Tenor by his recording company, EMI, Alagna was constantly in the news, especially now that he had found comfort in the thin arms of Angela Gheorghiu, a lyric soprano from Romania. "La petite Draculette" and "Vampira" to her colleagues, Gheorghiu also had a good career going, thanks much to Sir Georg Solti, the legendary conductor, who had insisted he absolutely had to record *La traviata* with her, even though this required the eviction of the previously cast Carol Vaness. I doubted Gheorghiu was surprised. A costume designer I know once came home from a dinner with the still-to-be-discovered soprano thinking it would take nuclear war to derail her career. How could you tell, I remember asking. "This is a true diva," she reported. "Convinced of her specialness and totally uninterested in what anyone around her was doing. Didn't ask me a thing. Divas never do."

Alagna had arrived late for rehearsals and then done his own staging, Miller reported. Gheorghiu amused herself miming Mimì's music from the wings while another Romanian, Leontina Vaduva, went through the bother of singing it. Vaduva was hopefully getting used to these appearances. "My dear, best be careful! Your high C is sounding a little low tonight," Gheorghiu was overheard telling her as the weary woman was sitting in her dressing room during a performance of *Roméo et Juliette* with Alagna a few months before at Covent Garden.

Miller guffawed, but thought it was the tenor who should be careful.

"It's very interesting," he mused. "I've been watching the Alagna effect. I think there's something happening which is unprecedented, an environmental influence which had not previously existed in quite the same way. I mean, fame has always had much the same effect on people. But the acute pressures of fame are much greater now, because the fame is much more explosive, much more sudden, and much more intense for all sorts of reasons: the effects of the media, the speed with which someone can become famous through records, television, and the vast multiplication of opera magazines. And this imposes on young people an explosive decompression which leads to psychological problems in the best."

He stopped to sit back in his chair.

"They get nitrogen bubbles in the soul. They travel too fast too far.

They finish in Rome one night, travel rapidly somewhere else, pop in and out at the last minute, encouraged by their agents because of the fee. The combined effects of greedy agents, greedy recording administrators, equally greedy magazine journalists, and editors looking for charismatic covers—all come together and have a dangerous effect on young people who have not experienced fame.

"It's especially true of singers, whose talent is often not related to any sort of educational culture."

"Fortune is capriciously scattered around, isn't it," I asked.

"Indeed," he agreed. "In the theater, this doesn't really exist. You find more rounded attitudes. There's no prodigious peculiarity of the voice which marks you out. My experience of working with singers is that it is rather like working in an Olympic village with these rather peculiar athletes. And they are often as banal as athletes."

He paused to feed Frieda leftover bagel crumbs and to acknowledge a gnawed slipper that had been dragged to the breakfast table for his inspection. Then he said: "They often seem to behave like lottery winners, in part perhaps because there is no rational explanation for how they came to do what they do. And that has disastrous results if they are badly educated from a poor background with parents who perhaps have not brought them up well. They don't know how to deal with it. Some spend, spend, spend and do what they like because they believe their publicity. They oversing, underrehearse, and think it's less and less important. Many are quite stupid and believe once they have played a part they have actually been introduced to the person they are playing."

Miller's aria had returned a healthy color to his hangdog cheeks. He took a breath and continued.

"They say, 'Violetta wouldn't behave like this' and so on. What they don't understand is that Violetta is a virtual character who can be endlessly reconstructed under different auspices. But they actually think they know her because they've played her and they have better access to her. So they don't need to rehearse if they played her once. And they really are quite stupid about that. They take possession of the character as known to them and therefore think they can travel with them, rather in the way that a concert cellist traveling on an airplane books two seats. They don't understand Violetta needs to be brought into existence every time."

In two years, Miller would be staging *Traviata* at the Bastille. "Who's the soprano?" I asked.

He snorted and looked a little sheepish as he reached for his coat. "Gheorghiu," he laughed gloomily. "Maybe she'll cancel."

THE SINGERS IN *Così* were pretty level-headed by the airy standards of Alagna and his maiden. Carol Vaness was singing Fiordiligi, whose principles put up a good fight against her heart. Tall and imposing, funny and hardworking, the California soprano made her name in the waning seventies as a tart-tongued Mozartean with a flexible, shimmering voice, style, temperament to burn, and a few extra pounds. Going home one night, Vaness had a flash that changed her life.

"I realized I was just another girl with a fat ass trying to get a taxi," is how she remembered it. Immediately, she discovered the benefits of aerobic exercise, transforming herself into a lithe fashion plate in a single season.

Fiordiligi's flighty sister, Dorabella, the role Cecilia sang in her extreme youth, was this time in the hands of Susanne Mentzer, a charming performer who resembles Winona Ryder. The tenor Jerry Hadley, chosen by the former Beatle Paul McCartney to star in his big-guns *Liverpool Oratorio* and a popular performer of show tunes, would portray Ferrando, the lyrical romantic. The baritone Dwayne Croft, homegrown in the Met's Young Artist Development Program and now the all-but-ubiquitous house baritone thanks to his gorgeously mellifluous voice and amenable manners, was Guglielmo, the goofy one. The pivotal role of the troublemaking Don Alfonso fell to an ex-Guglielmo, Thomas Allen, the suave fifty-one-year-old British baritone prized for theatrical savvy and elegance. They were all getting bored executing Koenig's tightly choreographed movements, which thwarted whatever impulse toward improvisation anyone might harbor.

"I've got a great idea," Vaness said at one point. "Let's get Kathy Battle to sing Despina. She could probably use a little work."

Vaness's dislike of the soprano was the stuff of legend. Battle had once thrown Vaness's gowns out of the dressing room she wished to occupy when they were both singing in *Le nozze di Figaro* at the Met. After Battle upstaged her during a performance of the same opera during a Met tour of Japan, Vaness shook her hand after the last curtain call, saying: "Working with you has been the most hideous experience of my life, and I will never do it again." To Battle's embarrassment, the line got a big ovation from the rest of the assembled cast.

Vaness and Mentzer, however, were friends who were spending so much time onstage with each other this season, they joked about taking their sister act on the road. After *Così* closed they were continuing on with Bellini's big "oogabooga" (Vaness-speak for *Norma*) at the Houston Grand Opera before proceeding to the Opéra Bastille. Not that hanging around with Mentzer was a lot of laughs all the time. One of the nicest people who ever stepped onto a stage, she was also prone to melancholia. Dorabella is meant to be the funnier of the two sisters.

"Lighten up, Susanne," Carol would say. "We're not doing *Hedda Gabler*."

Koenig kept plowing through act one. "If you don't have a sense of humor, you shouldn't be directing a comedy," she said, talking from her West Side apartment one Sunday afternoon. Things were starting to move along, she insisted. But now came act two, and if Bartoli wasn't there soon, she would lose valuable time explaining all the moves when she showed up. "Why can't she just get on that plane? She can't be contagious anymore," Koenig wondered. "She isn't required to sing at the rehearsals."

She thanked her father for teaching her a lesson she found useful in later life. "He said: Never make a grand exit without knowing how to make your reentry. Cecilia has to figure out for herself if it doesn't become more difficult the longer she stays away."

Was the Met going to demand a doctor's note? I asked Jonathan Friend. He laughed heartily. "What for?" he asked. "First of all, we believe she really is sick; after all, she also cancelled a recording session. And anyway, Italian doctors, well, you know they are known for handing sick notes to pink-cheeked singers who've double-booked themselves or just don't want to bother." He remembered Katia Ricciarelli showing up in Rovigo and Las Vegas after cancelling some Met performances with a doctor-documented illness. It helped end her Met career. The only time she was ever invited back was for *Otello* at the request of another famous canceller, the hermit-maestro Carlos Kleiber.

Slowly, the rehearsals petered out for lack of a Despina. Vaness announced she and Mentzer were planning to go on strike. Relations with Koenig were getting stiffer. Technically, Koenig was well prepared, but once she told people where to stand, she seemed to offer little advice about just what was meant to be going through their heads and hearts as they sang their songs and waited for Despina. Croft, being a newcomer to the piece, was in particular need of help, since Guglielmo's antics do not come naturally to a singer with the vivacity of Al Gore.

"I am sort of boring," he once explained to me. "I am not a great reader. I've taken up skateboarding."

Maybe a skateboard was what the show needed. "Right now, I would say that it has about the comic touch and bounce of a serial killer," Vaness said on the phone one evening.

I asked if Koenig had some fresh insight into an opera that on one level suggested women are feckless fools.

"Beats me," Vaness answered, before returning to the subject du jour. "This has got to be the longest-running case of bronchitis in medical history." She had just come home from another Despina-free rehearsal and wasn't feeling well herself. Jerry Hadley had sneezed on her during rehearsals and now she obviously had an inner ear infection. "There I was singing in the rehearsals and I had to ask someone, 'Did I hit that pitch?' I couldn't quite tell. Man!" She took some comfort in the production. "It's very pretty. Basically, if you are not going to do anything interesting, never mind weird, with *Così*, this is acceptable, nice. The one good thing about Lesley is that she listens, even though we sometimes have to use positive manipulation.

"We don't say: 'That's a truly dumb idea.' We say: 'We need some help here working this out.' Meaning I have to control myself, because you know what kind of a cut-to-the-chase person I am. Hold on a minute. Let me get this call."

A few seconds later, Vaness was back on the line.

"That was the Met. Miss Despina is coming in on the Concorde tomorrow. So we can all be half an hour late."

Jack Mastroianni confirmed Bartoli's arrival when I called him a few minutes later. The fever was gone. She was packing her bags. "By the way," he asked, "did you hear about the *Barber of Seville* last night?

"Just before Rosina, Ruth Ann Swenson, arrived for her entrance, the set collapsed. You could hear the turntable grinding to a halt as part of Rosina's house fell apart. A few seconds later, she would have been standing right in that spot. Hmmmm. Well, not my client."

There was more good news. The other reluctant debutant, Jane Eaglen, finally got out of bed, signed off CompuServe, and rumbled out the door just in time to join the season's last *Don Giovanni*.

Slowly, majestically, the Met's new Donna Anna made her way onto the set designed by Franco Zeffirelli, a set so enormous that even a partial collapse of the Don's palace would have decreased the company payroll by several dozen names.

CHAPTER SEVEN

Despina's Here

R EHEARSALS AT THE MET take place in subterranean rooms that look like bomb shelters from the Sputnik era. Visitors are not permitted, though the fire wall gets slightly more porous as the show migrates to the main stage some two weeks before the opening for the final rehearsals. Directors and designers begin chewing their nails and running manically from their computer-and-phone-equipped (but it's more satisfying to yell) desks in the darkened auditorium to the stage, where the tenor is usually standing in the wrong place.

By those standards, *Così* was running very smoothly now that Bartoli had been buttoned into her costume and was waiting in her dressing room for the first run-through with the orchestra. Stagehands were pulling the set into place, an elegant contraption outfitted with sliding doors and an invisible system of trolleys that would allow Don Alfonso and Despina to move the scenery around as they moved the plot along—a nice conceit, I thought.

Koenig, a slender blonde with a black wardrobe, was standing in the center aisle conferring with Duane Schuler, the lighting designer, on loan from the Lyric Opera of Chicago. The Met had only recently started paying attention to lighting, and Schuler, a tall, lanky guy with blond hair out of Botticelli, is one of the best. He had some three hundred light fixtures at his disposal, and had spent the last few days entering all the cues into a computer program that would gradually drain away sunny colors as Mozart's story took on a chilly tone.

Vaness sauntered cheerfully down the aisle, stopped, and tapped him on the shoulder on her way down toward the stage. She playfully tugged his ear and bussed him on the cheek. "I have only one thing to say to you: more peach lighting!" She grinned.

He laughed and gave her a fond squeeze. "That's what you all say." Peach is a friendly light that makes them look young, he explained.

She continued on her way down the aisle, waving grandly to retainers, finally stepping to the temporary catwalk that connected the auditorium with the stage. As several cast members and stagehands watched with amusement, she lay down on the prompt box and, winking like Marlene Dietrich, slowly raised one long and limber leg into the air. "And this, this is the way I will sing 'Per pietà.' "

Levine arrived in the orchestra pit, a tubby enthusiast with uncombable frizzy hair and his traditional blue towel draped over his left shoulder. He conveys a mixture of authority and friendliness, and the hall became quiet as he gave the downbeat for the overture.

Despina is usually first seen whipping chocolate to a fine froth for her demanding mistresses, who come running in to announce their decision to kill themselves with sword or poison because their boyfriends have gone off to the field of battle. But this Despina made a different first appearance: she brought the entire kitchen and house with her.

Back bent over in mock exertion, Bartoli slowly pulled the house behind her on a long rope. It was quite an entrance. Funny and surprising, it was guaranteed to bring the (big) house down.

But singers are rarely pleased.

"What's not to like?" I asked her as we sat down during a break in a corner of the depressing company cafeteria—also underground, to resist the next alien invasion. Never mind the gorgeous satin bodice and skirt this Despina gets to wear, she seemed glum, even more reticent than usual. I'd heard she'd been somewhat frostily received by the cast once she squeezed off the Concorde and hightailed it to the Met. Was that the problem? No, she said, not the problem. Levine had postponed the recording date for *An Italian Songbook*, which would include Rossini's melting "L'esule" (The Exile) and melodies by Bellini and Donizetti; she was late and he had understandably gotten busy with this show.

Just then, the show's three young assistant directors, Robin Guarino, Paula Williams, and Peter McClintock, walked in. They hurried over.

Assistant directors do what the title implies, cajole singers and chorus into the gestures and formations devised by the director, rehearse covers—understudies, who are usually rewarded with one performance—and maintain the black notebooks that are the memory of a show when the cast changes or the opera is revived. They're specialists in what is known as the park-and-bark school of direction (as in: "Hey, Tosca! Now go stand next to that table—and remember to pick up the knife!").

"Listen, dears," Bartoli said, addressing the adoring trio. "I have a problem." Just what assistants love to hear. They looked eagerly at her and moved their chairs a little closer.

"My accent. What should I do?" Bartoli was talking about Despina's disguise as the notary. In most productions the notary lisps, stutters, or sings through the nose in an attempt to be amusing. "I want to try something different," she informed them. "Some other accent.

"Any ideas?"

One of them suggested the accent of a German doctor. That was rejected. It's been done.

Why don't you put marbles in your mouth? No. What if she swallowed one?

"How about this: Why don't you try talking Italian like an American?" Guarino suggested, offering me as example.

"How about Winnie Klotz?" Paula countered, more diplomatically. Klotz, the Met's beloved photographer, turned English into Italian by adding "-io" endings. "Crossword," say, became "crosswordio."

Bartoli glowed.

"Hmmm. It's very good, I think," Bartoli said, absorbing the concept. "What an idea. I'm going to try it."

They finished their coffees and wandered back to the auditorium, leaving me to sit down with Michael Yeargan, the show's set and costume designer, a middle-aged cherub who was filling up with a pastrami sandwich prior to a meeting with Fiordiligi. Vaness had complained about her pumps; she wanted them to be as pretty as Despina's.

"Ever have to change an entire costume?"

"Not often," he replied. "Mostly, singers are happy if they don't look fat. So a lot of what I do is camouflage, and a little therapy on the side. You just have to listen to them as they come up with one bizarre ailment after another: 'There's mold on the wall and I can't breathe.' 'The conductor's wearing after-shave and I can't sing.' 'The costume has weird stuff on it and I'm allergic.' And so on. This bunch is fine, but sometimes it gets to be a long list."

He began to quiver. "I remember a *Traviata* at the Lyric in Chicago a few years ago with June Anderson. She was suffering from one thing or another, and Ardis Krainik"—the general manager—"practically had to get down on her knees and beg her to get onstage, and finally June said, 'Okay, but there has to be an announcement at the start saying I'm not well.' So that happened. An announcement was made: 'Ms. Anderson is not well but is graciously singing anyway.' Then the prelude started.

"Normally, as you know, the curtain goes up after the prelude. But in this production the curtain was already open as the prelude started. There was a tableau more or less vivant, with everybody onstage striking poses, including June, who was slumped on the couch as Violetta with the opera's Dr. Grenvil standing over her, checking her pulse.

"The people next to me were clearly at the opera for the first time. They were so excited. So they see the doctor onstage holding June's hand and they're in shock. 'Oh my God!' one of them gasps. 'She's brought her doctor onstage with her! She must really be sick!' "

Yeargan chuckled at the memory.

"With *Così* there are no real costuming problems," he added. "Only some adjustments for Carol, who's been pounding on the treadmill an hour a day. This is a show without what I call 'skunk costumes'—the ones with lots of black material and white trim in a V-shaped pattern to make you look thinner."

Once Yeargan even designed a slimming bed. That was in the 1980s when Jane Eaglen was singing Mimì—slimmer than now, but even so interfering with the sightlines when she lay down to die. One of the Bohemians was instructed to pull a peg out of the mattress so it would sink down with her.

Yeargan took another bite. He'd seen skinnier days himself, but he wasn't out there pretending to die of tuberculosis. He had a favorite movie, he said: *I Married an Angel*. "It's about a woman who can come back to earth but on one condition: she can never, never tell a lie. So she meets some humongous person who says to her something like: 'I look so fat.' And she says: 'No, you don't look fat. You *are* fat.' "

Yeargan crumpled his napkin and grinned. "Makes me laugh every time."

Edgar Vincent, Bartoli's press agent, came in with a lunch tray and sat down across from us. I stopped to ask when she would be appearing on the *Today* show. He sighed and rolled his eyes. "Not now. I got her on David Letterman and Charlie Rose, but the *Today* show people finally just wore me out. It wasn't enough that she is making her debut or that her Mozart album has sold nearly a quarter-million CDs. Or the fact that she is the most popular singer in the world. You know what they wanted? They wanted to shoot her shopping or in a deli buying a sausage."

"Buying a *sausage*?"

"Yes. Buying a sausage or cheese or doing something human that ordinary people could relate to," he sighed. After forty years in public relations, neither the media nor life holds many surprises for Vincent, but he admitted that he was mystified. "I just don't get it," he said, poking glumly at his salad. "The advertising community is perfectly happy using opera and arias to sell products. Clearly someone thinks opera is popular enough to appeal to the buying public. But as far as the talk shows go, opera is just off the screen. Is it that the people who book are dumbbells just out of college who don't know any better? Well, I don't know. But the woman who was booking the *Today* show wanted Bartoli to buy a sausage."

He shrugged and continued with his greens.

AFTER EVERY STAGE REHEARSAL, the director usually gives the cast "notes," comments on little things that still need fixing. Usually the conductor does the same with the orchestra, but more often than not separately.

Conductors don't say to the director: "That ensemble is a mess. Change it." And directors don't tell the conductor to pick up the tempo. But Levine liked to hold joint meetings and comment on the staging once a rehearsal was over. If Koenig had any problems with that, she wasn't going to say. After all, as artistic director, her conductor was also her boss.

Koenig had finally staged the crucial last few minutes of the piece. There was no happy ending: the couples stayed unhappily apart.

Levine wouldn't have it that way. "It's in C major," he insisted. "It's optimistic. The ending has to be up." And as the assembled singers and assistants fixated on the floor in embarrassment, he told Koenig to change the staging. To most of the assistants and singers, this was so provincial, so of another age—a prefeminist age—and also so irrefutable: who was going to question the music master of the Met?

What could Koenig say to him? Play it in C minor?

The scene was another reminder of Levine's instincts—musical more than theatrical. He rarely worked with directors who saw the stage as a symbolic world of suggestion. Sets to him were purely decorative, and direction a literal act of libretto reading. He had already let it be known that when *Così* returned the following season, he would like the singers even further downstage, just like in a concert opera.

But before that could be arranged, the show first had to open. February 8, 1996, had finally arrived.

. . .

In a co-op building a short walk from Lincoln Center, Despina was getting dressed. She was calmly taking her time while her manager waited for her to arrive so we could walk across the street to the Met.

"The moment we've been waiting for," Mastroianni jabbered, cradling his phone and struggling with his cummerbund. He'd been putting on weight this last month. "A very calculated debut. I've been thinking back to when we first planned this. She has an open door here, Levine said. But this is what we wanted. Now it's here and my beard is partly gray." He had just turned forty-seven.

"Oh, there you are," he said, as Bartoli picked up on the other end. He put her on the speakerphone. "Are you ready?" he asked, looking out the wall of windows on his high-rise.

"Almost," she said. "Wait. Can you turn your lights on and off? I think I can see you from here, but I'm not sure."

"Okay. I'm turning the lights on and off." Mastroianni started flipping a switch by the kitchen.

"Yep!" she yelled. "It's your apartment. Wave!"

He turned to his guests and ordered us to wave. We waved.

"Where are you?" Mastroianni asked. "I think we can see you too. Turn your lights on and off."

"I can't. I'm not wearing anything."

"You're half a mile away. How much can we see? Turn around and do it."

"Okay," she said, flickering in the distance like a star in the sky.

Twenty minutes later, Bartoli was in her dressing room, forty-five minutes to curtain up, looking relaxed, unlike her manager.

"Calm down already," she said. "What a mess you will be when I sing my first Carmen!"

Her door stayed partly open; every few minutes someone stuck a head in, or more. She signed programs for box holders brought by Sissy Strauss, the Met's dirndled house mother, who finds the top singers nice apartments and makes them feel less homesick at regular gatherings in her well-upholstered duplex across from Lincoln Center. Osele stopped tinkling on the piano and proofed the stage-door guest list. Bartoli's parents didn't come over for her debut. Her father stayed where he always seems to stay, in his little hideaway in Rimini; Silvana was needed in Parma to help her overextended mother care for her ailing father. If Bartoli thought they had very peculiar priorities, she kept it to herself.

Osele opened a Tiffany package containing a crystal apple with a gracious note from Marilyn Horne. "Bello, carino," Cecilia murmured. She opened an envelope and extracted a watercolor by Tom Levine, the conductor's brother and a visual artist of some repute. The sketch showed Despina pulling along the Manhattan skyline, with "Despina debuts, toting Manhattan" written underneath.

Robin Guarino of the directing team appeared at the door. "First, have a great opening night. And second, you know when you stir the chocolate—can you use the long spoon instead of the whisk? It's funnier. Also, maybe you should change."

Vaness's door was open. Her dapper fiancé and fellow exercise nut, Bruce Brown, was checking out her costume, sitting on a monstrous, three-canister humidifier left behind by Aprile Millo, who had just sung Desdemona—in well-lubricated if somewhat absentminded condition. It didn't seem quite possible considering the plot implications, but during one of the performances Millo had skipped offstage without dropping her handkerchief (for Emilia to pick up and Iago to grab and give to Otello, who kills Desdemona over this fictive evidence of her supposed adultery). Emilia and Iago improvised.

"Good thing Aprile doesn't work in props!" Vaness joked. "Think of *Tosca* without a knife. Think of *Walküre* without the sword or *Rheingold* without the gold. Nice and short."

Unlike *Cosi*, which would be performed in the no-cuts version preferred by Levine, who stepped into the pit at seven-thirty. He might as well have just skipped the overture as far as most folks were concerned. It was Despina that everybody was waiting for, and when finally she stepped into view with her house, the applause and bravos started, growing in volume as she toiled across the stage and held her pose, eyes lustrous with mischief but very modestly cast down, until the hall grew quiet and she could get on with her foot bath and some singing.

Next to Fiordiligi's and Dorabella's showy set pieces, Despina's brief solos sound slight, almost like musical-comedy interludes. The two sisters work much harder, especially Fiordiligi, who in addition to "Per pietà" has another hugely difficult aria, of mock seriousness, called "Come scoglio"—in which she insists she is not fickle at all but as steadfast as the rock of Gibraltar. Vaness dispatched it with such brilliance that the show briefly focused on her. But then it was back to Bartoli, especially when she put on the outfit of the doctor and walked off the side of a little cliff, working her legs in the air like an upside-down junebug and singing unperturbably all the while. In the next act, her Americanized notary outfitted with a huge nose, goggles, and a straggly clown wig flapped in just in time to rejuvenate an audience fighting off sleep during a show otherwise short on laughs.

The curtain fell and pandemonium broke out once more. Bouquets sailed across the orchestra pit and piled up at her feet. The line outside her dressing room eventually extended all the way down the corridor to the stage door.

I headed upstairs to the cast dinner in the Grand Tier restaurant. Joe Volpe was guarding the entrance with Bruce Crawford, the sardonic president of the Met Opera board. Once the Met's very effective general manager, Crawford had resigned for the greater challenges and rewards of running a global advertising agency. He told me at the time that he was sick of worrying whether, say, Kiri Te Kanawa would get out of bed in time to sing the matinee performance of whatever she was booked to sing.

Both men were in good spirits: Sold Out signs, no screw-ups, no boos. They looked like they might break into a soft shoe and shuffle any minute. "Say, Jimmy's gala . . ." asked Crawford, turning to his sidekick with mock anxiety. "Is it really true it's going to be longer than *Götterdämmerung*?" Wagner's *Götterdämmerung* takes nearly six hours before twilight sets on the gods.

"Oh, definitely. At least!" Volpe snickered.

"Makes you want to get a syringe with the flu virus!"

Levine appeared, dressed in a worn gym suit, though the sneakers seemed new. He sat down for a while with Koenig, waved to a few people, and left. People have stopped expecting him to acquire social graces, and nobody was surprised.

Bartoli arrived with Osele and Mastroianni, but left them both as she spied a dark-haired, handsomely tropical man standing by the buffet with a haute-couture model attached to his arm. "This is the most important person here tonight," she insisted, introducing the Cuban-born Alberto Vilar, the wealthy head of the Amerindo investment company headquartered in San Francisco. Vilar was turning into a sort of Alidoro figure in her career at the Met. He wrote checks that turned cardboard and cloth into the glittering realms of operatic myth. When he was a boy, his father, who had lost his sugar plantations to Castro, refused to let him listen to opera: he thought it was something for sissies. Now Vilar made up for the silence of his youth by buying himself shows he wished to hear, having smartly foreseen the boom in emerging technologies like semiconductors and molecular biology.

In a land whose politicians think that applying forty-eight cents per taxpayer to the arts is a criminal act of robbery, Vilar enjoyed the clout of a Medici and the slavish attention of the Met's worshipful development department. He had committed himself to giving the Met $20 million, which would pay for at least ten new productions over the next few years, including *Cenerentola* in the fall of 1997 and *Le nozze di Figaro* in 1998 with Bartoli, Fleming, and Terfel.

"I'm so glad she has no interest in Benjamin Britten. Or modern music," Vilar breathed. "I do good old-fashioned productions."

I figured he'd gotten his money's worth tonight, and followed Bartoli back to her long table. "Well, I guess we proved it," Mastroianni said, embracing her as she sat down across from Evans Mirageas, Decca's sleek VP for artists and repertoire, who had flown over from the London headquarters. "All those people who said your voice was too small for the Met. I guess they heard you." He poured himself a glass of red wine and opened his snug jacket. She smiled, happily clinking glasses with Mirageas.

Whether Bartoli's mezzo could reach the last row of the Family Circle had been the subject of much discussion among opera fans, some posting on the Internet messages claiming she would be miked. Contrary to popular fiction, the Met doesn't use mikes except on Fafner the dragon. The reason we all heard Bartoli is that she sings on the words and with perfect focus, while being sufficiently charismatic that you lean toward her and enter into an emotional commitment. You want to hear her, and you do.

"Say, Cecilia. What's happening with the Pope?" Mirageas asked.

Bartoli had acquired a new fan, who expressed the hope that she might give a concert in the Sistine Chapel. Decca was hoping to turn the event into a CD and possibly a video with Mastroianni's new company. Such a concert would boost her presence in Italy, where she was not particularly well-known. Mirageas was pleased to hear that His Holiness's emissaries had visited her.

"What did they say to you?" he asked.

"They wanted to know my views on abortion," she said.

"So what did you tell them?" gaped Mirageas.

"Well, what was I going to say?" Bartoli answered, shrugging her shoulders and pursing her lips. "I said, 'I like children and hope to have a few someday.' That seemed to satisfy them. They just don't want someone who sings in the Sistina to go on television making controversy."

"Smart girl," he said.

Vaness's sparkling Queen of the Night–style hairband drew me to her table, where she was presiding over a long table crowded with family and friends, including the evening's Alfonso, Tom Allen. They've known each other since the early 1980s, when they "bonded over Battle," in Allen's phrase, during those problematic Met *Figaros*.

"I guess we went off the diet for tonight!" Vaness noted deadpan, surveying the empty plates up and down the table. "Here, honey bunny," crooned her husband-to-be, proffering a forkful of pasta, "it upsets me to see you look so sad." Then they discussed an upcoming trip to a shopping mall in New Jersey with the excitement less fortunate travellers reserve for the chateaux of the Loire Valley.

Così BRIGHTENED the life of Joe Volpe, who could make his gut bleed thinking of the previous premiere, director Elijah Moshinsky's hideously afflicted production of Janáček's *The Makropulos Case*, staged especially for Jessye Norman. On opening night, minutes into the show, the veteran tenor Richard Versalle, cast in the small role of a clerk, had climbed up a dangerously high ladder to reach a filing cabinet and plunged to his death from a heart attack in full view of the horrified audience, which was sent home after a grim news-and-music-free wait. In his late fifties, Versalle was hardly right for such vertiginous exertion, but he was a pro, eager for work and eager to please after a frustrating career in which he'd never ever been quite in the right place at the right time to be properly recognized for his ringing heldentenor voice. Only his death was front-page news. A blizzard knocked out the second performance. All this generated publicity but few sales, even with the imperious Norman, now ever more inscrutable in her middle years and thus well cast as a mysterious diva obsessed with her voice. But in the drearily conceived show, Norman spent most of her time just sitting in large chairs smiling scarily under huge hats.

"One million," Volpe was saying over poached sea bass one morning. The curtain had just gone down on the last, long *Così* on March 14, and he was hosting a small dinner for Bartoli at his favorite hangout, San Domenico, near Lincoln Center. "One million bucks. I'm taking donations," he continued, muttering about his anticipated deficit, while most of his guests dozed uncaringly into their plates and Bartoli discussed her upcoming Carnegie Hall debut with the hall's executive director, Judith Arron. It was hard to say who was more tired. Bartoli had helped plug Volpe's deficit by singing at the Met's annual corporate dinner a few weeks before and by selling out all ten performances of *Così*—usually something of a box-office dud. That's why he was giving her dinner.

"You know, I've been thinking," he said, smiling and wide awake. "We need a smaller house, something for Mozart, the more intimate works. We could do a whole series with Cecilia. It would be my legacy."

CHAPTER EIGHT

Paris Prince

IN THE FOUNTAIN OF VICTORY, at the center of the place du Châtelet, chill waters dripped from the lips of glum sphinxes. Across the street, outside the Théâtre du Châtelet, the last stragglers pushed into the lobby and up the stairs, passing a model of the auditorium, the size of a doll house, each and every seat bearing a number—the number of a ticket long since sold. The curtain was about to rise on a hotly awaited *Don Carlos*, Verdi's grand opera about suffering mortals crushed by church and state in sixteenth-century Spain.

Like the even more opulent Opéra, the soggy lair of Andrew Lloyd Webber's Phantom, the Châtelet has had its share of illustrious guests and was about to have some more. It was here at the Châtelet in the early part of the century that Serge Diaghilev, Russian prince of impresarios, presented the legendary basso Fyodor Chaliapin in *Prince Igor* and *Boris Godunov*, reserving other nights for his high-flying love slave, Nijinsky. Anna Pavlova left behind a few feathers from her swan costume. Creaking to your seat on well-worn floorboards, you feel the ghostly frisson of history.

Now, in late February of 1996, it was Roberto Alagna we were waiting for. He was making the city go wild with magazine covers and TV reports. In a world full up with mezzos, lyric sopranos, and baritones, Alagna continued to reign as the heir apparent to Pavarotti. There were young tenors around by the dozens, but most of them inhabited the delicate world of Mozart, Rossini, Donizetti, and Bellini, singers like Ramón Vargas or Bruce Ford. What the opera world needed was a sexy, swaggering champ who could sing Verdi and Puccini and *Carmen*'s Don José with the charisma of Bartoli.

Was Alagna the answer? His voice had a recognizable coloring—clear like Pavarotti's, with a little ping on the top notes. And he brought a seductive swagger to roles often sung by people with the vitality of ham sandwiches. Self-taught—he learned from records—and not entirely well taught, Alagna had some shortcomings, but they seemed fixable. He did not have a perfect pianissimo (the opposite of fortissimo, which he did very effectively), and his pitch could be erratic. Neither did he go in for singing portamento—that way of sliding into a note for a little extra poetry. Purists found him a puzzle.

Alagna's brief stay at the top already seemed to be giving him the shakes. He had spent much of the fall threatening to cancel. The role of the Spanish prince in love with the French princess his father marries for reasons of state was longer and more dramatic than anything he had ever sung; and he surely harbored somewhere in the back of his agitated brain the memory of Pavarotti, who added the role to his small repertoire only to be booed at La Scala in the winter of 1992 for cracking on a few notes and forgetting others.

But Luc Bondy, the director of *Don Carlos*, took the time to build the tenor's ego, and Alagna got his courage back. He'd shown up for rehearsals and by all reports been courteous to his colleagues, all of them his artistic equal. Elisabeth was Karita Mattila, a striking Finnish soprano in her early thirties, who had just had a tremendous success at the Met in Tchaikovsky's *Pique Dame*, bringing a mesmerizing edge to dull Lisa, a towering achievement. The brainy American baritone Thomas Hampson was departing from his Mozart roles and gloomy Mahler songs for the Marquis of Posa, a role requiring a long line agitated by the fervor of a utopian free thinker who dreams of liberty in a land of prisons and auto-da-fés. The classy Belgian bass José van Dam and the glamorously aggressive German mezzo-soprano Waltraud Meier rounded out the cast as the aging, heretic-toasting king and his conniving mistress, Eboli.

Verdi wrote the opera in the five-act grand-opera style for Paris in 1867. But it made for a very long evening and these days *Don Carlos* is more often played as *Don Carlo* in a four-act Italian-language version the composer himself cooked up years later. The Châtelet, fortunately, was returning to the original French, which opens with a wistful scene in the snowy woods of Fontainebleau, where the Spanish prince meets his young bride-to-be, Elisabeth de Valois, only to lose her to the king, his father, before the scene is over. The sudden loss of happiness barely glimpsed sends the prince into abject self-pity and desperate political acts—though he remains likably romantic compared with the historic Carlos, a sadistic little man who once got so mad that his new shoes were too tight, he forced the shoemaker to eat them. For that matter, the real Elisabeth loved the king, who adored her. History relates (I hope not apocryphally) that Philip was so delighted with his princess that he adorned the barren trees on the wintry mountain pass she crossed from France to Spain with oranges from his gardens. But while the libretto (based on Schiller's play) departs from history, its emotional truths are no less compelling, and they became palpable in Bondy's staging, which was neither abstractly modern nor realistically period.

The curtain rose on a landscape of frail trees painted white, suggesting snow and bandaged wounds. Slowly, Alagna stepped from the shadows and into silvery light, dressed in fiery red doublet and ash-black boots. "Fontainebleau," he sang, "vast and solitary forest, what garden full of flowers can equal your frozen ground after happy Carlos sees his Elisabeth?" As he described their future under fair skies, he sang with such poetry, sound and words fused into pictures. It was just the beginning of a performance that would be hard to surpass in its dramatic power and melting lyricism. Mattila, in a clinging dress suggestive of red-hot passion, was equally astonishing, utterly convincing as a young woman who suddenly finds herself forced into the stiff robes of a queen.

As their future disappeared, so did the ground underneath their feet—a swirling white cloth that was suddenly pulled into the wings. The designs by the French painter Gilles Aillaud allowed for many such unforgettable moments. When van Dam sang his mournful "Elle ne m'aime pas"—"She does not love me"—he contemplated the sleeping Mattila, who slowly rose and drifted offstage, sleepwalking and even in dreams, it seemed, belonging to another. Usually the king sings as he labors at his desk alone in his room. Bondy's interpretation was heartbreaking. Their emotional distance seemed insurmountable.

It was a night when everything was special, from the conducting of Antonio Pappano, who revealed a remarkable feeling for the opera's epic structure, to the seductively charged encounters between Hampson and Meier, to the unusually lively ladies of the court, who danced through the gardens of Aranjuez holding elegant flutes of orange juice. In conventional productions, they just sit around the garden with glue on their bottoms.

DON CARLOS TOOK some of the sparkle out of another big opera event in Paris that same week. The Palais Garnier Opéra, which goes with *Phantom*'s chandelier, was reopening after a thorough restoration of its interior and backstage areas. Mysteriously devoted to ballet for many years despite sightlines so bad you had to be dead center to see both the swans and the lake, the Palais Garnier would now be used for opera again, the more intimate operas anyway, leaving the spectacle pieces to the new, space-age Bastille.

Both houses are run by Hugues Gall, who had recently won a power struggle with the Bastille's chief conductor, Myung-Whun Chung. It was the latest chapter in the Bastille's farcical employment sagas. Even before the place formally opened in 1989, Daniel Barenboim had been pushed out the door—deemed insufficiently industrious and overly high-minded to merit his amazing paycheck (about a million dollars for less than half a year's conducting). The place was then turned over to Pierre Bergé, Yves Saint Laurent's friend and business partner, who brought in Chung, an opera neophyte, who built up the orchestra's tattered reputation and his own nonexistent one in the course of five years. By the time Gall arrived, Chung had the final word on artistic matters and a Barenboimian salary that was scheduled to zoom up to around $1.6 million by the year 2000 (the pay package included a guaranteed forty performances, rising to an insane $35,400 a pop). The contract was arranged by Bergé, who had not been eager to depart and was probably being malicious.

But Gall, fresh from a highly regarded tenure at the Geneva Opera, thought he could run the Bastille by himself. The protesting Chung was finally sent away with a $1.8 million check to stanch his tears. Gall would soon hire a less costly but far more experienced opera conductor, the American James Conlon, prying him loose from his commitments in Cologne. Sadly, no one called for the public execution of Bergé as a fundraising event, though the Bastille's historic location would have been the perfect spot.

What did this mean for Cecilia Bartoli? She loved Paris and had been declared a *chevalier des arts et lettres* by the culture ministry. Not only had she concertized in Paris, Chung had also cast her as Cherubino and more recently accompanied her on a French-song recital tour through Germany that Decca would package as *Chant d'amour*. Now the amiable if greedy Chung was gone, and Gall so far seemed blind to her charms and very receptive to Jennifer Larmore, whose fee demands were also more in line with the frugal Frenchman's budget. He had hired Larmore for *La Cenerentola*, the opera Bartoli liked to call her own.

Gall was in his offices at the Garnier when I arrived. He had just finished a press conference devoted to his opening night, a concert performance of *Don Giovanni* conducted by Sir Georg Solti. When Gall was a young guy in the early seventies, he was the assistant to Rolf Liebermann, who briefly restored the fortunes of the Garnier together with Solti. Then the place fell apart again. Now it was Gall's to run, and he had asked the legendary Solti to return, in a sentimental gesture atypical of Gall, but one that clearly filled him with pleasure and pride. I found him in his anteroom eyeing sample opening-night flower arrangements that had been placed on a round table for his approval.

"They must be larger!" he declared after a few minutes, fiddling with the buttons on the double-breasted suit he favored and which now included a tiny red ribbon stitched into the left lapel—the symbol of the Légion d'Honneur, the highest of French distinctions.

The job came with a chauffeur and two offices, one in the Garnier and the other at the Bastille, where he had to attend a union meeting after a quick lunch. Settling into the backseat of his comfortable Renault, he reviewed his annoying morning as we inched along the crowded boulevards toward the place de la République.

ALAGNA MAY HAVE DECIDED to sing Don Carlos, but he seemed unwilling to see himself in the satin britches of a lesser nobleman, the Chevalier des Grieux. Gall had just received a letter from Alagna's agent saying the tenor was cancelling his appearance in a new production of Massenet's *Manon* planned for spring 1997. Gall was livid. "So then I had to pass the problem to Pål Moe, my administrator, who has to deal with it, and to the lawyers, who will give me what are my rights. I have to make up my mind whether I will sue him or not.

"I wonder if Angela Gheorghiu is confusing the poor boy," he mused out loud. "Think of my situation: we stage it for him as a showcase because he wants to sing it, now he doesn't want to sing it."

The cancellation made no sense: with his excellent French and active love life, Alagna would be perfect as the love-besotted young man who briefly checks himself into divinity school to hide from his feckless Manon, an eighteenth-century material girl.

Did Alagna hope to force Gall to cast his real-time girlfriend as Manon? If that was the game plan, it failed. Gall was proceeding with Renée Fleming. "Why should I change the program?" Gall asked. "A beautiful voice like that, I would be crazy. . . . Look at this mess," he suddenly ordered as his own opera house came into view, a shiny hulk rising up over the place de la Bastille like a large whale that got lost looking for the Left Bank. The medieval Bastille prison was centuries old by the time revolutionaries knocked it down in 1789. The name-sake opera house seemed to be collapsing all by itself, though it was just six years old. The facade's limestone plates were coming unglued;

engineers were about to cover part of it with a gigantic hairnet. There were no funds, he complained, for renovation and upkeep.

We had arrived at a small, busy restaurant around the corner from the Bastille toward the Seine. Gall wasted no time ordering the fish of the day, *lotte à la crème de saffron,* and a bottle of Perrier.

A handsome man in his early fifties with sardonic, icy eyes and little patience, Gall exudes a firm, no-nonsense manner that seemed to be working at the Bastille, where new productions frequently opened without sets and costumes because the stagehands were unhappy about something or other. Even better, his brand of populism—untraditional stagings of mainstream operas by younger directors like Robert Carsen and Francesca Zambello, plus a shrewd sprinkling of twentieth-century pieces like *Billy Budd*—was proving very successful at the box office and with the press.

We talked about the singers of the future. Who were they? I asked him. His list included the three Susans (Graham, Chilcott, and Mentzer), the baritone Simon Keenlyside, and the tenor Rainer Trost. I asked him who he wasn't hiring, and he mentioned Barbara Hendricks, the chic, lark-voiced American soprano, who lived in France, where she was very popular as a concert artist and fundraiser for good causes.

"Yes, so many disasters happening all over the world and there she is," Gall scoffed. He was still in a bad mood. "Destroy Sarajevo, she'll go sing there. Do you think she had it destroyed to get the publicity?"

He was amused by his thought and smiled faintly.

"Maybe she'll sing at my funeral! Ha."

Our lunch arrived to soothe his rage over Alagna's cancelling, which somehow had landed on poor Barbara Hendricks's head.

"I don't think they are that good," he said mysteriously, poking his fish with his fork.

"Who isn't that good?" I asked.

"She or that Alagna and his maiden. They are not very good, unlike your Madame Bacelli," Gall insisted.

Monica Bacelli is a mezzo who was singing Zerlina at the Garnier. I didn't know Madame Bacelli, however.

"Who?"

"Bartoli! I meant Bartoli. She is very good, actually. Very good indeed. But such a tiny voice!"

Gall put down his fork and made little flying gestures with his fingers. "Third row of the Palais Garnier, you could hardly hear her. It is a phenomenon like Barbara Hendricks, who used to be quite a good singer but also has a small voice. At least right now, I'll do my business with Susanne Mentzer and Jennifer Larmore. Larmore is good. She is pushed by her record company as well, but not that much."

Gall wolfed down his fish. His union meeting would take all afternoon; then there was a dress rehearsal of *Don Giovanni*.

THE NEXT DAY, I went to visit Donna Anna in her rental off the Champs-Elysées—rather far from the Bastille, but Renée Fleming had special needs. The Liv Ullmann lookalike was travelling with one of her two tots and a nanny and required something bigger than the usual crummy student-type lodgings opera companies find for singers who are not the Three Tenors or Jessye Norman. After moving once already, Fleming had finally secured a sizable duplex decorated in late-period Arab Oriental in a charmless modern building.

Rather like downtown Omaha, I thought, remembering the first time I heard Fleming. It was 1990, and she was there singing Donizetti's *Maria Padilla*, in a production that cost $14,000 and that included the sets and costumes for another equally obscure opera the next night. I remembered sitting down in the auditorium of the local art museum and thinking, I really don't want to be here. What have I done? Then this little-known beautiful blonde stepped to the makeshift stage in a black gown sprinkled with sequins and began singing in a dreamy voice that reminded me of the young Kiri Te Kanawa but with enough coloratura ability to recall Beverly Sills. I remembered walking back to my orange and blue hotel room in a state of enchantment.

Then came a 1993 concert performance of Bellini's *La straniera* at Carnegie Hall with Eve Queler's Opera Orchestra of New York, following in the steps of Montserrat Caballé, who had triumphed with the part in the same hall in 1969. Fleming sang the dame of mystery at the opera's empty center, a veiled French queen who skulks about a lakeside hut, where the tenor mistakenly stabs her lover, who falls into the water only to be rescued by the same tenor when he realizes the lover is actually her brother. Fleming sang with such a poetic line and a sound so incredibly round and luminous, it seemed to have a halo you could touch.

I rang the bell. The intercom wasn't working. I called her up. "Wait, don't go away!" she commanded. Her au pair, a voice student, retrieved me from downstairs. Fleming was feeding Sage, a crinkly, complaisant, and very quiet infant. Three-year-old Amelia was home in New York with Rick Ross, Fleming's actor husband.

We immediately began talking about the Bastille.

Gall's decision to stick with *Manon* came as an immense relief, she said. "I really thought, Well, I guess I'm not going to be singing Manon at the Bastille. Hugues Gall will call me in and say either 'I've got to give it to Angela and could you sing something else?' or I thought he'd just cancel it."

"Maybe he knows you opened the Met in the fall and sang a pretty fine Armida in Pesaro," I suggested. She gave me a puzzled look, as if I'd just offered unusual information. She wasn't kidding or being absurdly modest. A late bloomer, the thirty-seven-year-old Fleming was just awakening to the fact that she had finally, after several setbacks, reached the pinnacle of the opera world. For example, she survived a crisis of confidence and sadistic pedagogy by the legendary Elisabeth Schwarzkopf when Fleming was studying in Europe on a Fulbright. Told to sing like her teacher during a weeklong master class, Fleming returned home from Germany barely able to sing at all. "It took me two years to recover fully," she said. "Not only was I too young to sing in the finely controlled way she demanded, but she was manipulative. One day I was destined to be great; the next day I would have no career." Finally, Fleming emerged as the most fully equipped lyric soprano of her generation. Decca had just signed her up for a valuable and increasingly rare exclusive contract.

Fleming handed Sage to the au pair, sat back down on the ice-green leather sofa, and popped a Coke. Rubens would have rushed to his brushes. With her rosy skin and blue eyes, she exudes a seductive mix of sensuality, naiveté, shrewdness, and humor.

Her troubles didn't end with the German voice kommandant. With an honesty you don't often get from singers, she recalled a stressful *Don Giovanni* at La Scala in 1993, where she came very close to being fired by Riccardo Muti, the famously short maestro of fear. She was singing the nagging Donna Elvira, a role she has since dropped for the differently obsessive Donna Anna. But then, Carol Vaness was Donna Anna, while Cecilia sang Zerlina. All are survivors of Muti's Sala Gialla course in artist abuse. (The Sala Gialla is the yellow rehearsal room where Arturo Toscanini, another choleric puritan, liked to hold his music rehearsals, chasing down every sixteenth note and heretical interpolation.)

Muti typically hires two or three singers for the same part, sometimes keeping them guessing who will sing the prized opening night, a habit that fosters an atmosphere of insecurity that drives them crazy while empowering the maestro, who adores it. Everybody gathers around the huge table with their scores. "Now you sing the phrase," he will say, pointing at some shaking soprano. "And now let's hear how *you* sing it."

Sometimes the process identifies a shock-proof talent. A little-known Alagna so distinguished himself in *Traviata* rehearsals, he was bumped to the first cast and had one of his first great triumphs, partnering another Muti discovery, Tiziana Fabbricini, as Violetta. Lauren Flanigan, the unflappable and underappreciated diva of the New York City Opera, startled him with her perfect octave jumps in *Nabucco* and was awarded more than her expected number of performances. Jane Eaglen survived the hazing when she arrived for her first *Norma* rehearsal and was immediately tested with the taxing entrance aria. "Sing 'Casta diva,' " Muti ordered after staring at her intensely for several minutes. He soon found out that Eaglen was someone who absolutely cannot be bullied. She took a deep breath and sang the bloody thing, start to finish. "Hmmmm. We have a Norma," he declared, and continued with the rehearsal.

"Looking back, that was truly the lowest point, ever," Fleming said. "Thank God Cecilia was so friendly and supportive."

I remembered a joke that captures the conductor's legendary vanity that I first heard from Bartoli and now shared with Fleming. Muti has been banished to the desert as punishment for his lack of humility. After three days, he drops to his knees, hands outstretched, begging God for water. "Forgive me," he gasps, "I promise to mend my ways." So God sends down three drops of water. "O, thank you, thank you," Muti says. And uses the water to slick back his hair.

Fleming laughed, leaning back until she was practically lying down on the couch, then continued her tale.

One of Muti's associates came to Fleming's dressing room and said that the maestro was worried she might get booed on opening night and maybe she shouldn't sing the first performance.

"I got so mad," she remembered, "I told him, 'If I don't sing opening night, I'm going home.' At that point, I really didn't care if I sang at La Scala. I'd had enough. The stunned man conveyed the message to Muti, who changed his mind. Suddenly I was singing."

"So did you have a big triumph?"

"Nope," Fleming said, making a face. "I tripped on my dress making my entrance—not that that helped with the audience. Italians have no feeling for the underdog. But I didn't get booed, either. It just wasn't that great a success."

"Think you'll ever sing with him again?"

Fleming looked up and pursed her lips. "I think I would have to be feeling really generous," she said.

Already booking into the next century, she had few openings in her calendar anyway, with, for instance, the world premiere of *A Streetcar Named Desire* by Mia Farrow survivor André Previn looming on the horizon in San Francisco. Not so long ago, she'd left her long-time manager, a big bear of a voice buff named Merle Hubbard, for CAMI's Matthew Epstein, in a calculating move that startled quite a few. But CAMI, she explained, provides the kind of support staff, including a travel department, that makes life easier for someone with a complex schedule and a large household. Whether Epstein's aggressive booking pace and game plan was a good one is hard to say.

Just who is his client? A Verdi singer? A Mozartean? A bel canto specialist? Fleming can sing almost everything, even jazz, and at her most omnivorous she recalls Cheryl Studer, that other hugely talented soprano who could not make up her mind. Her manager wants her to concentrate on the Schwarzkopf and Te Kanawa repertoire—Mozart and Strauss, with only a little bel canto, and next to no Verdi and Puccini. Yet given the shortage of ample-voiced Verdian sopranos, wasn't that peculiar?

"We had a transatlantic tug-of-war just the other day," she agreed.

"I hate thinking about these decisions," she stated, getting up to hunt for Sage's rattle. "It keeps me up at night. What is right in the long run? I can't say I am really sure. I suppose someone like Cecilia sort of avoids the issue by singing not so many roles. At the moment I still tend to make up my mind on a project-by-project basis. There are conductors and directors I want to work with. One thing I do know is I will be singing more recitals, which would allow me to be home with my kids even more."

So many recitals, she thoughtfully keeps a list of her gowns on her PowerBook to remind herself not to wear the same one twice in the same place.

Nor is she budging on another issue that has brought her pressure from some of her image makers. She often concertizes with Helen Yorke—a female accompanist is still a novelty in the concert arena—and planned to use her for her Alice Tully Hall recital in May. "This notion of what looks correct is too ridiculous," she said. "We're making music together. I like singing with her. I wish people would leave it be already."

"So what's the program?"

"Lots of different things," she answered. "I like to mix 'em up. Strauss to Ricky Gordon, who writes songs for me. And maybe a piece by some friends of mine, Andrew Thomas and Gene Scheer. It's called 'Another New Voice Teacher,' and it'll strike a familiar chord with many people, I suspect."

She grinned.

"It goes something like this," she said, and, gesturing effusively, started to sing:

I just found a new voice teacher
and now I'm expecting great things.
I'm finding a place, a cavernous space
a spot in my forehead that rings.

I just found another new voice teacher
who thinks I have nothing to fear
who believes with her power
at a hundred an hour
it's certain I'll have a career.

She curtsied and fell back onto the sofa, laughing. It wasn't the end of the song, but Sage needed to be put to bed. Dinner was ready.

A FEW HOURS LATER, as I made it up the last crooked landing to my apartment in the rue du Temple, the phone rang.

It was Herbert Breslin calling from Montevideo, surely using someone else's credit card.

"God, I just had to call someone," he gasped. "That *Forza* at the Met! They had to bring in stretchers to take us out, what with everybody in a coma." He was still laughing about it two days later, thousands of miles away in the Uruguayan capital. The Fat Man was giving a concert in the stadium.

The Met's new *La forza del destino* with Domingo had turned into the tenor's own *Fille du régiment*, an act of vocal contortion and self-punishment for which there was no rational explanation. Alvaro, a half-breed Inca prince who ends up as a hermit monk in Spain living a few craggy holes away from his beloved Leonora, is an unrewarding role in an episodic work by Verdi at his gloomiest. If you need to hear *Forza* sung really well today, it is probably best to acquire the old Decca set with Tebaldi, Mario del Monaco, and Ettore Bastianini.

Cackling with joy, Breslin described Domingo lurching between two other miscast singers, the bulky Sharon Sweet and the pleasantly ineffectual baritone Vladimir Chernov, who tossed his shoulder-length hair as usual. The production, by del Monaco's cigar-chomping son Giancarlo, was dark and dreary. In Herbert's description, the principal threesome looked like two potatoes and a string bean ladled out of the soup tureen Fra Melitone hovers over in the opera's one intentionally comic interlude.

"I will refrain from comment on Mr. Domingo's contribution," Breslin continued grandly. "He is a serious artist. He tried his best. But Vladimir Turnoff and Sharon Sour. When are they going to change their names? 'Chernov' and 'Sweet' just don't quite catch the full dimension of their vocal splendor."

He took a deep breath to compose himself.

"How's Miss Butterball?" he asked.

Bartoli was getting a cold.

CHAPTER NINE

Get a Muffler

CELEBRATED Roman entertainer of another age, the emperor Nero, always wore a protective scarf around his neck and kept a voice coach by his side. He loved to sing, never missed his own recitals, and made sure nobody else did, either. Attendance was mandatory. Chroniclers tell us he gave freely of his time. As dusk turned to deepest night, and finally morning filtered through the columns of his golden house near the Roman Forum, guests would feign heart attacks just to be carried out the doors. Women sometimes gave birth waiting for the last encore.

I thought of Nero when Bartoli called one evening in mid-March. Released from maid duty at the Met, Bartoli had taken the train to snowy Minnesota for a recital with the Schubert Club. The weather proved uncooperative. The fuel froze on the train; the hall was a little chilly, too. Signing autographs afterwards, she felt a chill but couldn't bring herself to leave. She had a cold by the time she arrived in Washington, D.C., for a song recital with the Performing Arts Society, which was to be followed the next morning by a special concert in the chambers of the Supreme Court. Both events had just been cancelled. She needed time, she said, to recover for her Carnegie Hall recital debut just two days later, in the scheme of things a bigger event. A solo recital at Carnegie is the pinnacle of every artist's dreams. For most it never becomes reality.

She'd just had quite a surprise, she added breathlessly.

Last night, she arrived with Claudio Osele to find her New York rental disturbingly, mysteriously clean.

"I thought I'd been burgled," she said. "I walked in and it looked like someone had gone through everything." She seemed both amused and annoyed.

"This woman. Impossible! I still can't find my brassiere and a pair of heels I need for the Carnegie concert." The woman was the apartment's owner, who had come in to show the place to future tenants and decided to straighten things up a bit while there. Bartoli likes to save on maid fees, though her own housekeeping skills might not get her a job in Almaviva's household.

By the time I dropped by to see her a few days later, things were back to normal, with clothes on the beds, suitcases spilling out CDs, videotapes, and sneakers. The coffee table was cluttered with enough medicine to excite Florence Nightingale: eucalyptus bottles, aspirin, echinacea, cough syrup, vitamin C, Kleenex. An opened carton of tea was on the kitchen counter.

Things looked dire. They were dire. Returning to New York did nothing for her cold, and she had been forced to cancel the sold-out Sunday recital. But when it turned out that the popular hall was miraculously free on Thursday, she had decided to stay. Now it was Wednesday and the question was: would she be able to sing tomorrow night? Her accompanist, András Schiff, a teddy-bearish, ginger-haired pianist of Hungarian-Jewish origin with intellectual interests and intense work habits, had not been happy about the delay. He had his own busy solo career. But the two of them go back a long way. In his Haydn phase (preceding his brilliant harpsichord-be-damned grand-piano Bach period and his poetic, heavenly length late-Schubert period), Schiff had joined Bartoli, a mere novice, for the emotionally wild, twenty-minute solo cantata *Arianna a Naxos*. Their CD, *The*

Impatient Lover, an oddball but highly appealing assortment of Italian-language material by Beethoven, Schubert, and Mozart plus *Arianna,* won a Grammy. And so, for old times' sake, Schiff gallantly offered to stay. After all, *Arianna* was on the program again, and when else would he ever get to play it?

Looking distracted and bedraggled in her usual sweatshirt and stretch pants, Bartoli clearly wished she had simply gone home.

"What am I going to do?" she asked, looking gloomy. Judith Arron, the executive director of Carnegie Hall, had just called to say she was bringing over her doctor. Of course she would see the doctor, but this solicitude seemed to be getting on her nerves. "I'm already doing everything I can do," she said. Her lack of prudence at that drafty autograph session had landed her in a sticky spot. She could make everybody happy and just possibly hurt her voice. Or she could leave with another little black mark on her reputation as a reliable professional. Word travels quickly nowadays, and there was no one in the music business who didn't know she had cancelled long tours of Japan and South America in the last fifteen months.

"Why this pressure? Why risk the voice? Not for Carnegie, not La Scala—or God," Bartoli asked and answered, puttering around the kitchen, wondering if she should have another cup of tea. Like many singers, she tends to talk about "the voice" as if it belonged to someone else or existed separately in some other dimension.

The door opened and Claudio came in, dragging a new and huge green suitcase, though an investment in thermal underwear might have been more useful if this career was going to continue. He was in an affable mood and showed me pictures of his pretty vineyard near Verona.

The intercom started buzzing. A messenger was bringing up flowers—four dozen roses from James Levine. The vase joined the last delivery—three bottles of Chianti from Isaac Stern, the violinist who saved Carnegie Hall from destruction years ago and was eager to see her grace it.

Another insistent buzz. Bartoli looked puzzled. A surprise visitor. "Okay, send him up." A few minutes later, Frederick Noonan stood in the door with a small azalea tree. "Just so you have something nice to look at." He smiled, giving her a big hug. A quiet man with gray clothes and a mournful manner, Noonan used to work at Lincoln Center, where he pumped life into the moribund recital series, skillfully developing subscriptions that combined legends with nobodies. In 1990, when every other door was still shut in New York, he took a gamble on Cecilia and plugged her into the Mostly Mozart series during the summer, immediately following up with a recital at Tully Hall. Without Noonan, Bartoli's trajectory would not have been so steep here in America. And when he was fired by a jealous superior who found him insufficiently subordinate, Bartoli, who hates signing anything but contracts and photographs, wrote a protesting letter to Lincoln Center, which at least made Noonan feel better, though he still didn't have a job.

But then, she's often attentive to people who helped her on the way up: Noonan at Lincoln Center; Robert Cole at Berkeley; Charles Dutoit of the Montreal Symphony, who conducted her first orchestral concerts in North America; William Lyne, the respected director of the tiny, prestigious Wigmore Hall in London, who graciously let her step in for an ailing Nicolai Gedda in 1989, two weeks after she'd cancelled her own debut because of a throat infection. Yet at the same time, Bartoli's memory of what it is like to be a nobody appeared to be dimming. Or else why would she be so careless with her voice? Making sure you're well draped against drafts doesn't seem like a difficult task. Pavarotti, for instance, is so afraid of catching a chill after a sweaty performance that he usually only changes his costume from the waist down, toddling off for dinner improbably attired as Canio the clown or whatever role he's just finished, his head toasty in a wig yanked down on top of his ears and his bow-shaped legs stuffed into jeans and a pair of well-worn Hush Puppies.

"What do you think about this?" I asked Albert Innaurato over dinner that night, having left Bartoli sniffling into her Kleenex and facing another cancellation. The playwright, who shares his apartment with an enviable collection of opera recordings (including all the pre–World War I acoustical leavings of such insufficiently adored deities as Eugenia Burzio, who took sleeping pills when her lovers and her voice deserted her), might be expected to have insight into sudden fame. He was just in his late twenties when he woke up from poverty to celebrity and more money than his parents had made in their lives. *Gemini* was on Broadway, while his more controversial *Transfiguration of Benno Blimpie* played off-Broadway. By the eighties, critics started picking apart his newest offerings. Now he was starting to put his life back together again, finishing a new play and curtailing an appetite for ice cream that made him almost as big as Benno.

"No ash sitter ever gets all the grime out," he said.

"Meaning?"

"Meaning that great success when it comes early, when you're young, doesn't seem that way; life seems so slow, and you are sure every crisis is the end and reversals will do you in. You become morbidly aware of your limitations. Without comparing my success with Bartoli's, I sense in her a little at least of what I experienced myself."

Innaurato had interviewed the mezzo at stardom's gate for *Vanity Fair*, and felt a certain sympathy.

"My family was a little like hers, provincial Italians who knew nothing about contracts, networking, or the kind of behavior expected of high-flying professionals. I'd cancel meetings with important people, always claiming to be sick. I was hated for that, maybe rightly, but nobody knew how scared I was. I was unbelievably insecure."

Innaurato paused to study the menu. I could see his brown eyes glimmering and his big chest pumping air underneath his mulberry vest.

We both really wanted the special of the day, cappelletti with meat and cheese, but mournfully settled on chicken breast in a light sauce.

"Right I was!" he continued wryly. "It did evaporate. I think with famous young people, not only Bartoli, there is a paralysis which grows in direct proportion to fame. They may not even be aware of it. I also think Cinderella success postpones maturation. You are relieved of the pains and responsibilities of being a professional adult. A flock of people do everything for you and pick up the pieces when you misbehave. You rarely have to confront your immaturity and self-indulgence. You don't know what they are complaining about. Aren't

Finally here! Opera's most famous maid makes her Metropolitan Opera
debut as Despina in Mozart's *Così fan tutte* in February of 1996.

Luciano Pavarotti and June Anderson in the luckless 1995
Met production of Donizetti's *La Fille du régiment*:
the king of high C struggled for high B.

Two years later, and no wiser, Mr. P signed on for *Turandot* with web potato Jane Eaglen as the ice princess of China.

"Why is my fee so low?" Another phone call for manager Jack Mastroianni, a master of the "diva dienst," the twenty-four-hour service expected by opera's kings and queens, among them Cecilia Bartoli.

Joseph "That-wig-is-going-on-with-or-without-you" Volpe, the take-no-prisoners general manager of the Met.

The Bartoli apartment building not far from the Vatican walls,
in the pleasantly leafy neighborhood where she was
born and still spends most of her time.

The great days of helmet hair and high notes: Renata Tebaldi
and Joan Sutherland admire the Metropolitan Opera
before its opening in September 1966.

Tebaldi and Sutherland recorded for the Decca company, whose brightest soprano star these days is the American Renée Fleming (right). Mezzo Susan Graham keeps her company in Richard Strauss's *Der Rosenkavalier* at the Opéra Bastille in the fall of 1997.

Fleming entertains crowds as the eighteenth century's material girl in
Jules Massent's *Manon*, also at the Bastille in the spring of 1997.

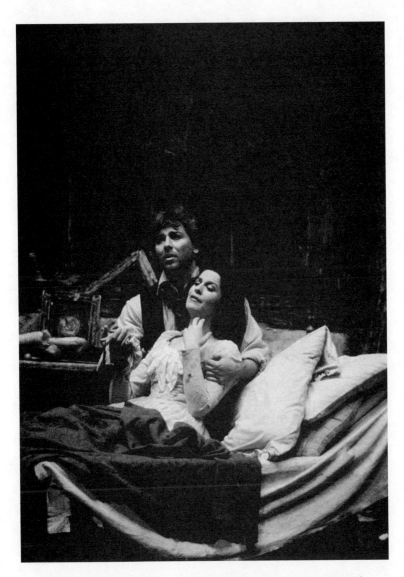

Roberto Alagna weeps over Angela Gheorghiu in the last act of
Puccini's *La Bohème* as the Love Couple make their first unhappy
joint appearance at the Met in the spring of 1996.

Angela Gheorghui, as Micaëla in the Franco Zeffirelli production of *Carmen*, wearing the blond wig she loved less than the Met's general manager.

Ach du Lieber! The strangest *Elektra* in recent history
featured a deconstructing Hildegard Behrens, along with
Deborah Voigt as Chrysothemis, the evening's big
surprise in the 1992 Met production.

Soprano Patricia Racette sings an offstage toast to the
Santa Fe Opera's *Emmeline*, a tonal opera actually written
by a non-dead composer (Tobias Picker).

Voigt poses with an admirer.

Happy ending: Cinderella eats her cake in the last scene
of Rossini's *La Cenerentola* (in October 1997 at the Met),
the signature role Bartoli's rags-to-riches rise . . .

. . . A transformation also captured in an official publicity photograph.

you an exception, after all? Who else from your class or background transformed themselves this way?

"That," he said, "is the dark side to quick success."

STANDING IN THE EMPTY BLONDNESS of Carnegie Hall the next day, Judith Arron tried to find something upbeat to say. "She seems to be coughing more early in the day than later," was the best she could do as Mastroianni walked over so we could all stare at Bartoli pouring herself a cup of tea from a silver platter placed next to the piano and approve of her toasty turtleneck sweater. Schiff was sitting quietly at the piano, staring into space. Osele, attired in a raincoat, was slouching around the hall as he usually did when she rehearsed, testing the acoustic from various places.

By now it was already twelve-thirty, and Bartoli was still unsure about singing that night. While singers often will show up for an opera with a minor sore throat or cold, armed with aspirin or echinacea to reduce inflammation and constantly sipping water in the wings, proceeding with an entire recital program when you're sniffling is pretty stressful. And lurking somewhere in every afflicted singer's brain is The Fear—that indescribable horror of losing the voice, of sudden, total shutdown in front of thousands of people. Waiting for Bartoli to start singing, I remembered Rodney Gilfry, a suave young American baritone featured on many of John Eliot Gardiner's Mozart recordings, and a onetime Figaro to Bartoli's Rosina. Last spring, I was sitting in a café on Neal Street near Covent Garden in London when he came running by with his gym bag. "What are you doing?" I asked him. "You're singing Billy Budd tonight." He explained that he always exercised the day of a performance to make sure he was totally fit. As we chatted, he told me about his encounter with The Fear. It came one night unexpectedly when he was singing Enrico in *Lucia di Lammermoor* with Alagna and the European superstar coloratura Edita Gruberova. "It wasn't quite my repertoire, and the role was probably a little big for me," he said, "and I hadn't been feeling tip-top but went on anyway. Alagna wasn't well, either. This was just around the time when Alagna's wife had been diagnosed with a brain tumor, and he had taken so many pills to calm him down he came close to fainting.

"Anyway, in the middle of the show, my voice suddenly just gave out. I could hear Gruberova gasping 'Rodney, mein Gott!' from somewhere in the wings and getting so agitated she missed her entrance. We continued until a scene change, and then I walked off to my wife and kids thinking, Well, it's over, but at least I've got them. I'd ruptured a vocal cord." Gilfry recovered completely and sings in all the top houses, but the incident left him with a sense of frailty he fights off with his workout routine.

Arron's stage whisper brought me back to Carnegie. "She'll make it, don't you think?" she was saying, bending down over Mastroianni, who had slumped down next to me in a seat close to the stage. A quietly determined woman in a pastel suit, Arron had turned Carnegie Hall into such a smoothly run institution, her efficient staff had called every single subscriber the weekend before to notify them of the concert's cancellation and rescheduled date within a matter of hours. She was clearly hoping the day would end without another phone marathon.

"Has she said anything?"

Mastroianni shook his head. Schiff whispered something to Bartoli that made her laugh for the first time. Putting down her teacup, she cleared her throat and began with one of Rossini's many settings of "Mi lagnerò tacendo" ("I shall suffer mutely"), which now took on an ironic undertone, though I heard nothing occluding the million-dollar pipes. I was sure she still felt under the weather, but she sounded fine.

"I can still remember when she first saw Carnegie Hall," Mastroianni murmured. "It was in the summer of 1990, and we were walking by this place and she got so excited. She really wanted just to stand on the stage, even though singing here was still a distant dream, at best. But she was so eager. So I called up a friend from the house phone and we got permission to walk on the stage. She stood right there where she is now and sang a few bits from 'Voi che sapete.' " He looked worried. He had invested so much time and energy getting her to this moment, this recital, and now for want of a muffler . . .

This wasn't the first time he'd been in this situation. For Bartoli's orchestra debut at Carnegie in November of 1992, he'd positioned her with Dutoit and the Montreal Symphony in a program of Rossini showstoppers. New York at that time had not heard her sing a big program with orchestra; the engagement was crucial to his career-building strategy. Everything progressed smoothly until two days before the concert, when a bumpy plane ride from Rome to Paris so unnerved the mezzo she refused to continue to New York. Calling from Charles de Gaulle Airport, upset and alone, she said she was going to take the train back home to Rome. Telling her to stay there, he rushed to JFK, forgetting his jacket, caught the Concorde, scooped her up in the airport lounge. The next morning, they flew back to New York, and the next night Bartoli triumphed as Carnegie vibrated with ovations. It confirmed the emergence of Bartoli as the international star soon heralded by *Time* and *Newsweek* magazines.

But the dynamics between the two seemed to have changed since then with the appearance of her personal companion and confidant, Osele, who was standing in the back of the auditorium as she tested a bit of *Arianna* with Schiff humming along. "Sounding good, right? We do it!" he exclaimed, getting up. "Okay," she replied. Arron climbed to the stage, her smile the size of the sun, followed by Mastroianni. Schiff picked up his music from the floor and seemed to freeze as he saw Osele coming slowly down the center aisle to the stage, dragging his feet and looking glum. Finally, he stopped in front of the stage and Bartoli knelt down to talk to him as everyone else pulled back nervously and a funereal atmosphere engulfed the stage.

"Why can't he smile?" Schiff whispered furiously, turning to Mastroianni. The two kept talking. After a few scary minutes, Cecilia got up, looking worried once more. "Okay. We try. See you later," she said, walking away. The concert was on.

And shortly before ten that night, the ordeal was over—not the greatest of evenings, but no disaster, either. What Bartoli occasionally lacked in tonal beauty, she more than made up for with an intense performance of *Arianna*, turning the abandoned princess's surprise, laments, self-recriminations, and outburst of fury into a compelling little opera.

Decca no doubt noted a nice uptick in sales of *The Impatient Lover*. Cyberspace meanwhile filled up with the postings of cancelled-out Washington fans, some of them three-time losers. One sent an "Open Letter to Cecilia Bartoli and Her Management" to the Bartoli home page on the Internet. "Dear Cecilia," he wrote. "My entire family was planning on going along with friends and co-workers. I bought those tickets last August, a full 6 months before your concert. I understand you could not control having a cold (although I would question the wisdom of your management team sending you to a concert in Minnesota in the midst of winter just a few days before your scheduled D.C. appearance). . . ."

"Got any answers for him?" I asked Mastroianni.

"He should try to organize a tour only in nice weather," he answered tightly. "They asked and she wanted to go."

SHORTLY THEREAFTER, the Alagna juggernaut hit New York, just as Mr. P was seeing if he could sing his way through Giordano's *Andrea Chénier*. It wouldn't take long to find out. Chenier sings the first of his four ardent arias in the opening scene, surrounded by frivolous aristocrats who wish to dance the gavotte on the eve of the French Revolution. Only Maddalena di Coigny really listens to his song of warning, and she will later die with him on the guillotine.

Chénier had helped open opera's doors for me, in 1966. The two singers onstage were neither young nor fair; they were plump and unattractive. Yet when they looked into each other's eyes and sang of love, the intensity of their song transcended the reality of their being and I was enslaved. I had thought love was reserved for beautiful people—popular people like prom queens and wide receivers—but it seemed to be much grander and mysterious than I had ever believed, and I became passionately attached to Zinka Milanov, who abandoned me immediately by retiring that very day. I had unknowingly attended her farewell.

A year later, Franco Corelli and Renata Tebaldi were even more thrilling than Richard Tucker and Milanov. He struck his typical contrapposto pose to sing of the beauty of life, of azure heavens and violet-covered meadows, "Un dì all'azzurro spazio," and then pumped a little extra volume into the final high notes because she would probably miss hers. Only a few years later, this clarion-voiced, handsome bag of nerves suddenly retired without singing the Otello everyone had expected.

Now it was Mr. P's turn, in a new production by Nicolas Joël that was low on energy right from the start, with aristocrats gathering stiffly under a huge, precariously tilted mirror no doubt meant to symbolize their perilous situation. At least the tenor fit in with his limited locomotion, stepping gingerly into the palace, where Aprile Millo hovered sweating bullets underneath a large wig, probably wondering which one of them was in worse shape. They had already transposed the last duet down to avoid the irksome high C, but while that was probably wise, the music that came before often sounded surprisingly good. Millo sang carefully and prettily, if not dramatically. As Pavarotti delivered Chénier's improvised poem, standing with his fists in his pockets and his eyes glazed, the sky turned blue and the meadow violet. There was no mistaking him for an ardent young revolutionary; but neither had he forfeited his crown to the terrier tenor nipping at his ankles.

Alagna was making his long-awaited Met debut in Puccini's *La Bohème* with Angela Gheorghiu as Mimì and his Paris Elisabeth, Karita Mattila, improbably cast as Mimì's pal, the shoe-buying, dinner-plate-dropping Musetta. Simone Young, a young Australian, was also making her debut, only the second woman to conduct at the Metropolitan Opera in its entire history, and still one of the few with a big career.

Posters affixed to bus stops and construction sites in the Lincoln Center neighborhood announced the arrival in our midst of "The Tenor of Our Generation" and his new recording for EMI. Outside the Met's lobby, scalpers prowled the pavement, circling the glass box displaying the cast list and a rare Sold Out sign. Even Hollywood took notice: a sitcom producer and his three guests gamely shelled out $2,000 in large bills to a hustler in a yellow bomber jacket for orchestra seats costing $125 each. Others importuned the fortunate many streaming through the doors, holding up handmade signs pleading for a ticket.

And after all that, Alagna proceeded to give an earthbound performance. Nervous and very possibly, as he claimed, not well, he reached for Mimì's tiny cold hand and started Rodolfo's first-act aria, "Che gelida manina." The world's riches mean nothing to me, the poet sings, moving ever higher on the scale; I dream of castles in the sky. Ideally, the castles are outfitted with the pinnacle of a high C. But Alagna couldn't reach that high that evening and seemed to wince. Many tenors transpose the aria down a half-step to begin with, but what was the poor guy going to do, stop the orchestra and say, "Simone, let's try it again in the other key?"

His voice had briefly failed him and he suffered visibly. As the scene changed to the festive Café Momus, where the Bohemians celebrate Christmas Eve, Alagna sat glumly at the table while everyone else enjoyed the antics of Mattila, probably the tallest, funniest, and loudest Musetta in many years. Gheorghiu, meanwhile, showed off steadier nerves and a freshly fragile voice that gently probed the tender details of Mimì's suffering phrases.

Reviews were mixed, and Alagna was said to be depressed for days before recovering his whimsical nature. One of the performances featured a different Mimì, and he realized he wasn't feeling well—no, not well at all. He was sadly, unavoidably sick, and would have to stay at his hotel with his favorite Mimì.

Solicitous retainers dropped in on the couple that night to see if anything was needed—chicken soup, perhaps. The couple was watching CNN, practicing their English. After chatting amiably for a while, Alagna suddenly got up from the couch and reached for his jacket. His visitors stared at him, perplexed. "So let's go," he said. "Where are we having dinner?"

Dinner! He was meant to be sipping champagne at the Café Momus on the stage of the Met right about then! Someone in his retinue had the wit to suggest eating in the hotel restaurant. If Volpe heard Rodolfo went out for dinner, his Met career would be over before dessert.

At the Bastille, Hugues Gall snorted as he heard about Alagna's troubled debut. Still mad over the *Manon* the tenor had cancelled, the general manager finally squeezed out a "so sorry to hear that." The offices of the summer festival in Orange in the south of France warmed up with similar feelings of schadenfreude. The Love Couple recently had caused a schedule change by withdrawing from a projected staging of Gounod's *Roméo et Juliette*. Gheorghiu had decided she did not wish to sing in a large, unamplified outdoor arena, though Orange had never been anything but a large outdoor arena (with superlative acoustics) since the days of the Romans.

CHAPTER TEN

Endless Night

JUST BEFORE NINE-THIRTY one chilly March morning, some twenty-five sleepy-looking people filed wearily into the Met's pleasantly bland board room. There were members of the wig and makeup departments, representatives of the stage, chorus, and orchestra unions, a person from wardrobe, another from the box office, deputies of the music and directing staffs, two press representatives, and the production team from the Met's media department.

And me, the scriptwriter. The time had come to think seriously about the Jimmy Levine gala that would galvanize the music world at the end of the next month. The gala was now so long, Nero could have produced it. Sixty singers, more or less, many of them pensioners, had been invited to celebrate the maestro's twenty-five years at the Met. Many, I was horrified to see, had accepted, meaning I would have to write their entrances and their exits, as in "And now, weeping and waving as she leaves the stage of her many triumphs, wearing a layered outfit sprinkled with sequins and dragging her train, is

Madame Grimgerda, whom we thought was dead/retired/singing Klytemnestra in Chile."

A meeting of such scale was unheard of at the Met, where people use e-mail to communicate if they do so at all. But Sarah Billinghurst had thought the time had come to mobilize a united front for what was unofficially called the March on Moscow. We'd be going down in snow and fire on April 27, 1996. Just the task of feeding and watering them in the undersized dressing-room areas boggled the mind. There was hardly a person—except the anniversary boy—who didn't think this gala thing was too much of a good thing, but by now there was no turning back.

Volpe had let it be known that "whatever Jimmy wants" he should get. This task was, however, made difficult by Levine's legendary unavailability and his even more legendary reluctance to make up his mind. In keeping with Met tradition—often very frosty to other talented conductors—Levine was conducting the entire concert himself.

"This is a nerve-wracking project we are embarked on," Billinghurst was saying, eliciting laughter. She presided over the meeting swathed in a scarf and a festively floral silken ensemble. Jonathan Friend brightened the other end of the long conference table with his yellow sweater and deadpan mien. Questions and problems presented by the gala were discussed for nearly an hour.

For starters, there was the opening number—the overture to a Wagner bomb called *Rienzi*, which drags on for thirteen minutes. Thirteen minutes! How many times could the camera show the trumpet section on television? All effort to get Levine to choose a chirpier, shorter overture had failed.

The discussion moved along to the gown problem. Some divas have less taste than others. Should they be asked to bring two gowns to the rehearsals so the less ugly one could be chosen?

Should they wear makeup? And if so, should they put it on themselves? Makeup assistance was not generally provided for concert appearances at the Met. A note was made to bring in extra makeup people as well as extra dressers.

A member of the chorus union spoke up. "What about the chorus? Do they wear concert garb all night long?" They don't want to! They too would like to flaunt their finery. This presented an obvious logistical problem, given the number of soloists already changing. And would the union consider such a change a costume change, adding to the bill? What about color clashes?

The unbelievably complicated rehearsal schedule now needed to be addressed. Not only was the program still changing one month before the event, but it included music that either hadn't been played recently or had never been played at all, a good deal of it sung by artists with complicated travel plans. For instance, Gabriela Beňačková, famous for her beetle-browed impersonation of the water sprite Rusalka, was still going to be airborne when the orchestra rehearsed her silvery Song to the Moon.

When scientists finally perfect the teletransponders previewed in the *Fly* movies and there is no longer any danger that the voice of Ben Heppner will end up in the body of Kathy Battle, singers will be first in line for their personal model. It will function like a fax machine that sends molecules instead of paper, so that never again will a diva have to be the prisoner of place and time.

The room fell silent as Friend identified a problem that would take weeks to resolve. His terrifying words were, "We may need a harpsichord."

Stunned looks all around. "For what?"

"For the *Così fan tutte* duet."

The duet is with orchestra, but apparently Levine wanted to start with the short recitative that sets it up and which requires a harpsichord.

"Where are we going to put the goddamn thing? There is no room in the pit. Wouldn't this problem go away if the two girls just did a different duet without a harpsichord?"

Everyone was talking at once.

"Yes. But this is not a logical event."

"Have we ever used a piano for this?"

"Yes, but it's way back in the pit and the singers can't see it, which they need to for the recitative."

Friend, continuing, remorseless: "Don't we also need a harpsichord for *Don Giovanni?*" Bartoli and Bryn Terfel were teaming up for the popular seduction duet. She was also doing the long rondo from *Cenerentola*. The Met would be extruding choice bits into a commemorative album, possibly a two-CD set, for Deutsche Grammophon, whose sales would be boosted by her participation.

But where to put the harpsichord?

"Why don't we put the thing onstage and roll it down when we need it?"

"Because by the time it gets downstage it will be in the key of D-flat minor. They're delicate."

Billinghurst, smiling pleasantly, playing with her lavender scarf: "Perhaps, Jonathan, you could emphasize the difficulty of the harpsichord when you speak with Jimmy?"

"I'll see what I can do."

No one seemed to think it possible to just pick up the phone and call Jimmy, who does have an office here at the Met.

Billinghurst now plodded on to the matter of seating. During regular performances, latecomers are herded into a viewing room.

"People paying a thousand dollars a ticket would like to be able to leave to go to the bathroom, don't you agree?" It was agreed that normal house rules would be suspended.

The discussion moved on to the matter of the special gala curtain.

Billinghurst, beaming: "And what *is* the special curtain? Will it be a surprise?"

Two people simultaneously infused with the same vision: *"A large photo of Kathy Battle!"* The room filled with chuckling and whooping at the thought of the banished minor divinity towering in effigy over the pit.

Billinghurst, after recovering her composure: "Mr. Volpe has asked that champagne be served backstage afterwards."

Friend, muttering: "It may be a champagne breakfast."

The next five minutes were spent on the backstage situation and traffic management.

Billinghurst: "I think we need to ask all managers not to come backstage. If Luciano wants to bring Nicoletta, well, I guess we can't say no. But can we try to keep Herbert Breslin somewhere else?" With his large ego, Breslin would have trouble fitting into a dressing room already occupied by his chief client and his girlfriend.

"What about dressing rooms?" someone asked.

"There will be sharing, obviously. Significant others and family members must either stay out or realize that someone might be changing."

"I am thinking of Ms. Bartoli and her friend. Should it be pointed out to Ms. Bartoli and her friend that she may be sharing with Ms. Bumbry?" said someone from the directing staff.

Laughter, lots of it, as people imagined Bumbry, a woman with big clothes and big hair, in the same room with Bartoli.

Billinghurst: "This is something hard to contemplate. Any news from the box office?"

"Our capacity is $2.6 million. Today we are at $1.8 million. All $500 and cheaper tickets have been sold."

A person from wardrobe piped up: "What about pressing? Gowns will need to be pressed."

Another voice: "What about furs? Where do they leave them?"

Someone else returned us to the matter of dressing rooms, of which there were clearly not enough: "Um . . . Ms. Norman won't share. Will she have her usual dressing room?" (Norman apparently insists on special, decontaminated quarters set up for her in the extra men's chorus dressing room and equipped as her contract specified, with several sealed boxes of Kleenex and bottles of mineral water. Maria Ewing, the other problem dresser, afflicted with a more generalized fear of the world, would probably be stashed into the office of Ken Noda, Levine's special assistant.)

A clueless person: "But Norman's in the third part. She could probably share with—"

A weary person: "Yes. But she always comes two hours early. She'll probably be there for part one."

Billinghurst, trying to move along: "She will have to have her own dressing room because she won't sing otherwise. Do we have timing estimates?"

Various staffers now entered the discussion.

"Yes. We have the *Meistersinger* finale starting at 12:46 in the morning. That's allowing thirty seconds between pieces."

"I doubt that's enough time," cautioned Friend.

"When and where do artists check in? And where should they be until they go on? Ms. Bartoli . . . where will she be between her two scenes?"

Billinghurst: "In the audience." (Cecilia, when asked about her whereabouts the next day: "In the audience? I don't think so. Isn't there time for dinner somewhere?")

"What about Alagna and Gheorghiu?" someone asked.

"They'll probably go home and go to bed and then they can get up and come back. Plenty of time."

The meeting dissolved after a discussion of bowing etiquette.

IT COULD HAVE BEEN a nice evening, with the maestro on the podium and at the piano, which he plays so beautifully, surrounded by singers who were fond of him and possibly even each other, reminiscing about their times together onstage and on the road. They could have projected nostalgic photos and popped champagne corks with the audience.

But James Levine's twenty-fifth anniversary was definitely going to be different.

"Why should it be intimate or fun?" asked someone who works backstage. "There's nothing fun or intimate about this place."

Days after that first meeting, the lineup and repertoire had already undergone wrenching changes. Austrian legend Leonie Rysanek horrified everyone by cancelling, even though her long career at the Met included countless performances with Levine, who adored her. She had just retired from the Met with an eye-popping performance of the old Countess in Tchaikovsky's *Pique Dame*, rising through cracking floorboards B-movie-style and clawing her way into bed with the tenor in her ghost scene. After the final show, she waved for half an hour to teary and loud admirers from a stage covered with flowers. Only later did it become known that she had been diagnosed with cancer.

Another old-timer and Levine favorite, the mezzo Christa Ludwig, suddenly noticed she was buying a house that day.

"Perhaps we could flash cancellations as surtitles," someone suggested at the next meeting.

An anxious wig person spoke: "They must do their own hair and makeup. We can do comb-outs, but that's it. If anyone is bringing hairpieces, we have to be informed."

With some headshaking, it was noted that Levine was still insisting on playing the *Rienzi* Overture. And while Volpe would be interviewed for the telecast in the last intermission, Levine was unsure he wished to be interviewed. Paradoxically, the man who was giving himself an eight-hour gala was camera-shy—not that this was surprising to anyone in the press. Mortified by unsourced rumors about his personal life, Levine long ago found refuge behind a beaming podium facade that shielded him from any possibly unpleasant scrutiny. He rarely gave interviews.

The discussion returned to the program. The athletic German soprano Hildegard Behrens had been threatening to sing not one but two scenes from that toe-tapping party favorite *Wozzeck*. But she had allowed herself to be persuaded to consider something more tonal, without revealing what this might be.

Billinghurst continued: "Margaret Price has asked to appear early in the program so she can get back to her dog, Contessa. She is arriving on the Concorde on April 26."

I was suddenly totally wide awake. *Margaret* Price? I'd scripted an entrance for the other Price, Leontyne, who shared the stage with me when the Met inaugurated Lincoln Center with the world premiere of Samuel Barber's *Antony and Cleopatra*. She was the Queen of Egypt; I was a mute woman of the bazaar who huddled near the prompt box selling trinkets with the other extras. Miss Price, as we all called the politely reserved diva, made her entrance inside a swirling little pyramid that during one rehearsal refused to disgorge her. At first we heard polite knocking; then came plaintive cries from within. Stage hands tried their best to pry open her walls but not before we heard: "You idiots! Get me outta here. Help!"

But for most folks, her signature role, though, was the Ethiopian slave Aida, the vehicle for her Met farewell in 1985, which Levine conducted. She was still at large, giving the occasional quite enjoyable recital. For mysterious reasons, the Met had invited Margaret Price of Wales. The silver-voiced Price had never had much of a Met career, though I remember her beautifully floated Desdemona, a role she sang everywhere—including San Francisco, in a gala evening Billinghurst probably wished to forget, since it turned out to be the longest night anyone has ever spent at the opera. (Though now it looked like the record was about to be broken.)

The day of the San Francisco performance, Otello became too sick to get out of bed. His cover had been allowed to leave early, something Billinghurst, then the company's artistic administrator, had cause to regret. It was the opening of the season, a very dressy social event in San Francisco. Of the few tenors singing Otello, none happened to be on the western seaboard. The desperate company finally tracked down Domingo, who was rehearsing at the Met. Would he get on a plane and fly to the rescue? Domingo is always up for a challenge and could not have failed to see the publicity value in rushing to a private jet with his makeup kit. Late in the afternoon, he was on his way to San Francisco. The opera ball, which was meant to follow Desdemona's strangulation and Otello's suicide, was quickly rescheduled to precede the opera. Terry McEwen, then the company's general manager, stepped to the stage and announced that drinks were on the house until Domingo arrived, a little after ten p.m., he reckoned. It was now a little after six. Bulletins of Domingo's progress were sent out over the PA system, as in "Mr. Domingo has left Chicago!" or "He's refueling in Nevada and eating a steak!"

Price, a jolly woman by nature, found the whole spectacle very amusing as she clomped around backstage in her billowy gowns and slippers. She enjoyed a little gin sometimes, and as the evening got longer and longer, a friend of mine was dispatched to keep an eye on Margaret. But Price was very famous and my friend too awestruck to deal firmly with the diva. By the time the tenor finally arrived with a police escort, dowagers were weaving in the aisles and the chorus was tipsy. Quickly pinned into his cloaks, followed by unstable choristers, he stepped from his storm-tossed boat without falling into the water—possibly the only totally sober person in the house. Price, meanwhile, slowly progressed from her dressing room to the stage without bumping into the scenery. She sang beautifully until finally, in the last act, just as Domingo finished strangling her—it was by now around two a.m.—she fell blissfully asleep on Desdemona's bed. Witnesses insist she was snoring as Otello grabbed his sword and sang his last.

I wondered how to compress that heroic evening into a non-libelous sound bite for her entrance when a voice asked: "Can Nilsson be asked to come to Friday's rehearsal? And can we have a body mike available just in case?"

Everybody was counting on the jolly Swede and famous postwar Brünnhilde to brighten the long evening with a witty speech. But she seemed to be out of pocket on her farm near the North Pole, and there was no arrival date.

Provisions were made to feed the orchestra during the intermissions by closing down the cafeteria to everyone else.

Box-office rep: "There are still 450 tickets left at $850 and $1,500."

Stage director: "This is still a work in progress."

A few days later, Behrens finally revealed her song.

What had she decided to sing, out of a soprano repertoire that is not exactly small? She had decided to sing someone else's aria: Jane Eaglen's "Dich teure Halle" from Wagner's *Tannhäuser*, the impressionable maiden Elisabeth's roof-raising salute to her favorite chamber in her castle, the music room. Not only that, she absolutely had to be the first singer on the program, because she needed to fly home immediately.

Behrens had never sung Elisabeth at the Met. And rather more to the point, she couldn't sing it, with her worn voice and ghastly technique. There wasn't a person at the table who didn't know that, but there was also nobody there who was about to say: "Frau Behrens— *Frau Behrens!* Have you lost your mind?"

Certainly not Levine, whose Brünnhilde she continued to be. Just locating him seemed impossible. Had no one ever thought to equip him with a box of cookies he could crumble like Hansel as he trundled through the Met's backstage labyrinth?

A stage director then pointed out that the Jessye Norman selection, from Berlioz's *La Damnation de Faust*, required an unseen chorus. Should this chorus remain unseen? Or appear onstage—and if so, what should it wear?

There were many moments when I wondered if I'd landed among amiable lunatics. This was one. At least the harpsichord issue was approaching resolution. It would be parked in the pit; there would also be an upright piano for the *Mahagonny* aria which Teresa Stratas would sing, along with a quartet from John Corigliano's *The Ghosts of Versailles*—if she showed up, which wasn't likely given her track record. "Couldn't she just cancel now," someone pleaded, "and save us a step?"

WE WERE NOW in gala week. Cecilia was in Rome after a brief trip to London to wrap up the recording of Haydn's *Orfeo*. She was feeling a little under the weather but was planning to take the Concorde from Paris on Wednesday. And Eaglen had announced her new song for the evening. Since Behrens had stolen hers, Eaglen had taken imaginative revenge. I'm so sorry the moment wasn't caught on camera when Eaglen informed Billinghurst & Co. she had chosen Brünnhilde's Immolation Scene from *Götterdämmerung*. Clocking in at nearly twenty minutes, it's about the length of five normal arias.

"Yes, I would like something. I would like a portatoilet put up right outside the TV truck and food services throughout," Brian Large, the TV director, told Billinghurst when she asked if he had any special requests.

Cancellations and repertoire changes continued. The *Don Carlo* duet suddenly lost Nicolai Ghiaurov, leaving Thomas Hampson looking for a substitute King Philip. Montserrat Caballé was not feeling well enough to travel from Spain. And Teresa Stratas had discovered she had asthma. There would be no need for the *Mahagonny* piano, and Hei-Kyung Hong, the charming, underrated Korean soprano, would take Stratas's spot as Marie Antoinette in the pretty quartet from *Ghosts*, the only successful new opera heard at the Met during Levine's reign.

Somewhere along the line, *Tosca*—Levine's debut opera and an obvious gala choice—also mysteriously vanished from the program.

So did Bartoli. On Tuesday afternoon she decided she really wasn't feeling up to another voyage across the ocean. "I am sorry about this. Of course, I want to be there for Levine," she said on the phone. But she also had a concert tour starting on May 5 in Monte Carlo. She sent him a fax wishing him all the best, adding a small drawing of a heart with wings.

I surely wasn't the only one who had seriously wondered whether she would fly across the ocean to sing one aria and one duet, but the lateness of the cancellation meant that Terfel suddenly required a new piece and the second half a different finale. Neither would the gala album sell as well without Bartoli's participation.

At least good news had come from Nilsson, who had been tracked down and was fit enough to fly. And Alagna and Gheorghiu were in such excellent health they cheerfully rehearsed their duet (from *L'amico Fritz*, a Mascagni operaletta) and showed up for the *Bohème* matinee they were singing the day of the gala. Just before the curtain rose that afternoon, Joe Volpe slowly trudged onstage looking like his dog just died. The audience groaned. But it was just a joke. "It isn't often that when the general manager steps out he has good news," he said, as the audience relaxed. "But our Mimì and Rodolfo were married yesterday at City Hall. And so when the curtain falls today, you know that they will, however, stay together."

A much-married man himself, Volpe wisely refused to suggest how long.

But as the Fourth Tenor revived, the First or Second, depending on your view, took to his sickbed. Luciano Pavarotti had the flu. Always competitive, Domingo turned up for his gala rehearsals coughing constantly and pulling at his dewlaps, but even so failed to sound convincingly sick.

The rehearsals were spread out over several days, with each selection allotted one rehearsal, about all that Levine really needed to pull into shape even pieces the orchestra had never played in living memory, like Georges Bizet's *The Pearl Fishers*, with Terfel and Alagna singing its celebrated duet for two fishermen who love each other but a Ceylonese priestess even more. There was a touching moment when Grace Bumbry arrived to run through an aria from *Samson et Dalila*. She was Levine's Tosca at his debut twenty-five years ago. The orchestra applauded when she bustled excitedly onto the stage she hadn't recently adorned. She got through her aria smoothly enough, and then, as everybody expected her to go away, she asked to sing part of it again. Time was running out, and Levine really needed to move on. But she clearly just loved being on that stage of many triumphs long ago, and after a second's hesitation he kindly indulged her. "Sure, Grace. Let's do it."

Other singers were still dropping like flies. Marilyn Horne sent her regrets, and Margaret Price stayed home with her old dog. Behrens, of course, cancelled. But Eaglen stuck with Brünnhilde even so and left Elisabeth's much shorter aria to, well, whomever. Finally, Pavarotti cancelled, and a revised program had to be inserted into the printed program the day of the gala.

By now it had also become sadly evident that I myself would never celebrate any kind of anniversary with the company. Except for the opening spiel delivered by the urbane Garrick Utley, who would utter only so much fluff, my script was scrapped as insufficiently lofty, by either Volpe or Levine, I never did find out. I was thanked profusely and handsomely paid, but "girls who couldn't keep their socks on" had to be changed to "tragic heroines who died for love" or something else more suitable to the dignity of the Metropolitan Opera. Billinghurst turned the script over to the flowery old host of the Met's radio broadcasts, who happily rewrote every single line.

In its weirdness the scriptwriting experience was like the gala itself—a baffling adventure whose perfect image was the special gala curtain, which merely inscribed his name on what looked like a huge place card. There was nothing to suggest the arc of the career, because about one-third of the pieces had as little to do with Levine as the performers singing them.

It was as if his life had happened to someone else and he was just here making music. Could there not have been some mention of Tatiana Troyanos, whose mesmerizing presence had galvanized so many of his shows until her premature death from cancer in 1993?

Levine still shared his large apartment on Central Park West with a woman who had been one of the mezzo's closest companions. They'd all been friends for years. What a strange guy.

I ended up sitting next to a harried-looking man with a stopwatch and the gala program. He kept crossing off names and adding timings to others during the first of the three segments. "God, this audience is so kind," he suddenly whispered, as loud applause rewarded seventy-something Carlo Bergonzi for singing the tenor aria from *Luisa Miller* in fading tones, but the kind of classy phrasing you wish could be decanted directly into the heads of a lot of tenors half his age.

He told me he was a producer who had bought the gala for Dutch television.

"Are you showing the whole thing?"

"No! No!" he gasped. "We're Calvinists! We like opera, but in moderate amounts. A two-and-a-half-hour compilation will be just fine for little Holland."

He still had five hours or so to go, but figured he'd be using Renée Fleming's ravishingly floated "Depuis le jour" from Gustave Charpentier's *Louise* and the soprano aria from *Tannhäuser*, which ended up with Deborah Voigt, who delivered it with golden tones and such a big smile that she briefly animated her morose publicist, Herbert Breslin, whose chief client had stayed sick. I found Breslin prowling around the crowded lobby during the first intermission. Rumor had it that Mr. P would rise miraculously from his sickbed carrying his vaporizer and putter over to the Met to say a few words about Levine to the audience.

A sight worth waiting for but deemed unlikely by his manager. "No, I wouldn't put your nickel on that," he said, leafing through the program. "My God, the entire fucking scene from *Eugene Onegin*," he muttered. "They really know how to punish you. Can you buy me a sandwich or something?"

But the Met's bars had already been swept clean of food, and I went home to eat and watch the rest on TV.

Mr. P apparently also watched the telecast—until he tumbled out of bed with rage during the next intermission, when Utley interviewed Volpe. The general manager was saying how disappointed he was that Mr. P had not found it possible to drop by for a few words. When Volpe later took a break from the ceaseless singing and went to his office, the phone rang. Pavarotti was on the line, yelling at him for embarrassing him in front of the world when he was so sick.

"Aw, come on," Volpe said, after taking it for a few minutes. "We're both Italian."

CHAPTER ELEVEN

Bartoli for Italy

"WHATEVER HAPPENED to the Pope?" I asked Mastroianni. Back in February after the opening of *Così*, a concert in the Sistine Chapel with Bartoli had seemed like a sure thing.

"It's been difficult to find a mutually agreeable date for the Pope and Cecilia," he answered, sitting down at Duomo, a small restaurant behind Lincoln Center. "Did I say that with a straight face?"

His Holiness was busy touring underdeveloped continents, and now in May her dance card was also full, with concerts and a recital tour that would culminate at London's Wigmore Hall.

The Pope news was disappointing all around. His marketing strategists were unrivaled on this planet and perhaps in the hereafter. Was there a Christian who wouldn't buy a Bartoli video that had been blessed, so to speak, by the Pope?

Now a new project needed to be found to identify Bartoli with Italy—a country where a cycling champ named Michele Bartoli got most of the attention. She constantly complained about her lack of recognition in Italy to Italian journalists, amusingly oblivious to the fact that this might change if she actually sang there: her last staged performance was the 1993 *Don Giovanni* at La Scala with Renée Fleming. La Scala called with some regularity, but by the time the fabled house came up with a date she was usually booked; Pesaro, site of the summer Rossini Festival, conflicted with her vacations. Admittedly, Italian opera houses have a hard time planning anything, because most are run by incompetent political appointees and afflicted with powerful unions. The Rome Opera was still recovering from its last general manager, who spent $50 million he didn't have on things like English lessons for the theater's thirty-five firemen.

One way Bartoli could achieve instant local fame was to appear at San Remo, the splashy annual February pops concert in the seaside resort that was watched on television by one out of three Italians. Some of the suits at PolyGram dreamed of this. San Remo had made a millionaire out of Andrea Bocelli, a charming tenor in his late thirties who lost his sight as a child, but had become a popular concert artist, singing pop and opera tunes with a mellow voice coached by Franco Corelli. But not surprisingly, Bartoli and her manager questioned the wisdom of singing crossover when she had been so unusually successful getting pops people to cross over her way and listen to classics. Why water that down? Her instincts seemed right.

"We need to break CB into Italy," Mastroianni explained, throwing extra peperoncino on his usual dish of eggplant parmigiana. "But in a classy way. Right now, she wants to sing a lot of Vivaldi and I want to make another video. Venice seems like the perfect spot."

Mr. Four Seasons spent a good deal of his life in Venice teaching music at La Pietà, the most famous of the four *ospedali*, or charitable organizations, that cared for orphan girls and illegitimate castoffs. Part of the complex still exists on the Riva degli Schiavoni, just around the corner from the Piazza San Marco, including the building that housed the music school, where the girls learned to play instruments or sing in the church choir. In the very early eighteenth century, Vivaldi wrote some of his most charming music for these *orfanelle*, who gave immensely popular concerts, usually on Sunday in the Pietà's chapel, sitting high up on the second story and slightly, tantalizingly obscured by a decorative grille.

Attending one of these all-girl concerts (the sturdiest played kettledrum) was a must for every foreign visitor. In his Vivaldi biography, H. C. Robbins Landon includes a description of just such a visit by the philandering political philosopher and part-time opera composer, Jean-Jacques Rousseau. Frustrated by the "accursed grills" which concealed "the angels of loveliness" he asked a friend to arrange for a surreptitious meeting with the barely glimpsed Sophie, Cattina, and Bettina. On close inspection, one had a missing eye, smallpox had disfigured the second, the third was just plain ugly. He went home crushed (if admiring of their spirit, or so he wrote).

The custom has yet to be revived, and the chapel was long ago replaced by a larger church, which was finished after Vivaldi's death but even so is closely associated in the public mind with the celebrated composer. That was why Mastroianni was strategizing with a mutual friend, Marilyn Perry, the chairman of the World Monuments Fund and a chicly energetic force in the preservation movement. A kind of World Wildlife Fund for endangered monuments and architectural heritage, the WMF provides seed money and expertise for ailing buildings of significance the world over. The church of La Pietà received some assistance years ago, and Perry knew who might open its portals for a concert.

"Venice is as rich as Rome in opportunities, it seems to me," Mastroianni continued. "The Fenice wants her to fundraise, but she was never asked to sing at the Fenice when there still was a Fenice. Maybe when and if they open, she can appear in some interesting opera. But there has to be something before that."

La Fenice, first home to Verdi's *La traviata*, went up in flames earlier in the year during a renovation (not WMF funded), incinerated either by a contractor who had missed a deadline and wished to create a diversion that accidentally turned into an inferno (the preferred theory) or by a worker using a defective coffee machine. By the time helicopters dropped enough water on the place, the beautiful house with its strawberry upholstery and gilt-edged boxes was a pile of rubble.

Perry pointed out that the WMF was not only involved with Venice and Italy. The fund was helping to restore a temple near Angkor Wat, for instance, and looking for celebrity assistance. The thought of getting Bartoli to Cambodia by train and oxcart for a fundraiser provided brief entertainment.

"Still, perhaps she could be encouraged to develop a global interest in monuments?" Perry persisted. She could see a whole video series in the making. WMF had just received a major grant from American Express to compile an annual list of one hundred cultural landmarks endangered by industrial pollution and natural disasters: the Taj Mahal, the isolation wards at Ellis Island, the Alexander Palace in St. Petersburg, Chaco Canyon in New Mexico, and the conservatory in San Francisco's Golden Gate Park are just some of the current projects.

A conservatory? Mastroianni looked interested. "Tell me about it." Bartoli likes San Francisco.

"It's one of the few glass conservatories still in existence, though the damage from a recent storm was severe," Perry explained. "But by some odd fate, many of the female plants survived, though without the males they too are doomed. We're looking to raise funds to restore the central structure."

Mastroianni's jaw dropped. Perry was talking about a plant conservatory.

He thought Bartoli's interest in plants was probably restricted to bouquets. But the monuments idea was increasingly exciting to him. He could see himself taping the great singers of the present and future in the great monuments of the past.

"The point of this is for her to be home and develop her presence," he continued. "It seems to me this is what should happen. First, she should do a public concert in Venice, venue unspecified. This could be for the benefit of the WMF. Second, follow up with a CD in a studio in Venice, and third, do a video recording in venues to be decided. Something classy that says, 'I am Cecilia Bartoli and I am here for Italy.'

"What I see is a campaign for Cecilia along the lines of 'the future looking at the past,' " Mastroianni said. "There is an integrity to this which San Remo doesn't have—history, culture, social conscience. The future and the past. Let's look at Vivaldi's church for starters."

MASTROIANNI WAS NOT the only manager in town exploring new adventures in music-making. "Admit it," Herbert Breslin yelled into the phone, "recitals are boring! Can you bear another helpless person standing in front of the piano with their hands folded?"

"What are you going to do about it?"

"I'll tell you. I've asked Robert Wilson to come up with some new recital concept for Debbie Voigt that would maybe do something with color and images. Something suggestive of either the subject or the mood or whatever," Breslin said.

Wilson, once very fashionable for a slo-mo directing style reminiscent of tai chi exercises, seemed like an odd duck for the job. His shows spurned conflict and drama and regularly turned auditoriums into dormitories. But once upon a time, he taught the hitherto immobile Jessye Norman a thing or two about using her body onstage, and concocted a sound-and-light spirituals show, *Great Day in the Morning*, which people in Paris liked a lot. She wore tentlike dresses splashed with summery hues and looked queenly. The vogue had passed, but maybe it was due for a revival. Several singers were trying to animate the staid song recital. Dawn Upshaw and Lorraine Hunt recently had performed a Bach cantata evening staged by Peter Sellars, who once memorably placed his *Don Giovanni* show in a drug-dealing Harlem neighborhood and *Le nozze di Figaro* in an apartment building Donald Trump could have called home. I remember Upshaw wore a blue dress of nunlike simplicity while rolling ecstatically around the stage.

Besides, Wilson does have a feeling for lighting, and that is what Herbert was shouting about. "*Something!*—" he was still yelling—"something has to be done to change the way we do recitals today, without destroying the musical values. Few singers have the commanding presence to stand there all by themselves and pull you in."

This wasn't the first time Breslin was scheming to bring to the world something it didn't realize it wanted. In the late 1980s, he announced plans to stage Handel's *Messiah* in a large stadium with hundreds of angels dropping from the ceiling. That was just for starters. In those days he also handled PR for Sir Georg Solti, already elderly even then, but never mind. Herbert had plans, big plans, for Sir Georg. He wanted the legend to conduct an arena *Ring* cycle in which the love duet from *Siegfried* would be acted out by a nude (non-singing) couple and the stage would burn down at the end of *Götter-dämmerung*. But New York's unhappily restrictive fire codes and Sir Georg's defection to a less demanding publicist derailed the project.

CHAPTER TWELVE

Cooked Pigeons

THE DOOR OPENED on Silvana Bartoli and Figaro, who was scampering at her feet. The Bartoli dog seemed to have endured a barbarous shave by a local namesake.

"Summer," she said, gesturing to her hairless companion. "The poor *bestia* had some skin problem." They share this shady ground floor in an apartment building near the Vatican with two cats and the occasional stray. This is Rome, after all, city of seven hills and seven million cats. Flower pots and bric-a-brac crowd the small patio outside the unassumingly furnished living room with its cooling tile floor. A house-sized piano—no huge concert grand—a bulky television, and a large rustic dining table just off the kitchen fill the space. Shutters thwart the late-afternoon sun.

Of Rome's hills, this green and pleasant incline up behind the Vatican may well be the sleepiest. It seems as if nothing ever happened here of consequence, though history is never far away. Across the road, a plaque marks the sinuously sculpted little fortress as the retreat of Garibaldi and his stalwarts during the month-long siege of

Rome in 1849. Behind the house, a little higher on the hill, is the imposingly durable Aurelian Wall.

The family has lived on this street since 1957, Silvana said, sitting down a little stiffly on the piano bench and picking at the folds in her floral housecoat. Bartoli and her sister were due back from shopping any minute; Silvana was filling in with coffee and stories. Bartoli was born across the street, and while she has her own little apartment nearby, she spends most of her time here, cooking and cracking open the occasional new score. After a foreign engagement, she always returns to her mother for what Silvana called "clean-up work." She'll sing her programs for her mother to keep things fresh and polish the essentials.

"*Golla aperta,*" Silvana stated firmly, "that's what it is all about." Asked to demonstrate, she walked to the piano and picked out middle C while opening wide in the manner of a panicked dental patient. "Aaaaah," she sang, pointing her lips. "You must open your mouth wide and relax. Like you are yawning! That is the secret! You cannot tense up or look down to the floor. Sing out!" she said, and did just that, rising up the scale and down in a pure lyric-soprano voice that must have been delightful many years ago as Puccini's Manon, the role she sang in Spoleto. "Aaaahahahaha."

Her daughter has a very physical voice production which includes raising her shoulders and, in rapid passages, the kind of facial distortions an American teacher would beat out of students at an early age. Her mother shrugged it off. "It's not a technical matter," she insisted. "More of an emotional thing, a kind of losing yourself in the music."

Would she like to teach others?

She sat back down and sighed. Right now, she said, her life was too difficult. Her father was ill and she needed to help her mother take care of him and their little garden in Parma where she grew up. But she has started coaching Federica, she said, and thinks she too has a promising light soprano voice.

"What about the singers of the past?"

She mentioned Tebaldi, Teresa Berganza, and, from an even earlier time, the silver-voiced Tito Schipa, a tenor of great refinement and charm, whom she once knew when she was young and he was already retired from an illustrious career. "A quality-not-quantity kind of a singer," she explained.

Alas, also a bigtime spender whose story ended in poverty far away from home in America. It is hard to make predictions, but this is not a fate likely to befall Cecilia, a frugal girl, who just then pulled up in front of the house in a small, easily parkable Fiat. She could probably visit her first dollar in her Swiss bank account and once startled me with her comprehensive understanding of fluctuating exchange rates between the deutsche mark and the dollar. She may sing of building a house made of peacock feathers, gold and silver staircases, and balconies of precious stones in the Donizetti song "Me voglio fà na casa," but so far she has only purchased a modest apartment in the tax haven of Monaco.

The door opened and she came in with Federica, both in Dolce & Gabbana T-shirts. A relieved Silvana scuttled off to make coffee while Bartoli sat down with Figaro and a book I brought—the illustrated correspondence between Madame de Sévigné and Madame de Grignan, a famous mother-daughter team of another time. This daughter loved her mother, but at a distance, from her chateau in Provence, while Madame de Sévigné sat at her desk in Paris, depleting vats of ink describing the romantic and political complexities of life in the era of Louis XIV. The letters seem possible song-cycle material for a clever composer and interpreter: Madame is funny and eloquent, her daughter more reserved and prickly.

But actually use her clout to commission new pieces, as divas of the past used to do? As she looked through the book, faintly amused by Madame de Sévigné's corkscrews, she put it aside and said, "How about something like this instead?" and began to describe what sounded like a monodrama with music. She was thinking it might be interesting to dramatize the lives of Schubert and Rossini, using letters and music to illustrate the fickleness of *fortuna* and the vagaries of fame. When Schubert died in 1828, he left behind ten pairs of trousers, one hat, a few jackets and shirts, and thirteen pairs of socks. The rest was on paper, some six hundred songs, nine symphonies, a few operas, many string quartets and sonatas. He was all of thirty-one years old and appreciated by only a small group of fiercely devoted friends in Vienna. Rossini, just five years older, lived until 1868, and though he composed only sporadically over his last four decades, his fame was immense and his funeral cortège very long.

"Don't you think this is fascinating?" she asked. "Such different fates, and yet they lived at the same time. It is incredible to me."

I wasn't sure where this idea would go without the ministrations of Tom Stoppard, but it was a start.

Looking at the wall behind her, I asked about the thank-you note from Prince Charles that was on display with photographs and drawings. "He sent it to me after a recital I gave at Windsor Castle a few years ago," she remembered, and looked to see if her mom had returned. Then she smiled. "My mother was with me and we knew we'd be presented to the prince and so we coached her how to say 'Your Royal Highness' in English. Finally, the moment arrived, and I could see my mother's eyes glaze over at the sight of him. She was staring at me, desperate. And she stared at him in mounting horror. Finally, it was her turn. What does she say? She says 'Buona sera'! We couldn't stop laughing."

Silvana emerged with coffee and cake, and we moved to the dining table. Bartoli said Decca had arranged for her to finally meet Renata Tebaldi in July when she would be recording a modern string version of Rossini's cantata *Giovanna d'Arco*. The company recently located an unreleased Tebaldi tape in its vault, a bunch of arias she had recorded on a lark to fill out some studio time left over from her *Tebaldi Festival* album. Tebaldi had asked to hear the selections on quality speakers, which she didn't seem to have in her Milan apartment. The two were planning to meet in the studio.

Bartoli's thirtieth birthday was in a few days. Any big celebrations or plans? None, she said, though she would like to arrange her schedule to sing even less than she does, say, half a year, spending the rest studying music and "having a life." Meaning? She frowned, fork in the air. It seemed to mean not getting older without enjoying being young. She missed staying out late.

Before that plan could be put into motion, though, she was heading to Zurich for a revival of a *Cenerentola* directed by Cesare Lievi, who had also been chosen to stage the Met's production in the fall of 1997. Older and better-known contenders like Franco Zeffirelli, Giorgio Strehler, and Luca Ronconi had all been dropped, for reasons including age, expense, drunkenness, and poor phone etiquette.

As I left, Federica trailed after me bearing a saucer of milk for a friend who was waiting in the bushes outside the entrance.

TWO DAYS LATER I was in Venice where Bartoli's manager's video team was meeting to scout out a suitably historic site for their "Bartoli in Italy" project with the World Monuments Fund.

La Fenice was obviously not a candidate. I stopped by the rubbled remains of the once exquisite theater early in the morning. Bits of old newspaper blew around the fire-seared shell and twisted heaps of ash and blackened timber. Cinderella would wear out several brooms just sweeping the lobby. Even four months after the fire, La Fenice was still a pile of burnt rubble, open to the sky and periodically probed by investigators looking for answers that seemed awfully slow in coming. It took great effort to remember the stage glittering with Rossini's *Armida* starring Katia Ricciarelli as a sorceress who could make gardens and palaces appear with the wave of a wand.

Where are these sorceresses when you really need them?

Optimists point out that the Fenice was quickly rebuilt the last time it burned down, in the nineteenth century, but in those days the Veneto was run by the Austrians, whose mania for music overcame their own natural inclination to bureaucratic lethargy. Knowing something about Venice, where I spent the occasional summer, I expected to be dead by the time the curtain rose.

The day was already heating up as I walked toward the Piazza San Marco to meet the video crew. Locals have the right expression for days like this: "So hot cooked pigeons are falling out of the sky."

Mastroianni was standing in front of the basilica looking over a list of places he expected to visit with his team: the director, Brian Large; the producer, Judy Flannery; two sound engineers provided by Decca; and an Italian to translate and handle the logistics. Instantly recognizable and occasionally available for concerts, San Marco with its four bronze horses high up on the loggia led the list of desirable sites. In the morning sun, San Marco's white domes and colorful stonework glittered like heaven's treasure chest.

"Have you thought about the floods?" asked Marilyn Perry of the WMF, who had just arrived, topped off by a straw hat and trailing a multitude of summer scarves.

"Christ," said Mastroianni. "No."

On *acqua alta* days the water can rise up to your knees, and people teeter along on elevated *passarelle* that look like long picnic tables for midgets. Bartoli's availability in late April of 1997 happened to coincide with the spring floods, which could add an adventurous touch to the taping.

Maybe she could accessorize that swimsuit-and-hat combo she wears on the Bartoli Internet site with a pair of designer galoshes and a swamp pump.

We walked to the basilica's offices behind San Marco. A thoroughly modern monsignor was waiting for us in his small office. Docksiders added a spiffy touch to his shortsleeved priest suit; a small crucifix looked down on a credenza with a fax machine and computer terminal. He had carefully gone through the proposal and loved the idea of the concert in his beautiful basilica.

"But I must ask you a question right away," he said. "How loud is it?"

Mastroianni, who was translating, looked puzzled. "How loud? . . . You mean the signorina Bartoli?"

"No. I mean yes, the whole thing. The concert. I have to ask because the Fenice orchestra, well, you know they were playing here the other week and it was a bit problematic. Indeed, we had to ask them to leave. It was the music, a Mahler symphony. Our conservators worried the mosaics might be hurt. It was very loud." He laughed.

Hearing that Cecilia would be singing with a chamber group, he was much relieved, and he proved quite informed in his understanding of conservation, music, and fundraising, especially if a small donation could go to San Marco for one of his own projects. He showed us a photograph of a dirty column.

"What about the water?" Flannery asked, concerned about flash floods sending the diva out to sea.

"Ah, yes, the *acqua alta*," he sighed. Then he shrugged. He thought this was not a major concern. At its highest, the water only seeped into the atrium, and furthermore, a helpful calendar showing lunar movements and projected tides for 1997 would soon be available.

Things were looking pretty good; we enjoyed an animated discussion about the state of Italian opera singing, which the monsignor seemed to find reflected in the ruins of the Fenice. Suddenly, he stopped and began rifling through the pages of his desk calendar. He slapped his head and groaned. "Wait a minute!" he exclaimed. "When did you plan this video?"

"Last week of April," Mastroianni reminded him.

"Oh no! How could we forget!" exclaimed the monsignor. He looked troubled. He was troubled. April 25 is St. Mark's Day at San Marco, and with all the festivities it would be impossible to have the concert. Maybe another time?

"Well, that's a disappointment," Large said, emerging from the sun-shuttered rooms into the blazing confusion of the Piazza San Marco. He led the way toward the lagoon, taking a left on the Riva degli Schiavoni past the Danieli Hotel, where Richard Wagner once stayed, and onward to the church of La Pietà, forever associated with Vivaldi's orphan girls. We stepped inside and admired a radiant *Coronation of the Virgin* by Giovanni Battista Tiepolo. But down below, matters were more pedestrian and depressing. "We need more things on the walls, a better altar," said Large, gesturing with his sunglasses. The altar's pillars were covered in red velvet leggings.

Over the next few hours, we saw the sites of Venice. I don't think we missed a prominent church: San Giorgio Maggiore, Il Redentore, the Salute, Santi Giovanni e Paolo, all either acoustically challenging or visually problematic. In every one of them Large and Decca's sound men performed their arcane ritual: standing in the nave and snapping their fingers or clapping, listening for the echo that would reveal the liveliness of the acoustics.

By eight p.m. we wandered exhausted down the Zattere and stopped for dinner at a small restaurant owned by a handsome giant named Fausto, who custom-tailors his pizzas. The night was filled with stars; cooling breezes blew our way over the water from the Giudecca. This is the island known to opera nuts as the resting place of La Gioconda, who spends her last unhappy moments there before stabbing herself after one of opera's great exchanges.

Gioconda to the baritone villain she despises: "You wanted my body, accursed demon? Here it is." Baritone to soprano, who has just dropped to the floor: "Last night I killed your mother. Aarrgh."

Perry introduced us to a familiar-looking man in a denim shirt sitting at the table next to us: John Berendt, millionaire author of *Midnight in the Garden of Good and Evil*, a murder story set in Savannah that has gone through enough editions to pulp several ecosystems.

He was here searching for a new subject, he told us, and Venice with its gloomy *calles*, wistful air, and collection of eccentric expatriates had been quite forthcoming. He'd befriended a descendant of an old Boston family who conversed with aliens on the *piano nobile* of his palazzo, which he has renamed the Spaceship Barbero. His answering machine said: "You have reached the earth liaison station of the democratic republic of the planet Mars." Berendt said he had to offer up a toeprint before entering the spaceship's library, where Henry James once wrote (without having to remove his shoes).

By now Berendt had spent many weeks in Venice and knew every corner. "How about doing the recital in the splendidly ornate grand ballroom in the Ca' Rezzonico?" he suggested. Not only is the Rezzonico one of the most expensive palaces ever built in Venice, but it was filled with good stories. "In the nineteenth century, Penn Browning, Robert's hopeless son, who could not get out from under his father's shadow, purchased the palace, which is big and baroque, to make a statement. 'Don't be a little man in a big house,' his father snorted." Berendt stopped for a minute to sample our wine. "Then, finally, he goes to visit his son, and what happens? He dies there, and Penn's house becomes known ever after as the house where the great poet died."

Perry made a phone call right away. The palazzo was under renovation and wouldn't be ready in the spring.

"Do stay away from Santi Giovanni e Paolo," Berendt counseled.

"I saw a dead person there the other week." He was looking for a bathroom, he said, when he took a wrong turn and discovered an old woman laid out on a table, quite dead. The local hospital was right next door. Maybe there was an arrangement? He hoped so.

"Okay, quiet, everybody," Mastroianni requested as he fished out his portable phone from his jacket and dialed Rome.

"Mamma! How's Cecilia," he bellowed. "She's out? Okay then, tell her we all wish her happy birthday!" It was June 4, Cecilia's thirtieth birthday. Her mother said she was having dinner with her brother, Gabriele.

The next day, our group finally wandered into the right church—Santa Maria Gloriosa dei Frari, built by frugal Franciscans in the very early Renaissance. But the plain facade only served to heighten the effect of an interior eye-poppingly outfitted with sculptured tombs, statues, and two Titians. There was even a sober memorial to Claudio Monteverdi, composer of *Orfeo*, the world's first opera that matters, and countless motets increasingly adored by Bartoli and her musicologist boyfriend now that she was slipping from the glittering realms of the bel canto into the ascetic confines of the Renaissance.

"Yes, this is it," Large muttered, wandering between Titian's *Pesaro Madonna* and his majestic *Assumption of the Virgin* in the chancel. The singing angels welcoming her arrival in heaven once reminded the moneybags art historian Bernard Berenson of the rapturous outburst at the end of Wagner's *Parsifal*.

A sacred site that was also a temple of Italian civilization: the Frari church looked like a winner. "Do you think we can use the altar area?" Large wondered. So far, church officials had shown an agreeably pragmatic interest in the prospect of renting the Frari for a lump sum, provided that the shooting did not impede daily access to tourists and worshippers. Their only request concerned the program, which could not be excessively secular (nothing too ornamental or funky—say, Rossini's "La regata veneziana" songs, about a macho gondolier and his panting girlfriend).

Exact details were left for the Italian associate to work out. He'd be a busy man. The generators, for example, would have to be rented in Milan and then disassembled to fit on barges small enough to negotiate Venetian canals. Then the reassembled generators needed to be placed in the piazza outside the church, which, unlike the Frari, was city property and thus required a special permit.

I stayed an extra day to visit Bartoli's *Cenerentola* director, Cesare Lievi. Also a playwright of some acclaim, Lievi is artistic director of the Teatro Grande in Brescia, a small town with a big reputation for making arms, beginning with high-quality assassin knives in the Renaissance. He was waiting at the train station, dressed in a salmon-colored shirt which brightened up his sad face and watery blue eyes. A short drive took us into Brescia's strangely sullen center, whose palazzos and piazzas recall the paintings of Giorgio De Chirico. Franz Kafka and his friend and future biographer, Max Brod, once spent an agreeable day in this town in 1909, watching an airshow featuring Louis Blériot and other early conquerors of the air. Kafka's report, "The Aeroplanes of Brescia," appeared in a Prague newspaper. Puccini was among the celebrity spectators; Kafka thought he had a "drinker's nose." Brescia doesn't get many tourists today, Lievi said, though he figured a few would soon come straggling in: a poster inside the restaurant where we sat down for lunch announced a Luciano Pavarotti concert in the local sports arena.

I ordered meat-filled ravioli, a local speciality, and asked about the tenor.

Lievi said he had never worked with Pavarotti and generally avoided celebrity singers. He almost hissed as he mentioned an Italian diva whom he refused to greet on the streets of Brescia, even though the creature lived here, because she once demanded that she be fitted for her costumes in the comfort of her apartment. Bartoli, he thought, was exceptionally collegial—"a collaborator," in his words. He had only happy memories of their *Cenerentola* collaboration in Zurich in 1994, which I'd happened to see. It included a food fight funny enough to extract smiles from the Zurich audience, a miraculous achievement.

The libretto makes no mention of spaghetti (even though Rossini loved his pasta). But the libretto is just meant to provide the director with a gateway into the realm of the imagination. At least the good ones know this is so.

How did you think of it?

"I really didn't know how to solve the problem of the first-act finale," he answered. "Usually everybody is just standing there singing as fast as they can before the curtain comes down after the father comes in and says 'a tavola, a tavola'—which means 'to the table,' as you know. And when I listened to the music, I heard six different chords, and I thought to myself, Maybe they are for the six people heading for the table. But then Cenerentola comes in. That's when I thought, There's no chord for her and also no chair. So that started the whole joke about seven people trying to sit down in six chairs. Finally, they begin shoving each other out of the way and throwing spaghetti at each other." Lievi praised Bartoli's spaghetti-flinging skills, while picking at his own lasagne with the sad and thoughtful demeanor of a man who thought seriously about comedy and had a degree in philosophy.

Right now Lievi was trying to figure out how to inflate his Zurich production without losing the sense of whimsy. He preferred smaller theaters and mostly directed plays, including his own. His last play, *Between the Infinite Points of a Segment,* he said, was inspired by Zeno's paradox (which demonstrates how a turtle can win a race with the swift Achilles) to contemplate the unsurmountable distance between two people. A man who has lost his friend struggles vainly to recapture the sound of his voice and the conversations they shared. Over time, his memory becomes ever more fragmented and fragile. Lievi looked so sad as he told me the story that I wondered if it didn't reflect a personal tragedy of his own.

But we had finished our pasta without incident, and he rose abruptly to show me around his theater. It was a surprise: of the same vintage as the Fenice, and hardly less beautiful, with a doll-house auditorium and a well-preserved lobby embellished with playful frescoes. Peering down on us from behind a painted balustrade was a permanent audience of rococo gents and ladies. They have welcomed visitors since the mid–eighteenth century. Lievi smiled briefly as he pointed to this charming play of reality and make-believe provided by a general manager of long ago.

He had a rehearsal and I walked down cobblestoned streets to see a show Lievi had curated about the Brescia-born Arturo Benedetti Michelangeli, a recently deceased piano legend remembered for his black turtlenecks, unsmiling disposition, incredible virtuosity, and cancellations—he found the audience component of recitals an affront to his fastidious solitude. He once pulled out of a concert because insolent travel agents had marketed package trips from Italy to London so people could hear him play. The idea! He was offended, he said, to be treated like a clown. It is a pity no one sought out his views on the subject of the Three Tenors while it was still possible, but he also disliked interviews.

It was hard to avoid thinking about the Fat Man anywhere in Italy, where local dailies provided ongoing updates on the tenor now that Nicoletta Mantovani had graduated from ex-secretary to live-in girlfriend and Adua Pavarotti was proceeding with the divorce. *La Repubblica* devoted a half-page to a comparison of Pavarotti and Alagna, with a helpfully filled-out scorecard. Mr. P got higher marks for diction but lost out to Alagna on appearance. In the text, Alagna explained that singing had become like a drug to him in the aftermath of his first wife's death and that he had overextended himself with assignments that no longer seemed to make sense. That was why he cancelled so frequently. It sounded believable, while not explaining his nutty behavior once he actually appeared onstage, since he now professed great happiness with his new wife, Angela Gheorghiu.

At the airport, picking up a pile of newspapers for the trip back home, I cut out a diet program London's *Independent* proposed for Pavarotti, thinking I might try it myself. The suggestions borrowed heavily from a diet book just published by Margaret Thatcher's chancellor of the exchequer, Nigel Lawson, who used to travel around making long speeches about how British industry had to become leaner, fitter (while he himself got fatter, fatter). His suggestions included avoiding treacle tarts and pork sausages.

Perhaps a meeting of the two gents could be arranged when Mr. P and his friends appeared at London's Wembley Stadium next month. This would be the second outing for the Three Tenors since the first concert at the Baths of Caracalla (now in such a parlous state it could use a fundraiser all its own). Back then, it was Carreras who needed money and a platform after his long battle with leukemia. Putting aside their long and sometimes acrimonious rivalry (especially between Pavarotti and Domingo), all three donated a portion of their ticket revenues to charity and took a flat fee of $300,000 each from the recording company. Nobody expected the album to make much money.

All three nearly had strokes when the concert became a money machine for Decca. By now, in 1996, the video alone had sold some 600,000 copies in the United States. Worldwide in all possible configurations (compact disc, cassette, laser disc, and video), the number was around twelve million. And they got no royalties! Domingo, apoplectic, liked to claim that Pavarotti eventually received a special signing bonus when he renegotiated his contract with Decca, and though the company always denied any special arrangement, who would be surprised? When the three gents regrouped at Dodgers Stadium in Los Angeles in 1994, it was with a different record company and a foxier promoter, Tibor Rudas, who had led a nervous Mr. P by the hand to his first outdoor concert, in Atlantic City in 1982, and on to the bank. Rudas was sitting out this global tour—Matthias Hoffmann, whose German agency handled the megaconcerts of Carreras and Domingo, was the promoter.

Having never attended a Three Tenors concert, and missing Herbert Breslin's mellifluous voice, I made sure to get myself a ticket to their appearance in Giants Stadium in July 1996.

CHAPTER THIRTEEN

Giants in the Stadium

"WINDY OUT THERE," Luciano Pavarotti said, looking up from a plaid couch in his trailer not far from the backstage entrance to Giants Stadium. "I need a little help with my coiffure." Nicoletta leaned over him, arranging his thinning locks horizontally, bar-code style. I'd never met her. Dressed in a long skirt, white blouse, and sneakers, she seemed more secretary than siren, a pleasant-looking woman with straight dark hair, no makeup, and an unpretentious manner. Finishing her task, she went to the fridge and poured out glasses of Pellegrino.

"You don't have anything stronger?" Herbert Breslin sighed.

The tenor grinned and quaffed his water with great gulps, looking a bit tired, though his lively brown eyes had their usual sparkle, and he sweetly remembered a great lunch we ate at his comfortable farmhouse in Modena. He himself supervised the tortellini in brodo and a fricassee of chicken with polenta followed by fresh strawberries from someone's kitchen garden. Wife Adua took care of the wine. That was in 1986; he was celebrating the twenty-fifth anniversary of his debut, as Rodolfo in *La Bohème*, and old friends kept popping through the front door, yelling their approval of a new car.

From what I'd heard, Mrs. P hadn't gone quietly into domestic exile, though no one seemed to know just how many millions the divorce was costing him, and Breslin always turned into a deep-sea mollusk when the matter of the tenor's wealth was raised.

"We shall see how it all turns out. I hope they like," Pavarotti said, adjusting the gigantic Hermès scarf he had draped over his torso like a portable tent. "It'll be just fine, Luciano," said Breslin, handing him his windbreaker as he got up. He added a porkpie hat and slowly stepped out of the trailer. A golf cart was waiting. He got in and rolled off to the stadium for a touch-up rehearsal and sound check.

Following on foot into the stadium's murky backstage area, I remembered something the tenor once told me. When he was a kid, his tenor father often took him to the opera, and he noticed that the same performance would provoke booing on his left and enthusiastic applause on his right. The tenor concluded that if he ever became a singer, he would settle for the approval of half the audience.

It wasn't such a bad concept.

Inside the stadium, stagehands were still putting up enormous screens for the poor folks stuck in the bleachers. I'd never been to a Giants game. Stadium architecture seems to have slipped a bit since the days of the Romans. The Three Amigos stepping to the stage might as well have been concertizing inside the mixing bin for a nuclear reactor.

James Levine was on the podium with a purple towel over his left shoulder, laboring over a few details in the Bacchanale from *Samson et Dalila*, as if anyone cared. Maybe the maestro's subconscious was bubbling up. Once the dance is over, the temple falls down. Pure-minded admirers of the maestro—who fought hard against surtitles at the Met for a decade—couldn't believe he had sunk to accompanying Mr. P in "Mamma." The task used to fall to Zubin Mehta, two-time survivor of the Three Ts. But I suppose a grotesque fee, said to be $500,000 a concert, would help anybody over any aesthetic hurdle and travel problem.

Levine was actually meant to be in the Wagnerian burg of

Bayreuth conducting the *Ring* cycle, but this obstacle had been overcome by having a stand-in handle the first rehearsal and then air-
lifting Levine out of Germany and into New Jersey. Why he would
bother was hard to figure, but his immense popularity among musicians and Met audiences had never translated into a high profile,
because he was rarely seen outside the orchestra pit; perhaps he
entertained a quixotic hope that the tenor tour would turn him into
a household name. If so, he would go home a disappointed and
much richer man. His picture wasn't even on the cover of the program book.

Why Matthias Hoffmann, the tour promoter, was paying a middle-
aged and serious conductor with no sex appeal such a large sum when
a trained dog would do the trick and probably move more tickets
was a mystery. Apparently Hoffmann was fulfilling Domingo's wishes.

"Look, Sarah. All these seats will soon be filled by people coming
to hear your conductor," Breslin smirked cheerfully, standing near
the fifty-yard line, where teamster boss Jimmy Hoffa's ground-up
remains are said to be buried. The concert had not been selling well,
and this afternoon there were enough tickets at the box office to
make dunce caps for all those who had actually bought seats. One
hundred dollars put you way up in the bleachers. One zero more
included dinner with the tenors, meaning they might snatch a meat-
ball from the buffet on their way to the Lincoln Tunnel and their next
stop, in the Swedish citadel of Gothenburg.

"Herbert, do be quiet," Sarah Billinghurst answered, stalking off
to observe the "Maria" medley from a spot closer to the stage. The
Met's stoic assistant manager had already sat through two previous
Three Ts concerts. Was there combat pay for these outings?

The gents warmed up. The Pavarotti tenor came through bright
and clear from underneath his hat. Domingo sounded darkly limber.
Carreras worked hard to control his huge wobble when he wasn't
beaming at the conductor in whose house he never sang anymore. This
was not because he knew an entire opera role was beyond him, but
because he thought Met fees, capped at $13,000, were beneath him.

Breslin hummed along as he pulled plastic armbands out of his
pockets and dangled them in the air like dog treats. Special passes

for fat cats who wished to enjoy refreshments in the suspiciously named Italian Garden, they bore a weird resemblance to hospital tags.

"Maybe we can send José out for a voice transplant," one of his friends suggested.

"You know," Breslin guffawed, outfitting himself with an arm-band, "that's not a new idea. Mickey Rooney once sent us a script for a movie in which through some hospital screw-up he ends up with Luciano's voice in his body."

"Sounds great. Why didn't you do it?"

"I don't remember. Of course we were interested. But then we never heard from him again," Breslin said, still smirking.

It was time for some refreshments. The Italian Garden! Herbert led the way into an Astroturfed enclosure set up behind the trailer encampment. The bill at the local superette couldn't have been very high; I hoped Mr. P had already eaten, and wished I had. All that remained on the platters were a few bits of cubed cheddar and a mountain of toothpicks. But our annoyance was probably nothing compared to that of ticketholders still in the Lincoln Tunnel when the concert started because the bus dispatch system had broken down.

THE ITALIAN GARDEN was the closest I came to Italy that July. A crisis at home forced Bartoli to cancel her appearances in the Zurich revival of *Cenerentola*, her recording, and the meeting with Tebaldi. Her brother, Gabriele, had suddenly become ill, suffering from headaches so intense he finally went to the hospital. A CAT scan revealed a brain tumor. He needed to be operated on as quickly as possible, and his Italian doctors suggested a brain surgeon at a Los Angeles clinic. Cecilia, with little time to lose, called up her friend Maria Montas, who works for Sony Classical in New York, to help with the arrangements while she transferred enough funds to pay for the operation—estimated at about eighty thousand dollars—into her American account. On a Wednesday afternoon she flew to New York with Silvana, Cecilia, Federica, Gabriele, and his fiancée, Antonella, expecting to continue on to L.A. as soon as Gabriele felt up to it. Montas, a resourceful, motherly type with a teenage son, suggested the family get a second opinion from surgeons she knew at Columbia-Presbyterian Medical Center in New York. Montas's sister had also been recently operated on for a brain tumor.

In one of those coincidences that usually happen only in operas by Giuseppe Verdi where the monk in the hut turns out to be the baritone's sister, the doctor who had operated on Montas's sister turned out to be a close colleague of James McMurtry, a patron of the Metropolitan Opera. Montas had discovered this when she had gone with Bartoli to an Opera Club dinner during the *Così* run. While the mezzo engaged in table hopping, Montas had tried to make conversation with the imposing older gentleman on her right and asked him what he did. He said he was a brain surgeon, and they talked about brain research for the rest of the evening.

Now hearing from Montas that Bartoli's brother was ill, McMurtry offered to see Gabriele when he arrived in New York. Two days later, a team of surgeons including McMurtry and the doctor who had operated on Montas's sister removed a malignant growth the size of a walnut.

Not quite forty-eight hours after his operation, Gabriele was already eating, walking, and bravely cheerful.

A butler had just finished removing dinner as I arrived with Mastroianni. Cecilia had installed her brother on the private-patient floor, where meals are served on Villeroy and Boch china and a pianist plays afternoon concerts in a salon with upholstered tête-à-têtes usually seen only in Zeffirelli productions of *La traviata*.

"What a plant!" Gabriele exclaimed in Italian, standing up and reaching for the miniature azalea we brought him. "I will take it to Italy to our terrace. Look," he said to Antonella, a thin girl with masses of terrific, unruly hair.

"I love flowers," he said. A slender, bearded fellow with soft brown eyes, he looked as if he'd just stepped out of a Titian portrait. Tiny stitches running from ear to ear like a headband were the only visible signs of surgery. His mother was sitting quietly by the window overlooking the Hudson River, looking tired and gray. She had a *Corriere della Sera* in her lap, but it was neatly folded. She hadn't been able to concentrate. Federica and Antonella fluttered about with an assortment of paper cups and trays. Cecilia looked up from a heap of forms. "The beefsteak was pretty good," Gabriele joked, looking at his mother, "but what I really want is a plate of your pasta."

It was hard to think he'd just had major surgery.

"Miracle boy," Cecilia said, standing up and patting him lightly on his head. "That's what you are." He grinned. "In two days' time, I'm out of here. We need to practice!"

Both Gabriele and Antonella are members of I Delfici, a string quartet Cecilia organized to accompany an evening of cantatas by Vivaldi and Pergolesi she wanted to sing on her upcoming tours. She, too, was sensing a need to add some variety to the typical piano/soloist combo.

"I only have one brother," she demurred when Mastroianni praised her for the way she had galvanized the medical community on Gabriele's behalf. She pulled us into the hall. "Now listen. This thing with Gabriele . . . it's not something the world needs to know. I don't want it dramatized into something very sentimental, like some family disease epic starting with my mother's illness." Silvana had needed a cancer operation a few summers ago, but seemed fully recovered. The American habit of cheerfully airing all kinds of intimate information to whoever happens to be in listening distance has yet to catch on in Italy. The Italians prefer *bella figura*—meaning they think it is good form to keep up appearances.

By the time Gabriele returned to Italy, his sister had firmed up a fund-raising recital for the fall of 1997 to thank the doctors at Columbia-Presbyterian for her brother's care. McMurtry suggested a private club he belongs to in Manhattan. "Too small," she replied, showing her typical business sense. "Let's do it in a bigger place. You will make more money. How about Carnegie Hall?"

The rest of the summer was free except for the recording in Bayreuth of her *Italian Songbook* album with James Levine, who had returned to the Wagnerian citadel. Renée Fleming would also be there, to make her debut as Eva, the goldsmith's daughter, in *Die Meistersinger* in a production directed by the composer's seventy-six-year-old grandson, Wolfgang Wagner.

A few days before leaving, she was still coaching the role. "Don't tell anyone!" she yelped on the phone. "It's . . . well, it is a little *langsam!*"—meaning slow, in the Wagnerian manner. But she wanted to sing in Bayreuth at least once in her life, and so she finally dragged herself, the kids and nanny, and the very heavy score—the opera is nearly six hours long—to the airport. Wagner's Festspielhaus is still a sacred spot for singers as well as the testing ground for the true opera fanatic: in the unbelievably uncomfortable, un-air-conditioned auditorium, the temperature sometimes reaches one hundred degrees. Weaker pilgrims are carted off to the Red Cross station right outside the portals. I went instead to Santa Fe, where the opera company's many attractions include a complete absence of the master's epics, comfortable seating, spectacular sunsets, a pool, and a premiere every summer.

CHAPTER FOURTEEN

Old Tunes

USIC FROM *EMMELINE* drifted up to the cafeteria from the open-air rehearsal stages at the bottom of the garden and to the right of flowerbeds blazing with roses, hollyhocks, delphiniums, larkspur, and Indian paintbrush. It was late in the afternoon, when the surrounding mountains turn the color of terra cotta mixed with lavender hues. A short walk up a steeply winding road is the theater itself, a small masterpiece of simplicity, set high into the Sangre de Cristo mountains, and partially open to panoramic views that extend at night all the way to Los Alamos, bomb city, twinkling eerily in the distance.

Down a few steps from the cafeteria is the swimming pool, the Santa Fe Opera's social centerpiece, where apprentices mingle with established stars and rest up for the weighty productions of Richard Strauss, the amiable obsession of the festival's conducting founder, John Crosby. Right then, two of the deck chairs were occupied by Dwayne Croft, soaking up sun, a *Don Giovanni* score on his lap and a bandanna on his head, and Susan Chilcott, soprano fixture of the opera theater in Brussels, where people go around in galoshes all the time.

I was waiting for Patricia Racette, who was singing the title role in the world premiere of *Emmeline* at the end of July in 1996. The audience would probably sit down hoping for a short evening. For most people, a modern opera has all the appeal of a large pill that must be swallowed on the orders of an unseen sadist. That's the legacy of fifty years of music that often sounds like water drips and surgery without anesthesia. Championed by a critical elite, nurtured by subsidies and tenured professorships, the epigones of Arnold Schoenberg turned out miles of music in the aridly intellectual style called serialism or twelve-tone, for the mathematical numbers game that took the place of melodic inspiration.

People just don't want to hear it anymore.

Fortunately for Santa Fe, the composer of *Emmeline*, the forty-year-old Tobias Picker, is part of the new wave of composers who don't think a melody is a sign of a weak and pandering character.

"Plates to the kitchen, hearts to heaven," the mill girls sing in one of the work's catchy songs.

Set in the mid-nineteenth century and based on a true story, the opera opens with fourteen-year-old Emmeline sent off by her impoverished family to work in the looms of Lowell, Massachusetts. Seduced by her boss, she returns home in despair and gives up the child she will unknowingly marry many years later with tragic consequences. Judith Rossner—remembered for the somewhat steamier *Looking for Mr. Goodbar*—wrote the original novel, which the poet J. D. McClatchy adapted for the stage.

Unlike most modern operas, which disappear after the first staging, Picker's would be moving to the New York City Opera and a PBS telecast. He had bunches of commissions. Cheerful Susanne Mentzer of *Così* had just asked him for a song cycle based on a long poem by feminist saint Adrienne Rich about a group of women who freeze to death climbing Mount Everest.

Finally, things are changing in the world of classical music now that the stern tastemakers who thought the world needed to be reordered in new ways have lost most of their power in music, just as they did in politics. But as with socialism, their effect was pernicious: Stravinsky's *Rake's Progress*, Poulenc's *Dialogues of the Carmelites*, and Benjamin Britten's two masterworks *Billy Budd* and *Peter Grimes* are among the few highly melodic operas that squeezed past the thought police and into the international repertoire after World War II. "It seems my Carmelites can only sing tonal music. You must forgive them," Poulenc once said facetiously, a proudly, imperturbably old-fashioned composer until his death in 1963.

American composers with melodic flair often ended up in Hollywood, though a few soldiered on writing song cycles and operas that told stories and spoke from the heart. I am thinking of Samuel Barber, Douglas Moore, Ned Rorem, Dominick Argento, and Carlisle Floyd, whose *Susannah* has turned into a star vehicle for Samuel Ramey and, lately, Renée Fleming. In today's increasingly temperate climate, there's room for ingeniously traditional operas like John Corigliano's *The Ghosts of Versailles* as well as the shimmering, minimalist sound-scapes of Philip Glass and the inventive eclecticism of Aaron Jay Kernis, Michael Torke, Richard Danielpour, Thomas Adès, or Jonathan Dove. And Picker's rise has been swift. Margaret Carson, a legendary New York publicist who used to represent Leonard Bernstein, remembers asking him whether he had a manager after he approached her for counsel. "No," he said, "but I have a therapist, a lawyer, an accountant, and a maid."

The rehearsal broke for fifteen minutes and Racette climbed up from the gardens, a dark-eyed, casual thirty-year-old who resembles Kiri Te Kanawa before she discovered industrial-strength hairspray. She sat down with a soda, tossing her vocal score on the table and exuding the kind of self-confidence that quickly moved her from a small town in southern New Hampshire—very much like Emmeline's—to the better opera houses. Racette's dad delivered Pepsi; her mother worked at the grocery store. "Blue collar all the way," she said. "And hardly musical. We didn't own a stereo.

"But I was always mysteriously drawn to music," she continued, telling me a strange little story of how she passed by a music store one day when she was maybe seven, and pointed to a guitar. "I want that!" she told her startled parents, who gave her an accordion instead. She refused it. "I finally got the guitar and would lock myself in my room singing and playing. The sensation I got I would later identify with love."

Racette suddenly started to laugh.

"I was so naive about classical music, when my teacher at college tried to get me to join a chorus, I said, 'No, really, I just don't do that. I only sing alone.' " But it was then that she started listening to opera, and became so obsessed with the sound, she decided she had to become an opera singer. Racette was admitted into the San Francisco Opera's apprentice program and went on to sing her first major role, Madama Butterfly, without ever having seen the opera.

Like most opera singers, Racette had never worked with a live composer before. I asked her if it was odd to have someone there who actually could tell her—and Picker wasn't shy, from what I'd heard— how the music should go.

"Right. We've had our . . . conversations. He's actually changed a lot to suit my voice. But at the start, well, I wasn't sure I really wanted to do this," she said. "You know what we all think: modern music will shred your voice. But *Emmeline* has all the elements that can make opera such a profoundly affecting experience: an epic, emotionally involving story supported by an arching score and well-defined characters. It's theatrical and moving and singable.

"It's also weirdly liberating. Nobody has sung this before. No way someone can write: 'Ah, but you should have heard the way Maria Callas—Renata Tebaldi, name your diva—sang that phrase with the violins.' "

Usually Racette spends her time advancing to the front lines of the lyric repertoire, singing Puccini and the lighter Verdi roles for which her flexible soprano—a steely core wrapped with silk—is ideally suited. But a world premiere attracts journalists and critics from all over the world, and that was another reason she took the job. Lyric soprano is an overpopulated voice category in an era when every opera house would pay gold for a Wagnerian heavyweight or a dramatic soprano who could belt out the ice princess Turandot. The number of singers competing for some of Racette's repertoire is so great she would need a pool much bigger than the Santa Fe Opera's to drown them all. Barbara Frittoli, Amanda Roocroft, Elena Prokina, and Angela Gheorghiu are all in her age group, and the list grows longer every day.

Right now, she wasn't feeling all that charitable about Gheorghiu. Racette had just learned that she wasn't making her Covent Garden debut that fall in the role she thought she was singing.

The Love Couple had struck again. Racette had signed a contract to sing Mimì, but then Alagna and Gheorghiu, both box-office magnets, volunteered, and an embarrassed Covent Garden asked Racette if she would accept being demoted to Musetta, a role she was just retiring. Tenor Paul Charles Clarke, meanwhile, was evicted from Rodolfo's garret. Clarke is also married to a lyric soprano and a rather good one, Nuccia Focile; but Covent Garden had failed to recognize the promotional possibilities in presenting "Love Couple: The Sequel."

What was Racette to do? Sipping her soda and putting her cowboy boots on the next chair, Racette stared into the clouds and contemplated her options, such as they were: "Make my debut in a role I don't want to sing and have my agent get a Mimì-sized role in some later season. Not make my debut in a role I don't want to sing, take my fee, and tell the Royal Opera House to drop dead.

"But what would I gain by annoying Covent Garden? Then again, what if there is no bigger role for me in the coming seasons even if I sing Musetta? I mean, I don't even know if they'll be in business."

Set to close its house for at least two years of renovations, the company still hadn't identified a temporary home, and furthermore had become the laughingstock of London, thanks much to Jeremy Isaacs, supremo of both opera and ballet. In a decision that struck the entire opera world with incredulity, he opened up the house to a very snoopy British TV-documentary crew, inviting them into board meetings in which he and his staff got dressed down by pompous aristocrats, into staff meetings where his subalterns plotted the ouster of other subalterns, and into chorus dressing rooms where choristers (stuffed into grotesque costumes, daubed with messy makeup, harried by hot wigs, and directed to disport themselves like robots) bad-mouthed the show they were in as only Cockney choristers can.

In one memorably absurd scene suggesting the company's disorganization and weird priorities, the American mezzo Denyce Graves—increasingly a big star on the opera circuit—was seen getting ready for the opening night of *Carmen*. She had made a modest request: that her family be given a table at the popular "crush bar" during the intermission of her next performance. But never mind the fact that she was about to step onstage in a rather important role; the mezzo just could not be accommodated, a secretary came in to tell her. Sorry. All booked. Could her folks stand? Graves was too preoccupied to strangle her. She wasn't feeling well already and then proceeded to lose her voice (temporarily) before Carmen lost her life by the time the curtain dropped. Then, on camera, she fainted, and it didn't look as if anyone rushed over to help.

Paradoxically, the miniseries ended up boosting interest in opera and Covent Garden as even confirmed opera-haters got hooked on the comic backstage travails, not to mention a large public for whom opera had been nowhere on the metaphorical screen. Suddenly the documentary, with its scenes of divas in disarray and tenors sweating made opera look real to ordinary TV-watching people, and they loved it. With the airing of the series, the Covent Garden box office (shown as woebegone and underachieving) reported a nice upswing in sales.

Look at it this way, I said to Racette: "You'll be at a historic opera house in the center of London. Not exactly a hardship."

The dread of all singers on the rise is to end up in a second-class hotel doing a dull role in Essen—the German Pittsburgh, but less scenic.

All things considered, Racette decided, Covent Garden was not a house she wished to alienate.

"Who knows? Maybe I can steal the show," she joked, retrieving her score and heading back to the rehearsal of *Emmeline*.

Chances were good. I remembered the first time I saw Racette. It was a production of *Barber of Seville* at the San Francisco Opera in 1992 with Frederica von Stade as Rosina, a singer who could steal the spotlight from a chorus line of orphans clutching large cats. But Racette caused such a diversion stripteasing as Berta, the maid, she jump-started her career.

WHILE A WORK like *Emmeline* is good news to those who have come to tire of the ceaseless repetitions of *La Bohème* and *Carmen* that have turned opera houses into mausoleums, the lack of new repertoire has already had a cataclysmic effect on the recording industry. It's really amazing if you think about it: no other arts area has such a fear of the new. Think how odd it would be if we only saw nineteenth-century story ballets or dramas written before the Second World War.

What's there to record? The same public that thinks twice about attending a modern opera is also not rushing into Tower Records to spend seventeen dollars on a recording by some guy with a roomful of synthesizers. It's quite a quandary. By now, standards have been set for just about every important opera ever composed, and basically there is little reason for most recordings to be made. The picture only gets darker when you realize that large stores balk at giving bin space to classical albums when these could be much more profitably filled with pop product. Throughout America, there are perhaps 150 retailers willing to take a three-CD opera set. The classical slice of the industry pie shrinks every year.

Even Bartoli's *Cenerentola* for Decca, released in 1993, had not yet paid for itself. Unlike aria albums, complete operas sell slowly and in small quantities. Thirty years ago, companies assumed their pop divisions would subsidize classical releases and were resigned to taking a longer view of the bottom line. Decca's *Ring* cycle conducted by Sir Georg Solti—still unrivalled in cast and sound effects—took more than two decades to pay for itself. But it set a standard.

I always thought record companies were dim not to charge more for the oldies and discount the new arrivals and once suggested this to Decca's Evans Mirageas. He laughed into his soup. "The dead are paid for," he said. "Unions are very much alive." Orchestra unions cling like barnacles to their sense of entitlement. For companies like Decca or DG to record a single CD with a major orchestra costs at least $150,000. A budget outfit like Naxos can record the same music in Bratislava for about one-tenth the cost.

"What's been a fortunate boost to the Bartoli recording career is that while she is not interested in modern music or crossover, she is a wonderfully exuberant promoter of less familiar composers or forgotten pieces by popular composers. With Bartoli we are expanding the repertoire in other ways," Mirageas added. "We are not constantly rerecording pieces we've already done."

One summer afternoon, Bartoli's accompanist for gala occasions, Jean-Yves Thibaudet, gave an informal short recital in the lobby at Lincoln Center's Alice Tully Hall in front of a group of visiting music journalists, and I found myself standing next to Mirageas's ultimate boss, Chris Roberts. A round-faced intellectual and part-time composer, he runs both PolyGram Classics and Jazz—apparently more successfully than the guy charged with PolyGram's Motown label. Andre Harrell was in the process of losing what *Forbes* magazine estimated was as much as $100 million in less than two years on the job. When he finally resigned, he reportedly walked away with another $29 million. But that kind of grotesque largesse never filters down to the classical labels, which are held up to profit levels increasingly hard to achieve.

"I don't even want to think about Decca without Bartoli. Here is someone who at her Met debut met thirty German retailers during intermission," Roberts said without smiling.

A young guy himself, not yet forty years old, Roberts spent a lot of his day looking into the future, and what he seemed to see there were fewer old-timers taking up studio time making records good for their ego but not good for his bottom line. He mentioned putting more money into Argo, PolyGram's contemporary-music label, and figuring out a way to bring the MTV generation to the convoluted stories and baroque imagery of opera. Maybe that was one way to build audiences; promoting offbeat projects and artists who have the kind of look and magnetism appealing to a younger generation in an era focused on personalities was another.

One answer to his millenarian dreams was Thibaudet, who was standing near the piano talking to Lowell Lieberman, a young composer whose new opera based on Oscar Wilde's *The Picture of Dorian Gray* had just been well received at the Monte Carlo Opera.

Thibaudet had commissioned him to write him a sonata. Fashionable, extroverted Thibaudet looked as if he'd just stepped out of Annie Lennox's *Medusa* video for a little shopping at Barneys en route to a Merchant Ivory shoot. As he started his short program, we admired the latest in men's suiting from Versace, his trademark red socks, and a serious musical intelligence.

After a bit of Debussy, he turned to music from his latest release, *Conversations with Bill Evans,* a crossover disc conceptualized by Roberts, who loves Evans's music and had set aside a considerable advertising budget. I'd never heard of Evans, a jazz pianist and composer whose shimmering idiom evokes Ravel. I liked it enough to buy a copy, and so did some thirty thousand other people over the next few months—about three times the number typically racked up by classical albums.

As an exclusive Decca artist, Thibaudet had just become part of the "Bartoli for Italy" campaign Mastroianni and Co. had been cooking up in Venice in June with his video company and the World Monuments Fund. That hadn't worked out as planned. Hearing that he wished to film in the Frari church, his European coproducers were aghast. A concert in a church cluttered up with pictures of suffering saints and tombs sounded pretty depressing to them, and they demanded something more upbeat. Why not film her in Rome, where she could roll out of her bedroom and fall on a ruin?

And so the new plan, which involved two sites: a concert at the Teatro Valle, original setting for the premiere of *Cenerentola,* and a gala at the Palazzo Farnese, where Puccini's Tosca stabs to death Baron Scarpia with his dinner knife. The biggest and most expensive palazzo ever built in Rome (with a cornice by Michelangelo), the Farnese was now the embassy of France, and while it was in no need of restoration, it would certainly provide a handsome setting for a banquet given by the ambassador and attended by a French pianist and a local mezzo, all united in their concern for the Eternal City's crumbling heritage.

When Mastroianni called Bartoli in Rome and Mirageas at Decca in London in August of 1996, both were enthusiastic. The singer had just received an offer of the type she disliked from the promoter of the Three Tenors. He wanted to arrange a series of arena concerts at around half her usual fees.

Was Matthias Hoffmann watching his pfennigs? The Three Tenors had just been tepidly received in Gothenburg. Maybe if they'd invited the very senior Swedish songbird Birgit Nilsson, born in 1918, to join them in their tiresome rendition of "America" from *West Side Story*, there would have been fewer empty seats. During a Swedish television show debating the merits of the Three Tenors, she hurled out a high C all three would have given a million bucks for. She said she sang it for her cats every morning. The TV panelists seemed to conclude the Three Ts did not significantly increase opera's popularity among people who didn't like it already.

This was hard to prove, of course, though there were the Olympics in Atlanta to suggest that at least as far as network television in America was concerned, opera singers ranked about even with the kayaking team from Latvia. At the closing ceremony, when Atlanta native Jennifer Larmore sang the Olympic Hymn, mikes were picking up the nonstop babble of the local NBC anchors, though Europe heard and saw her. We got to see a lot of Gloria Estefan, Stevie Wonder, and Little Richard, whose song choice (would it be "Long Tall Sally" or "Good Golly Miss Molly"?) kept the announcer mad with anticipation.

CHAPTER FIFTEEN

Renée to the Rescue

"*I*HAVEN'T BEEN at a dinner this past year where they haven't been the topic of discussion. Am I too boring? I'm thinking of calling up Angela and saying some cutting things. We could start a feud. What do you think? In the meanwhile, we're moving."

Tomorrow morning the Fleming/Ross family would be leaving Manhattan, moving to sylvan Connecticut, where toddlers don't drag rocket launchers to preschool. Fleming had almost finished packing and was making a few phone calls before going to bed.

"Or maybe I should cancel a few things in the next ten years," she mused. "Would that be interesting? Gotta come up with something!" She laughed, but she was thinking, Does my reputation as a dependable colleague and a nice person have some drawbacks? . . .

"Guess who I saw in Salzburg," Fleming continued. "Cecilia. We ran into each other after *Moses and Aron*. I mean, can you think of two people less likely to be at *Moses and Aron*?"

Schoenberg's name is laced with garlic for the queens of song. Just looking at the tune-free score makes their vocal cords want to wither and die.

"I thought you're meant to be in London recording with Simone Young?"

"Well . . . yes. Officially, I have a cold. Unofficially, someone didn't get her the music on time, so she couldn't prepare. Soooo, it's been postponed."

In September 1996, Fleming had just returned from her long, hot summer in Bayreuth. Her debut went beautifully. The reviews I read praised her summery singing along with her pretty frocks. But she wasn't planning any return visits very soon. You sign up for Bayreuth, you're there the entire summer. For entertainment, Fleming said, she spent one long weekend driving over to the Czech Republic in a van filled with family and friends to save a castle.

I told her that monument-saving was the newly chic thing to do. Bartoli was all set to glue Italy back together. Fleming was fascinated to hear this; she had no idea! She had met the American heir to the ramshackle Lobkowicz properties and offered to sing a free recital at Nelahozeves Castle in exchange for putting up the clan travelling with her in the van. Dvořák was born on the estate grounds. Fleming is of Czech ancestry, and Rusalka's Song to the Moon is her theme song.

"What a scene!" she exclaimed. "Paparazzi everywhere, the moment we arrived. I guess not much happens there. I thought I was a celebrity. Right in the middle of my first Schubert song, there were so many flashes I got lost. Then it rained. Five hundred people squeezed into a hall built for one hundred. Then it stopped raining and I said, 'Let's all go back outside.' Then it rained again. I didn't get much singing done, but we all had a good time."

Fleming went back to her boxes. The toy collection still needed to be scooped up. In a few days, she was off to England for *Don Giovanni* with Sir Georg Solti and Bryn Terfel—a short concert tour that would finish with a Decca taping at London's Royal Festival Hall. Then it was back to the Met for the fall revival of *Cosi fan tutte*—without Bartoli, however, who was planning on singing only two performances in the spring.

. . .

THERE WAS TROUBLING NEWS from Mr. P. He wasn't where he was supposed to be, in New York, taping *La forza del destino* and brushing up on *Andrea Chénier* for the opening night of the new Met season at the end of September. Not feeling well, distracted by the Tenors tour and his new romance, he had not finished memorizing Alvaro's music and had asked that the *Forza* recording be "postponed." Till when? you had to wonder. The next life? He was meant to be singing it in the spring revival at the Met! And while the opening of the season was still nearly three weeks away, it would be reassuring to have him in New York. Fortunately, the reliable and always-eager-to-sing Plácido Domingo would be in the house by then, rehearsing *Fedora*, which he was singing, and *La traviata*, which he was conducting. Maybe he could brush up on *Andrea Chénier* before starting rehearsals for the new *Carmen* and assuming his new post of artistic director at the Washington Opera. In this capacity, the ceaselessly striving demigod decided repertoire and hired singers, sometimes himself. Washington was about to experience *Il Guarany*, by a forgotten Brazilian contemporary of Verdi's, in which Domingo had reserved the Indian chief's feathery head-topper for himself.

But if the Met was nervous about Pavarotti, Joe Volpe didn't show it at a rare press conference in early September. Unlike most other companies in the United States and Europe, the Met doesn't bother with press conferences. The last press director, David Reuben, considered it his job to keep the company out of the press, which wasn't so hard given how few papers actually remained in this great literary capital and how little interest there was in cultural news without a sex scandal or a dead tenor at its center.

But the Met's new press director, François Giuliani (no relation to the opera-mad mayor of New York, Rudolph Giuliani), had yet to lose his enthusiasm for the few surviving members of the print media, and he offered lunch with Volpe and Levine in the August Belmont Room, where the more generous Met patrons get to spend intermissions in the painted company of the tycoon's widow, who had a preference for pearls. A fine buffet awaited underneath one of the towering paintings by Marc Chagall. The mostly freelance gatherers of useless information were either well-behaved or hungry like me.

Questions were perfunctory. No one grilled the twosome about hiring Zeffirelli for the next month's new *Carmen* production after dismissing film director Liliana Cavani because her sets were too weird. Well, what did anyone expect from the director of the glass-chewing exercise in sadomasochism, *The Night Porter*? But Zeffirelli? His last two productions, *Don Giovanni* and *La traviata*, had been clunkers. Once a charming provider of suitably flamboyant shows, including a picturesque *La Bohème*, he was now recycling sequins and non sequiturs. A *New Yorker* magazine profile mentioned—en passant, as if it were so perfectly reasonable—that the director had suggested women who have abortions should be executed. Just the kind of guy for Carmen! Perhaps Zeffirelli could stage Bartoli's event at the Sistine Chapel, whenever that might take place.

Still, the meeting did bring forth some facts. Levine let it be known that the Met orchestra would stop making studio recordings because of costs. I guess recording for less extortionate rates was not an option. And it seemed that the small theater, the projected Bartoli palazzo, was also not going to be possible, on those same grounds. Then Levine bounded off for a rehearsal, leaving Volpe as the lunch entertainment. Holding a piece of bread, the general manager needed only a little prompting to deliver his latest monologue on the subject of the Love Couple. Gheorghiu had asked to be excused from some of the *Carmen* rehearsals because of the Covent Garden *Bohème*s. Both had also acquired a new agent, who was eager to sell them to arenas at $100,000 a pop.

"Now, now, who knows when she will come, because from what I heard they cancelled the *Bohème*s," he said. "Not that it matters. She'll just do what she wants anyway."

This was news. This was the *Bohème* whose garret Patricia Racette and Paul Charles Clarke had hoped to grace.

"I've given her an ultimatum," Volpe continued, as his listeners drew ever closer to hear just what it might be. Divorce the Tenor of Our Generation? See a shrink?

"I told her she's got three days to make up her mind if she is going to do the Japan tour with us next spring. Else she's out. That's not all. Now Alagna is changing his schedule too." He'd signed on to sing both the philandering Duke in *Rigoletto* and the lovesick, Bordeaux-swilling bumpkin Nemorino (literally "little nobody") in *L'elisir d'amore*. "I told Roberto, 'Maybe you shouldn't do the Duke,' " Volpe reported. "It's too different. 'No, no,' he said. 'I can do it. I can do it.' So we scheduled him for two Dukes and three Nemorinos. Now I hear he doesn't want to do the Duke but is offering five *Elisirs*. But we don't want five Nemorinos. No, that won't do. We've announced it and we have a tenor for the other two. I won't pull Stanford Olsen out of the cast just for Alagna. It is not fair."

Volpe paused for a second to chew his piece of bread and survey his audience.

Then he said: "I am getting a little tired of working with these young singers. Could I please get some singers who are old, with two great years left?"

SOMETIMES ALAGNA AND GHEORGHIU got around to the business of singing. Just then in September, Lyon was flocking down cobblestoned streets to a production of *L'elisir d'amore*. Not that the performances proceeded without the expected eruptions. Alagna startled the management by suddenly objecting to a live radio transmission that had been planned all along. Finally, a "live" broadcast was arranged of an earlier performance. The scene reminded me of a Pesaro performance many years ago featuring Montserrat Caballé. Hearing that some people were coming to boo her next performance of *La Druida di Gorgonzola* or some other obscurity, which was being broadcast, she cunningly arranged for a transmission instead of the dress rehearsal, which had been taped in front of a jubilant audience.

"You know what amazes me about those two?" a manager friend said after hearing that the Covent Garden *Bohèmes* were in doubt. "They never seem to have any good excuses, like inner-ear infections, which mean you can't travel. Or food poisoning. Or dead grandmothers, like Caballé." The absentminded Spanish songbird once cancelled Covent Garden because her granny had died and then cancelled again not long thereafter with the same excuse. When informed her ailing grandmother was already dead, she giggled and said she had meant her grandmother-in-law.

Thoughtful in her own way, Caballé always went to the trouble of inventing truly wonderful excuses, especially for getting out of rehearsals, which she found a waste of time. The contralto Sheila Nadler remembered a rehearsal of *La Gioconda* at the San Francisco Opera years ago erupting in happy laughter when Caballé called in saying she could not possibly rehearse that day because her chiropractor's mother had suffered a heart attack. It was such an imaginative excuse, no one thought ill of her.

But this was an art the Love Couple needed to perfect. In the meanwhile, their sign-in cards were making the cancellations of Bartoli seem like minor lapses in etiquette.

Cecilia was in the midst of another family crisis. Federica, her younger sister, had been driving home from her boyfriend Piero's summer house south of Rome when a car went through a stop sign and hit them front-on. Piero suffered several broken ribs and Federica a badly crushed leg and fractured pelvis. Always a fragile girl, thin as a needle, she was so weak doctors delayed operating on her leg for a week. Mastroianni, who happened to be on a business trip in Italy, drove down to Nettuno, where he found Bartoli sitting on a little stool in a provincial hospital, watching over her sister. Silvana spent alternate nights in the hospital, especially distraught. On top of this latest trouble, Silvana's father, who suffered from diabetes, was not getting any better. Doctors had already amputated one leg and were worried he might lose the other.

Finally, reassured that Federica was improving, Cecilia returned to Rome. She was starting a short Scandinavian tour at the end of September, and the London Philharmonic was expecting her for a benefit concert in Glyndebourne, which she had offered to sing at a reduced fee. Founded by Sir Thomas Beecham, the LPO had fallen on hard times and needed a bit of boosting in the ego and budget departments. In a town with half a dozen financially troubled orchestras, even locals have trouble remembering which group plays where and with whom. Not so long ago the LPO made an attempt to define itself by becoming the orchestra-in-residence at the Royal Festival Hall on the South Bank, though it cannot be very uplifting to call home a building that looks like a showroom for used cars. More appealing is the orchestra's summer venue in Glyndebourne, where the LPO is the pit orchestra for most of the operas and where Bartoli would be appearing on a Saturday afternoon.

The program looked interesting—lesser-known arias by Mozart and Rossini (including a little-heard showstopper from *The Siege of Corinth*). But Bartoli had caught a cold sitting at her sister's bedside, and on Wednesday night she phoned Mastroianni saying she was probably going to cancel, which in fact she had done by the time I was at the airport the next morning en route to Heathrow with an unrefundable ticket.

"If she travels now to London, she might not get well in time for the Scandinavian tour, which in the broader realm of events is probably more important," Mastroianni explained calmly. Did he take Prozac for breakfast?

Who could the orchestra get on such short notice? Mastroianni amenably went through a list of locally available talent, trying to remember who was singing at Covent Garden just then. Ann Murray? Amanda Roocroft? Gheorghiu? "Say, isn't Renée meant to be recording in London?" he asked. Indeed she was. Fleming had just left Connecticut for London and *Don Giovanni* with the same orchestra.

"Renée to the Rescue" might be a theme the panicked LPO could play with success.

UNFORTUNATELY, she didn't like the tune.

"Oh, really. Is that what you thought." Fleming was on the phone the next morning calling from her London rental in the Covent Garden area, before heading out for a rehearsal with Solti. She was laughing. "They did call yesterday. But tomorrow is my one day off and I'm not feeling my best and so I said no, as in no, no, *no!* Shocked everybody. I guess nobody's heard me say that word. But I thought I should start somewhere," she explained.

By the afternoon, the orchestra's dazed manager had gotten lucky.

Thomas Allen and Susan Graham had agreed to appear as long as they could sing stuff they didn't need to rehearse. Allen was in London celebrating his twenty-fifth-anniversary season at Covent Garden. Graham happened to have two free days before leaving for Munich to sing the excitable Composer in Strauss's *Ariadne auf Naxos*.

Singing in Glyndebourne is not a hardship. There is hardly a more idyllic spot for opera than this privately run East Sussex estate belonging to the Christie family, where heifers gaze on Brits lolling on the grass dipping strawberries into pots of cream and sipping champagne. Even after the latest, highly praised renovation and expansion, the house still only seats just over eleven hundred—ideal for the Bartoli voice if not the bank account. Glyndebourne pays even its stars very little, though many come to spend the summer anyway, attracted by the setting and lovingly chiseled productions of an ever-widening repertoire. Janáček, for instance, is a big favorite here, sung in the original, impenetrable Czech. Mercifully, Mozart and Strauss are also cultivated. Strauss's *Der Rosenkavalier*, in fact, was the occasion of a historic misunderstanding on the part of Caballé, that pear-shaped floater of pianissimi and wonderful excuses. She had arrived having prepared a different Strauss opera. Undaunted, she announced herself as ailing, retired to her bedroom in the Christie mansion, and successfully settled in with a phonograph and score.

But the festival was over by now, and I regretted coming the minute the taxi left. There is something depressing about summer places out of season, and Glyndebourne was gray and cheerless.

In the abundant flowerbeds, the last blooms were dropping off in the brisk wind; dark clouds pressed down on the meadows and cows.

Peter Horne, Glyndebourne's technical director, spread more gloom over tea in his office. He was sitting at his terminal inputting cost estimates and looking as if he'd spent the entire summer underneath a dropcloth. Bureaucrats in Brussels busily creating the Euro-nannynation had recently passed new regulations mandating a forty-seven-hour work week in all sectors with no allowances for overtime. As TD, Horne is responsible for getting a production onstage and overseeing the crews of carpenters, electricians, props, and wardrobe. It is the third-most-important job in a company, right after general manager and artistic director. It was about to become more difficult.

"Who dreams up these dumb rules?" he wondered morosely. "There's no way a theater can function like a nine-to-five insurance office." Costs were bound to go up. Glyndebourne has an active touring program, for instance. Who would pay the per diem rates for extra stagehands? And what about furious employees who counted on overtime to make a living? There was the possibility of substituting a system of annualized hours (per year instead of per week), but the thought of figuring it all out made Horne's head hurt, and we went backstage to the dressing rooms.

Susan Graham was fighting with her hair.

The last time I'd seen Graham, she was at Covent Garden, rehearsing the world premiere of Alexander Goehr's *Arianna*, a new setting of an old libretto written for Monteverdi. Wearing her usual snappy baseball cap, she was eating her typical meal of nachos with extra cheese in a dive around the corner and wondering if she could really convey an abandoned woman's boundless suffering. Graham, as her culinary proclivities suggest, grew up in Texas, and is of cheerful disposition. She Rollerblades in her spare time and sings a lot of pants roles, though she also was a funny Dorabella in Jonathan Miller's most recent production of *Così* at Covent Garden. Tall and almost thin, she was able to fit into the couture outfits by Giorgio Armani that served as the show's costumes by temporarily altering her junk-food diet. Quick to see the amusing side of life (and opera especially), but highly professional, she had rapidly become a favorite in European houses for her easygoing attitude and luminous, high-flying mezzo voice.

Graham had powerhouse representation, equal to Bartoli's, and was moving fast: Matthew Epstein at CAMI in New York and Tom Graham (no relation) here in London. They had forged big plans for her: a short U.S. recital tour in a few months followed by Cherubinos at the Met and then Dorabella in the *Così* revival with Cecilia as Despina. A few seasons away was a Charlotte in *Werther* and a Met *Rosenkavalier* with Renée as the Marschallin.

"It takes two mere mortals to replace La Cecilia," Graham said, grinning as she put down her brush and batted her eyes. "But we will try our best."

Horne left, probably for the local pub. I lingered in the chilly hall for Allen's fluent *Barber* aria and Graham's show-stopping "Parto, parto" from Mozart's *La clemenza di Tito*, in which a love-besotted Sesto spends a very long time telling the unworthy woman he madly adores that he is leaving, leaving, leaving, before finally moving out the door. Which is what I did.

COVENT GARDEN in the morning was more cheerful. Never mind the company's constant financial difficulties, the Royal Opera still showed considerable imagination and even daring by Met standards, mixing new and unfamiliar works into its repertoire of golden-age oldies, and steadfastly signing up adventurous directors and designers. Just then, Richard Jones was freshening up a revival of his puckishly mod production of Wagner's *Ring* cycle. Rhinemaidens in outsized rubber skin suits; Fricka, Freia, and Froh growing long beards when the gods lose their golden youth-apples; Brünnhilde in a cheerleader's skirt: these were just some of the touches that made musty Wagnerians quiver longingly for the master's twiggy forests and long-tailed dragon.

I was eager to see the unusual Brünnhilde, Deborah Polaski, an athletic veteran of many *Rings*, most memorably a Bayreuth production I saw eight years ago by director Harry Kupfer, an East German with a dim view of our ecological future. Polaski carted Sieglinde around on her back as she picked her way through a nuked-till-it-glowed landscape littered with bomb shelters and defunct air strips. Maybe the exceedingly physical production tuckered her out, because it wasn't much later that she entered opera annals with one of the most interesting cancellations ever recorded.

Polaski was in San Francisco for *Der fliegende Holländer*, which she was not finding easy to sing. There were signs during the rehearsals that she might not be well, though how unwell wasn't clear until God visited her in her dressing room and she disappeared into the night, early in the run, clutching a Bible.

"That wasn't me singing, that was God," she had informed Sally Billinghurst, who was then still at the SFO and had stopped by her dressing room to do a little ego boosting, not realizing she would soon be looking for a new Senta. "Well," Billinghurst was overheard muttering as she left the dressing room, "it wasn't *that* good."

Fortunately, by the time the soprano came to her senses, Brünnhildes were still as rare as dragon's teeth, and Polaski had no particular trouble picking up her spear. If anything, a year or so of silent prayer had only benefited her tired voice, which now sounded plummier than ever before, though even God hadn't provided her with a secure high C.

As I watched from the first balcony, Polaski was so charismatic, I wished I could drop down to help with the cooking. A small oven range with a big pot had just appeared onstage, and Brünnhilde was gathering around it with the other Valkyries. Usually, in productions that insist on illustrating every word the composer scrawled into his long-winded libretti, this is where the girls gather on a mountaintop after picking up slain warriors for induction into Valhalla. In this production, the Valkyries scour the battlefield picking up different body parts—hands, feet, heads—and then bake them into perfect warriors suitable for life in the hereafter.

If only Covent Garden could also cook up a perfect tenor! Roberto Alagna and Angela Gheorghiu had indeed cancelled the *Bohème*s they had offered to sing here on the stage of the Royal Opera House. Now what? Paul Charles Clarke, the original Rodolfo, was no longer available. But the evicted Mimì, Pat Racette, happened to be just on the other end of the chunnel, singing Musetta at the Bastille with—hold on to your helmets—Clarke's wife, Nuccia Focile. The head spins. The world is so small. Racette was now invited to upgrade herself to the peerage of Mimì.

"So how do you feel about all this?" I asked Racette.

"Well, okay, I guess. At least I got my manager to extract a few more pounds so my voice teacher can fly over and work with me," she said grumpily on the phone from her rental near the Bastille. She wasn't feeling well. She'd just sung Musetta with a fever and then argued with Jonathan Miller, who had dropped in to see how his production was doing. He thought her Musetta wasn't vulgar enough and told her to imagine Musetta as one of the whores Toulouse-Lautrec loved to sketch, someone who would squat down in public.

"I said, 'Excuse me, Dr. Miller, I've got to go pee now.' That seemed to shut him up for a minute. Anyway, Covent Garden, here I come. You know me. Nothing will separate me from my fee." It's a favorite Racette line others might like to borrow.

A few hours later, a fax slithered to my desk from Renée Fleming, who must have been toiling away past midnight on her laptop. Cecilia, still sick, had just been forced to reschedule her concert in Copenhagen, and Fleming had once again been asked to fill in for her.

"An old friend of mine," Fleming wrote, "works for the orchestra and just called me in a panic to see if I could sing there Thursday night. One could have an entire career just picking up these cancelled performances. Maybe that's what I should do—not actually schedule anything—just say yes or no to these last-minute engagements and be the designated 'savior' of the Gala industry. Pinch hitter to the stars. Hmmmm."

CHAPTER SIXTEEN

Senior Songbird

IN THEIR MANSION just outside Paris, the world's most famous opera couple are having a quiet afternoon. She is reclining on a chaise longue doing her nails and singing along with a Maria Callas album. Lady Macbeth . . . she is musing. . . . Nice tunes! Maybe I should try it next month.

He is standing by a potted palm, shyly fondling his new album of *La Bohème*.

"Beloved, look, my new *Bohème*. Isn't it nice?" he asks.

"Oh, do show me, my darling!" she coos, putting down her nail file and extending a thin arm and a tiny hand.

Kneeling by her side, he presents it.

A second later, the album goes flying across the room. Or so I heard.

And minutes after that, the Tenor of Our Generation is on the phone. The cover is simply unacceptable! he fumes. Why wasn't he consulted? It must be changed!

What was the matter with it?

The cover showed Alagna embracing Leontina Vaduva, who

happened to be the Mimì on the album but the wrong Romanian in reality.

The cover had already arrived at the warehouse. At great cost, a new one was printed up, showing two hands touching, a key between them.

You just couldn't pay these two to be any more diverting; they were nutty enough to feed a forest of squirrels.

Just about then Luciano Pavarotti slipped back into town, late enough to distract everyone at the Met. Did he remember enough of *Chénier* to sing it for opening night on September 30, 1996? To make sure, he endured a few brush-up sessions for the final tête-à-tête and then put on his brown outfit to join the aristocrats gathering stiffly in the château of the Countess di Coigny, no moldier than five months ago and no livelier either.

But just when we started to wonder yet again why he was torturing himself singing a role meant for a huge-voiced dramatic tenor, he would stop the show with a gorgeous phrase, even an entire aria, or indulge in some captivating stage business that took our mind off his bow-shaped legs and pain-wracked body. Was there something special about or in Maddalena's wig that made it so magnetic? A glass of water? An apple? Whenever possible, he buried his face in it.

Maybe Mr. P was merely telling the soprano to pipe down. Maria Guleghina seemed to be competing for the loudest-voice-at-the-Met award, a trophy only reluctantly relinquished by Ghena Dimitrova of Bulgaria, who used to call home without a telephone. This new woman didn't need to open the windows.

But the New York opera world was already on to another footnote in the annals of operatic adoration. Senior songbird Mirella Freni had arrived in town, and her fans were starting to cut up the funnies into confetti and write love notes on white bedsheets which they hoped to sneak in past Joe Volpe's gestapo. Picking up a killjoy tradition periodically enforced since general manager Rudolf Bing's tenure, he was trying to forbid extravagant forms of enthusiasm, like the tossing of bouquets or the dropping of glitter paper, on safety grounds, though given the rarity of these outbursts, the cautionary measures seemed more a matter of obsessive control.

Long, long ago, so long ago it could almost be a fairy tale, Freni and Pavarotti shared the same wet nurse in Modena, while their mothers toiled in a cigarette factory. (He got all the milk, she liked to joke.) Now, many decades later, she had expressed the desire to sing the befuddled Russian princess Fedora, and the Met had obligingly borrowed a musty, much-travelled production from Barcelona so she and Domingo could adorn it.

Mastroianni had been counting the minutes. Managers the world over got their diva dienst training as young pups advancing toward the stage door tremblingly holding flowers, programs, and half their record collections for the adored one to sign, terrified she had failed to inscribe their names on her guest list and they would have to wait outside in the dismal subterranean car lot with ordinary people who had not chosen a life of worship. He's adored Freni since she sang her first Mimìs at the old Met and was nice to him and his friend David, another member of the Scarsdale High School orchestra.

I'd dropped by his office to pick up client Angelika Kirchschlager's first recording for Sony, featuring Viennese music by Erich Korngold, Gustav Mahler, and Mahler's wife, Alma (whose music-making annoyed him until he got her to stop: There can only be one composer in this household, he declared). The manager was in a talky mood.

"David came home one day and said he was in love with a soprano, an older woman with a daughter. So we'd go to *Bohème* together and then visit her backstage. He'd secrete one of her gloves when she wasn't looking. Or wait in the lobby at the Hotel Navarro, hiding behind a newspaper with a hole in it so he could sneak a look at her when she left. He was possessed.

"Finally, they had a talk. She was singing in the Met tour of *Figaro* in Philadelphia and he went down to hear her and was just hanging around as usual; so she took him back to New York in her car. 'This is not going to happen, David,' she said. 'I am old enough to be your mother.'"

But Mastroianni, whose devotion was purer, kept in touch with Freni even after she stopped singing at the Met. In the mid-1970s, Renata Scotto was the house diva and Freni had gotten caught in a tax scandal with a few other foreign singers, like Birgit Nilsson. Typically reluctant to pay local taxes, they gravitated to an accountant whose miraculous math got them into deep trouble with the IRS. While the singers were not accused of any wrongdoing, they still had to pay up, and with penalties. The tax bill for Nilsson, a notorious tightwad, was so staggering, she refused to return to the United States. Finally, a music lover helped arrange a settlement, and Levine immediately invited her for a special gala concert, followed by *Elektra* with Leonie Rysanek.

By the time Freni reappeared, she was already into her late forties, but finding continuing sustenance in shiny operatic chestnuts she had stored up like a squirrel in winter. She repaid Mastroianni's long years of devotion by becoming one of his first clients, first at CAMI, then at his own agency. The mutually beneficial arrangement probably added more than a decade to her career, as he shrewdly linked her up with the right vehicles and the properly doting companies.

For the youngsters out there, the Freni career offered a valuable lesson in longevity. By 1996 she was into her fifth decade of singing, having made her debut in Modena in 1955 and sung her way through menopause, whose hormonal changes affect some women and others not at all. Only Leonie Rysanek had enjoyed such a long career. Two years after she retired and not long before her death in the spring of 1998, I asked her how she had kept her voice, and she quoted Tosca's big aria, "Vissi d'arte." "I lived for art," she said. "I never smoked, I never drank, I watched what I ate within reason. It was hard and simple."

Small and shrewd, Freni had also retained a good deal of her youthful looks and sound, saying no to extra helpings and outsized roles (except for Aida, which she soon wisely dropped) and wearing a variety of draft-deterring shawls and hats. Occasionally, she extended herself to learn a new and challenging role, like Tchaikovsky's Tatiana in Russian, but when offered *Chénier* at the Met with Mr. P, she turned it down: too heavy, long, and high.

Fedora, short and low and by the same composer, was perfect for both Freni and her manager, who knew every unbelievable line by heart and could have picked up a few extra bucks as her cover.

Sending the office into near delirium was Billinghurst's suggestion to cast piano client Jean-Yves Thibaudet in the nonsinging part of the foppish Lazinski, who plays a Chopinesque nocturne while Fedora lurches around her potted palms furiously interrogating the tenor about her lover's murder back home in St. Petersburg, which she happened to be investigating from her spacious apartment in Paris. Old-time divas and their people obviously consider *Fedora* only slightly below *Parsifal*, say, or the entire *Ring* cycle.

By the time Freni reached for the poison-filled cross Fedora dangles around her neck in case she needs to commit suicide, her worshippers were overcome with emotion. For them Freni, however stumpy, was the last link to a great tradition of larger-than-life personalities, and they basked in her autumnal glow while cheering Domingo's stentorian delivery of "Amor ti vieta," the opera's only hit tune and a very short one too. He looked as if he'd spent the last months at the gym, watching his fat *Forza* on tape and pedalling madly. Once Fedora rearranged the stage furniture one last time in her final delirium, the leather-lunged troubadour left the matinee performance for a quick nap and returned to conduct the evening's *La traviata*, featuring Victoria Loukianetz, a tiny songbird escaped from the Ukraine, and one of his many protégées.

I caught up with him in Chicago a week later, where he'd just arrived by private plane, so he could cohost a Sunday-afternoon gala honoring Ardis Krainik, the Lyric's beloved, ailing general manager, who was leaving in the spring. A Christian Scientist, she had refused a cancer operation and was now a mere ghost of her former self, trapped in a wheelchair and increasingly frail. Once capable of squeezing dollars from a stone, a radiant, motherly type with a dimpled smile and great artistic vision and integrity, Krainik had inherited a renowned company from her predecessor Carol Fox and turned the Lyric Opera into one of the world's best. Singers loved coming to the Lyric, where the backstage atmosphere was warm and the productions were well rehearsed.

Well, most did. Krainik made headlines for firing Luciano Pavarotti when he cancelled an opening night after a long history of nonappearances. Her subscribers deserved better, she said, and Mr. P never set foot on her Chicago stage again. That was gutsy, given Mr. P's box-office appeal, but the Lyric under Krainik could afford to be ballsy and adventurous.

Domingo took care never to fail Krainik, and here he was again, even if his timing was a little off and he arrived backstage with a whole half hour to fill. He patted his black, curly hair, took off his camel-hair coat, looked admiringly around the newly renovated backstage area before checking his gold watch. Unlike Pavarotti, who looks pretty much the same off and on the stage—well, a little more unkempt actually, once out of brocaded vests and rhinestone-studded costumes—Domingo is much more finely built and poised in person than his stiff and scene-filling TV and stage presence would lead you to believe. Telecasts don't do him any favors. Since he is also easily approachable, with graceful manners and melting eyes, we talked a little about his travels as he waited.

Does he learn new roles intravenously? I asked. He leaned against the wall and laughed. A charming concept, he agreed, but didn't I think he already knew so many?

The backstage area slowly filled up with Krainik favorites: Catherine Malfitano, Frederica von Stade, Samuel Ramey, Carol Vaness, Dolora Zajick. In a while, they would start filing onto the stage for a program that was just a warm-up by Levine standards—estimated at less than three hours. A bone-chilling scream revealed the presence of Eva Marton down the corridor. I looked in to see the Hungarian Wagnerian in the last stages of her toilette. A dresser was teasing her hair into the traditional diva look: up high with a little flip. We New Yorkers hadn't seen much of Marton since her falling out with the Met, which had awarded the *Ring* cycle and video to Hildegard Behrens.

Another door opened and June Anderson stepped into the hall, looking transparent and gaunt, like a Pre-Raphaelite ghost.

I'd seen Anderson only twice since the Met *Filles*. At first things seemed to go well for her: Volpe rewarded her with new assignments, and Breslin took over her management from a sleepy agent. But she began to feel poorly, and when we spoke in the spring she was already being treated for a rare thyroid disorder. The medication had made her feel dry and tired, though a new doctor had devised a different treatment that did not seem to dry out her vocal cords. Her mood seemed even more wistful than usual. She had only discovered her need to sing, she told me then, after nearly losing her voice.

An hour later, Anderson offered one of her familiar showpieces, Amina's sleepwalking scene from Bellini's *La sonnambula*. The amazing technique was there, but that special, crystalline Anderson sound had lost its shimmer and a good deal of volume. She hadn't wanted to sing that afternoon, but couldn't bring herself to cancel a tribute to Krainik, who rose daily determined to get the best out of God's creatures and had been particularly sensitive to Anderson's many moods and chronic self-absorption. Yet by singing she had probably darkened her future. The auditorium was jammed with managers and agents the world over, and they would start writing her off as another expensive and annoyingly complicated fortysomething with an attitude, easily replaceable with, say, Ruth Ann Swenson or Andrea Rost, two highly competent coloraturas. In sports, a pitcher can spend a season nursing a damaged arm and return to the game. It's not so easy in opera. The voice is more delicate; the world in which it is heard, less forgiving. A few months later Anderson had regained a good deal of her old flair in a finely sung Norma at the Lyric, but it didn't seem to matter.

"KNOW WHO THIS IS?" Joe Volpe asked, rising from his tapas-heaped table.

I was back in New York, just like Domingo, leaving out a detour to San Francisco, where he sang a fundraiser for the company. Between performances of *Fedora* and *Traviata* and rehearsals for the new *Carmen*, the tenor had fitted in the opening of his new Spanish cantina, and invited the opera world and the mayor of New York. Domingo and Rudy Giuliani were watching the World Series on a TV set up on the restaurant's second floor, where Volpe was also holding court.

In a moment of besotted delirium, the general manager had cast as Carmen Waltraud Meier, whom he now introduced, extending a French-cuffed arm to a glum woman in a dark dress who seemed to be having major indigestion and gestured weakly. The source of the German mezzo's discontent was the little Puck with the big gut who was standing near the TV, Franco Zeffirelli, the designer and director of her first Met *Carmen*. The two of them had spent rehearsals locked in a life-and-death battle rivalling Carmen's with Don José. Zeffirelli had made it obvious that he didn't think she could sing Carmen; she didn't think he could direct it and had just threatened to quit because he was not helping her move around the stage in that seductively carefree fashion Germans find so challenging.

Judging by the opening a few days later, I guessed they were both right. Usually all it takes is one homely mutt or two horses to save a show. This one had seven horses, three dogs, and two donkeys and it was still a bust. Zeffirelli must be a walking case of attention-deficit-disorder syndrome. There were so many overdressed Spaniards, lurching cripples, cavorting urchins, and raggedy beggars milling around the plaza, Maria Callas herself could have come and gone unnoticed. Meier worked hard, even lying on the floor at one point for the wild-woman look. But this is a role you really must feel, not analyze to bits. Unlike Domingo, with his generalized earnestness and pleading manner, Meier didn't have the force of personality to carry her through a vacuous production. Like the toreador, Sergei Leiferkus, her companion in miscast misery, she looked uncomfortable, edgy, and unalluring.

Then came the third act. Angela Gheorghiu, who indeed had arrived late for rehearsals as Volpe predicted, made a beeline for the footlights and brightened the night with Micaëla's aria.

But who goes to *Carmen* for Micaëla? Someday Bartoli would probably sing the Gypsy, but that day was far in the future and would probably take place at a smaller locale, like the intimate Opéra-Comique in Paris, where the opera opened in 1875. So far, the closest she'd come to the cigarette factory in Seville was a forest in Darmstadt, where she filmed a commercial for Fuji Bank of Japan in 1990. It showed her dancing flamenco and singing Carmen's Seguidilla in a sun-dappled German bower.

CHAPTER SEVENTEEN

Micaëla's Picnic

HE KNOCKED AGAIN. "I don't know where else she could be. We made the appointment," Peter Clark said, looking mystified. The Met's press liaison was standing with me in the narrow corridor outside the dressing rooms at the Metropolitan Opera, a short walk from the stage.

"Maybe she's napping."

I'd asked to meet Angela Gheorghiu and he'd suggested the second act of *Carmen*, when "Ms. Gheorghiu says she gets kind of bored and doesn't mind company." Micaëla spends act two in her dressing room waiting for act three, in which she sings her long, arching aria as she picks her way down a perilous ravine, looking for Don José and the Gypsy who stole his heart. For sopranos who knit, a run of Micaëlas usually amounts to at least one sweater or a few pairs of winter socks, which might have come in useful in New York in the middle of a brisk November in 1996.

Gheorghiu, admittedly, didn't seem like the knitting type.

Finally, the door opened, and her husband leaned into the hallway, a friendly, questioning look on his boyish face. Gheorghiu was neither napping nor knitting; she was nibbling with a few friends off a platter balanced on the piano bench. A few slices of ham and melon, a wedge of cheese, a bunch of grapes, and a baguette—it looked like a fine *repas* for Micaëla.

She came to the door, looking surprised.

"Come in," she commanded. "Who are you?"

Clark began to explain.

"Oh, it doesn't matter. It's fine. Please come. Have a seat. Welcome. Roberto. Do something." She gestured to the Tenor of Our Generation and former waiter, who whisked the platters to the radiator.

"Please, you sit down. We do not wish to disturb. We go," he announced and started toward the door with their pals.

"You want he stay?" Gheorghiu asked. "Sure! He stay!" she answered.

"Please!" I exclaimed. "I would love for him to stay."

The other couple followed Clark out the door.

We sat down, Alagna perching on the piano bench. Slender, nicely proportioned, and beautifully dressed in a hounds-tooth suit, a light gray shirt with a black-and-gray tie, and shiny black ankle boots, he looked like a rich waif, like Pip about to regale Miss Havisham with an impromptu Sunday-afternoon piano recital. Gheorghiu reclined prettily on the chaise longue, a delicate, doll-like woman with tiny hands just like Mimì's and opaque brown, whimsical eyes. She appeared to be enjoying a private joke.

"I guess you don't need to stay in character?"

She looked even more amused. "I'm singing Micaëla," she replied, as if to say: Character? Micaëla? You do know I am not singing Carmen?

"Roberto, you know, is also singing. He is singing *Elisir*," she offered.

"Indeed," I beamed. "It was lovely to hear you sing Nemorino the other night, Mr. Alagna. And see your handstand. But that aria? Where did you find it?"

For many listeners, the reward of sitting through *L'elisir* is to hear the tenor sing the sweetly melancholy aria "Una furtiva lagrima." Alagna, however, had been full of surprises in recent weeks. First of all, he showed up. And not only for the Donizetti piece, but for *Rigoletto* too, the opera he didn't want to sing anymore. And in *L'elisir* he showed his happiness with the elixir of love by executing a limber handstand that delighted the audience. It was nearly as startling as the famous song inspired by the tear in Adina's eye. Had he forgotten it? I briefly wondered as a slightly strange tune more embellished than the original wafted into the hall.

"What was that?"

"It is another version," Alagna explained. "We are young. I wanted to do something different. If not now, then when?"

Gheorghiu added: "Donizetti rewrote the aria many years later for another singer. Doesn't that mean he liked it better?"

Of course not, but it was hard to argue with two enthusiastic charmers. We talked a little bit about politics instead. I had travelled to Romania in the dark decades of the Ceauşescus, when the Conducator, as he liked to call himself, had so totally destroyed not only Bucharest's historic center but the country's agriculture that people were collecting tree bark for soup. Gheorghiu had studied at the Bucharest Conservatory, and I asked what that was like.

She said she got very good instruction but remembered being cold a lot, though it was not clear if she meant this physically or metaphorically. Both tenor and soprano speak an emphatic and enthusiastic but limited English.

I asked Alagna how he learned music. Was it true he worked alone?

Alagna nodded. "Absolutely. With a machine, a tape recorder, I learn everything. I tape and listen."

"Do you ever hear anything you don't like?"

Gheorghiu laughed. "All the time. All the time he is making criticisms."

I asked him why he no longer liked hearing himself as the Duke. Hadn't he been planning on dropping the part? But here he was singing it at the Met!

He professed surprise, but then shook his head. "It's not a good role for me," he explained. "I don't like it."

"What's the matter with it?"

"It is not rewarding," he pleaded, leaning toward me with his soft puppy eyes. "It's very hard. 'Parmi veder le lagrime' is a very difficult aria and not good for the audience. They don't understand how difficult. And the character, he is not interesting. He stays the same from the first act to the end."

"But you've got two other arias that are very nice!" While "Parmi veder le lagrime"—the Duke's puzzled reflection on Gilda's disappearance—lacks bounce, he does also get to sing "Questa o quella" and especially the infectiously jaunty "La donna è mobile." Caruso, for instance, liked them well enough. Pavarotti still seemed pleased to have them around when the production was new.

But Alagna would not be deflected from the unloved aria. Verdi really let him down with that song.

"Well, then," I asked. "Micaëla doesn't change, either. Do you find her rewarding, Ms. Gheorghiu?"

"It's not the same," responded Alagna, eagerly continuing with his point. "You sing it well and you must have an audience success. The Duke is different."

He was meant to be singing the Duke tomorrow. I sensed a cancellation coming.

That made me think of the problem *Bohèmes* at Covent Garden, and I asked them why they didn't sing in that show and cancelled *Roméo et Juliette* in Orange. Gheorghiu furrowed her brow and said that was wrong. There never was a contract for Orange. Then Alagna leaned forward and said they had a good reason not to sing at Covent Garden. He looked sadly at his wife.

"Were you not well?" I asked Gheorghiu.

Alagna answered for her. "Her sister died. Tell me, do you think that is a good excuse not to sing?"

Silence fell. Gheorghiu's sister had appeared with them in the Lyon *L'elisir* some two months ago in the smaller role of Giannetta. I'd heard she was beautiful and talented. How she died has remained something of a mystery.

We turned to lighter subjects. Food. Yes, they enjoyed cooking in their rented flat but didn't go out much, though they found New York exciting.

"I hear you have new Rolex watches!" I remembered.

Finally, a bright moment. Both were pleased by this badge of success. They had just spent an afternoon getting their pictures taken for a Rolex ad.

"You know, this is the first time Rolex has done two people in one advertisement," he said. "I like the brand. I have four Rolex watches."

"How many do you have, Ms. Gheorghiu?"

"Just one," she laughed. "But I also like Cartier—so feminine!"

"You have everything—watches, recordings, fame, fortune. What's left? Do you still dream?"

Alagna looked reflective and even more sweetly vulnerable.

"Dream? Of course we still dream. For instance, I dream of being with Angela." He reached over to touch her tiny hand.

"Our dream is that tomorrow is like today. We love life," said Gheorghiu.

I was getting worried about the song Micaëla sings in the next act.

"Don't you have to warm up now for your aria?"

"No," she said. "Why? It's good, isn't it?"

"Yes! It is! Your voice is wonderful!" I exclaimed.

"No. Yes. I mean, thank you!" she responded, laughing. "This production is good."

I thought she was being facetious. "You like this production?"

"Yes, really. It's wonderful. We hope to do more things with Zeffirelli. Maybe a *Faust* soon."

But I guess there was no reason for her not to love it. She was stealing the show.

Sure enough, the next night, just before *Rigoletto* was about to start, a spot illuminated the curtain and a straight-faced Met representative came out to tell us that Mr. Alagna had suddenly required a dental procedure and was uncomfortable from the effects of the anesthesia. A dental procedure! But he'd been picnicking with Micaëla the night before! Fortunately, however, the speaker continued, he was going to sing anyway, begging our indulgence.

Maybe Alagna should consider having root canal whenever a performance threatened. He might have hated singing every note, but he hid it well enough as the booted scamp, singing even the annoying

"Parmi veder" with the bright, punchy tough-guy delivery that made him riveting, if not always elegant.

Even so, the Alagna/Gheorghiu Met sojourn had its down moments. After a *Carmen* performance, Gheorghiu opened the card attached to a flower bouquet tossed her way during the curtain calls and discovered a long letter—not an epic love poem, either, but a description of what the writer considered to be Alagna's vocal defects. Alagna's bloodlines are Sicilian, and he's touchy. At the next performance he kept a sharp watch on the flower tossers, thinking he might recognize his critic. And sure enough there was a suspicious gent crowding toward the curtsying Angela. The same guy! He was sure of it and had the house manager detain him. Opening the wrapping paper, they found another letter. "I really wanted to punch him," Alagna later told a friend. But he didn't. Instead, the tenor pulled him aside and told him how life was hard enough without reading letters like that. The man was so astonished, he apologized profusely.

But never mind her great success, Gheorghiu arrived for the last *Carmen* of the fall feeling unwell. She requested that an announcement be made to that effect and then did her first act nicely enough. But as the second-act intermission started, her strength ebbed badly and she announced she could not manage the only thing she had left: the third-act aria. Nothing could persuade her otherwise. Her tearful cover, Ainhoa Arteta, was seen being pushed into a dressing room to be kitted out for Micaëla's mountain walk. Then Jonathan Friend stepped in front of the curtain to explain the change in Micaëlas, adding just as he was about to leave: "I am delighted Micaëla does not appear in the fourth act, because we have run out of sopranos."

CHAPTER EIGHTEEN

Hat Hair

"Doesn't your mother make you wear a hat?" I asked, feeling elderly, as we walked along a wind-whipped street in Amsterdam toward the Concertgebouw on a grim, wintry day in early December. The huge bird nests atop the Dutch elms lining the street quivered in the wind underneath a threatening sky. I could hear a cold coming on as we walked from her hotel to Amsterdam's famous concert hall for a rehearsal. "My hair is too long," Bartoli explained. "A hat will make it look strange. Anyway, I can sing over this. It's nothing. I'll be fine." Otherwise she was windproof in a big parka, black gym pants, and white boots.

Tonight she was singing a selection of Vivaldi arias and motets with her brother's ensemble, I Delfici, supplemented by the presence of György Fischer, her frequent accompanist, who had been ordered to brush up on the portative organ, a cumbersome keyboard instrument that looks like a beat-up lecture podium. After the intermission, Fischer would return to the piano for a traditional program of Italian and French songs. Claudio Osele, the project's music researcher and author of the liner notes, was walking with us and also sniffling.

"What's happening with András Schiff?" I asked. The pianist, last sighted at Carnegie Hall waiting patiently for the latest Bartoli health bulletin, was also in town, for a concert with the Royal Concertgebouw Orchestra, the building's primary tenant. I'd seen a flier in our hotel and wondered if he might be coming tonight or she to his concert tomorrow night. Neither. Their warm longtime association seemed to be cooling down. There were no plans for a meeting, was all she could say.

"Did he feel let down by the Carnegie problems back in the spring?" I asked. She shook her head. "There are other problems." She wondered if he wasn't fed up with the accompanist role.

"He sent me a letter saying he just wasn't happy and it wasn't working out, so I thought that was it. But just now he called me twice in Rome. Once I was out and then the next time we spoke. He is doing this Schubert concert at Wigmore and wanted me there."

Embracing Schubert's two hundredth anniversary with his characteristic openhearted eagerness, Schiff had invited his favorite singmeisters for a six-hour tribute. An ad in the British magazine *Opera* announced Bartoli's presence. Given the important part he'd played at the beginning of her career, I figured she would torture him awhile and then show up at the last minute.

She didn't think so. "No, I can't. It's not possible," she said firmly. "I already have something during that time, a *Don Giovanni* recording with Claudio Abbado. The dates conflict." Abbado, the head of the Berlin Philharmonic, had selected Simon Keenlyside for the title role and Bryn Terfel as his comic notary and servant, Leporello. Abbado wanted Bartoli to sing Zerlina, the flirty peasant girl whose wedding party is interrupted by the Don.

It was nice to hear Abbado had recovered his faith in the recording industry, a faith recently bruised when his company, Deutsche Grammophon, released an Abbado compilation called *Adagio*. The classical music industry does not always put out albums nobody wants, even though it often seems that way. Adagio compilations are an audience favorite, and Gustav Mahler, forward-looking in so many ways, thoughtfully included slow movements in all of his symphonies, and they are so soul-stirringly sad, it's a wonder that no one has thought of commercial tie-ins with the manufacturers of Kleenex. So, sales slumping, DG compiled a CD of adagios from the Mahler cycle Abbado had previously recorded, but apparently without informing the maestro, who has a finely developed sense of his artistic position. He considered *Adagio* an affront to his reputation and demanded that the album be withdrawn.

I could see why Bartoli would wish to leave a record of Zerlina, a role she had sung most memorably in a strikingly dour production by Patrice Chéreau at the Salzburg Festival in 1994. Chéreau, renowned for his provocative Bayreuth staging of Wagner's *Ring* cycle as a capitalist nightmare, had injected an unusually dark, malevolent atmosphere into Mozart's quasi-comedy. Ferruccio Furlanetto, a fierce and fleshy Giovanni, sang one love song while circling his own shadow, a nice way of presenting a narcissist who loves himself more than his many women. The peasants who arrived for Zerlina's wedding scurried away in terror at the sight of him, and her reluctance to give him her hand in the famous duet "Là ci darem la mano" was, for once, more a matter of fear than of coyness. While the show was not universally praised, Bartoli had received excellent press.

I could also see why Abbado might want to record the opera many consider Mozart's greatest.

But why on earth would DG wish to spend at least half a million dollars to record it with a conductor whose CDs often gather dust? And at a time when downsizing had ruined the lives of dozens of employees at PolyGram, the parent company? Abbado's recording of Brahms's First Symphony had sold three thousand copies in five years; other releases with the Berlin Philharmonic, a few hundred. More weirdly, PolyGram's other classical label Decca had just recorded the opera with Renée Fleming and Terfel, this time in the role of Don Giovanni. By now, there were so many *Don Giovannis* in the Schwann record catalogue that Leporello, the Don's personal historian, would need another huge volume to list them all. If the Don's conquests are one thousand and three in Spain alone, the Don's recordings (excluding those mercifully allowed to slip out of print) count in at nearly forty. How many people on this planet are ready to buy a three-CD set with a baritone who is hardly a household name when Cesare Siepi, who owned Don Giovanni's tights in the 1950s, is available on several budget sets? Consider the folly: Terfel, "exclusive" to DG, was rented out to Decca for the lead role, and now Bartoli, "exclusive" to Decca, was about to be loaned to DG. Why didn't anyone have the foresight to just dump everybody in one place for one recording?

Bartoli had no answer. We had arrived at the Concertgebouw, a grand arrangement of Dutch bricks and Greek-temple facade, topped off by gray mansard roofs, that fills a square not far from the Rijksmuseum. Fischer, a thin intellectual with silvery hair, was standing by the stage wolfing down a sandwich; the four Delfici members were sorting out their seating requirements. Gabriele was helping to position the organ. He had shaved his head and looked like a Turkish warlord.

"So, *ragazzi*," Bartoli said, "let's go through the motet. And then a little bit of *Griselda*." That's the "Agitata dei due venti," or battle of two winds, the concert's vocal triple jump, a display piece from one of Vivaldi's many forgotten operas.

Pushing back her hair, she unleashed a stream of runs that took her all the way to high C as she mimicked the winds buffeting the heroine's heart—pulled up and down like a sailor at sea, in the text's extended simile. It was incredible. Even if Vivaldi seems to offer little sense of an emotional world stirring underneath the surface glitter, the opportunities for singing of the most exhilarating virtuosity are endless, and I found myself almost laughing as she looked out into the nearly empty auditorium and sang one perfect bunch of scales after another. I had a sense of being precipitated into an immeasurable, even infinite space sparkling with sixteenth notes and silvery trills.

"Think she can bring these works back?" Martijn Sanders whispered, sitting down during a short break. He's the Concertgebouw's savvy executive director, who returned the house to fiscal health, setting up an endowment, fixing the building's crumbling foundations, and bringing a fresh approach to programming. He doesn't run the famous orchestra, but decides everything else in the house, and as he picked at the crisp creases on his blue suit, he admitted he had been skeptical about the whole show. Because an earlier illness required a scheduling change, Bartoli had just been here singing a recital, and Sanders had worried about selling out yet another appearance so soon. Well, the concert was sold out, and he now could put away a little change to subsidize some unknown singer he might wish to showcase.

"So she proved me wrong. And this music? If she can't make Vivaldi matter, then surely no one can. Consider it a warmup," he said. "Even now with no one here, she radiates the pleasure of performing. An audience responds if the artist is eager to please in the best sense. If she wants to sing this music, she does have a gift for communicating."

Anyone else as popular?

"Only Jessye Norman has as many fans waiting for her after a concert," he told me.

"What's different is this: we've hardly ever had a star mezzo in Holland. Marilyn Horne was never really known here. Teresa Berganza a little more, but neither she nor Christa Ludwig ever sold out the house. Maybe eighty percent. Bartoli is the first mezzo to fill the house."

That night, this being Holland, it wasn't at first easy to tell whether nothing could please the polite Dutch more than a steady diet of Vivaldi marginalia. Applause was moderate for the first two selections, two quiet motets; but then came *Griselda*, clearly surprising the audience with its nonstop display of nearly impossible vocal challenges, every one of them met with startling ease. "Paaa!" exclaimed the dour-looking man next to me in the balcony. And suddenly, barely had Bartoli stopped singing when the whole audience stood to cheer and whistle. Drifting through the doors for intermission, the Dutch looked as if they'd all won the lottery.

Perhaps Bartoli's seductive enthusiasms will indeed help restore Vivaldi's vocal music to greater favor. Who would have foreseen the revival of equally obscure and far less lively pieces by Louis XIV's noodle-wigged favorite, Lully? Not I. Maybe taste has changed enough since Claudio Scimone and his ensemble, I Solisti Veneti, exhumed Vivaldi's *Orlando furioso* two decades ago for Marilyn Horne in Verona and then followed up with a first-ever recording. This was yet another of the countless musical entertainments drawn from the once popular pages of Ariosto, whose endless chivalric romance in very choice Renaissance Italian teems with wizards, knights, and witches. In particular, Horne's part of the hero crazed by love was a real stunner, with numbers combining the vocal equivalent of high-wire, trapeze, and tumbling acts. What a send-off! Yet no Vivaldi rush ensued. When the encyclopedic *New Grove Dictionary of Opera* appeared in 1992, *Orlando furioso* didn't even rate its own entry.

But before *Griselda* made it to another town, Amsterdam's own lashing wind claimed two victims. I flew home the next day with a fever, and Bartoli succumbed to a cold by the time she was meant to be in Berlin with Abbado and his Philharmonic. Her future *Don Giovanni* conductor was probably not pleased at the last-minute cancellation. The program featured Debussy's *Le Martyre de Saint-Sébastien*, a piece she learned for the occasion, and not something many singers could do at the drop of the hat she had not worn that day in Amsterdam. Forced as well to cancel her next recital, in Wiesbaden, she'd taken quite a hit at the bank, but recouped some deutsche marks and goodwill a few weeks later when, in an amusing turn of events, she stepped in for Bryn Terfel, who was too exhausted to sing his New Year's Eve gig with—who else but Abbado and the Philharmonic.

CHAPTER NINETEEN

Wiener Schnitzel

ISING UP over the Ringstrasse, its lofty porticos and ornate dome sprinkled with snowflakes, the fabled Staatsoper shimmers against the slate-gray sky like a local cakemaker's dream of Valhalla. The interior is an equally imposing arrangement of staircases and arcaded loggias embellished with statues and chandeliers—all available for admiration by properly dressed opera fans. A plaque in the lobby requests that you wear "clothing appropriate to the surroundings."

To most of the contented-looking people strolling past me in their loden coats and felt hats topped off by smart little feathers, their beloved and well-funded opera house is the center of the universe. After American bombs destroyed all but the facade and stairway, the Staatsoper's reconstruction was put on the fast track, and the house reopened in 1955 looking almost exactly the way it had in 1869. The Viennese take comfort in the past, and they are happiest when the costumes are inhabited by familiar and famous singers in conservative productions. Here I've heard Agnes Baltsa and Edita Gruberova duel in Donizetti's *Maria Stuarda*; *Tosca* with Caballé, who brought her pocketbook onstage for her encounter with Scarpia (maybe not accidentally: she often liked to take her fee in cash after the first act); and an amusing *Rosenkavalier* during which Octavian and Sophie got their buttons caught and could not disembrace.

Now I'd slithered in from snow-packed Prague (an unavoidable business trip), hoping to catch Jane Eaglen as Amelia in *Un ballo in maschera* in January 1997. She had cancelled by the time I got to my hotel, but fortunately I'd also made an appointment to visit the Staatsoper's general director, Ioan Holender, whose reputation as an entertainingly manipulative and seductive ogre extends across the ocean. In a contest for most autocratic opera manager he would probably edge out the Met's Joe Volpe and the Bastille's Hugues Gall, both friends and gold-star graduates of the take-no-prisoners school of management. The course is required to run the Staatsoper, which previously scared off the nervous Gustav Mahler, the imperious Herbert von Karajan, and the pompous Lorin Maazel.

It's not the only show in town, though. There's the dowdy Volksoper—the People's Opera—with its mix of populist fare, local talent, and low prices, and a jewel box called the Theater an der Wien, where Beethoven's *Fidelio* was first heard, mostly by newly arrived officers of Napoleon's army of occupation, in 1805.

This is, or was, Bartoli's house. At the Theater an der Wien, she charmed the locals with a rare production of Haydn's *Orfeo ed Euridice* conducted by Nikolaus Harnoncourt and staged by Jürgen Flimm for the annual spring festival presented by the city of Vienna. But the festival's enterprising director, Klaus Bachler, had just left to spruce up the Volksoper, where international stars rarely appear, while the Staatsoper's Holender is known as a guy who watches his schillings and dislikes Rossini. Lately, he's also been favoring a young mezzo from Salzburg, Angelika Kirchschlager, whose repertoire overlaps slightly with Bartoli's and who could sing the trouser roles for which Bartoli seemed curvily unsuited. For Jack Mastroianni, who manages Kirchschlager, too, the Austrian's rise has added a challenging layer to his management of Bartoli, and he is also heading here for an appointment with Holender in a few days' time.

The Herr General Direktor did invite Bartoli to sing Despina in a

Così conducted by Riccardo Muti, but that was in 1994, when renovations briefly relocated the company to the Theater an der Wien. So she has in fact never stood on the stage of the Staatsoper. The Viennese who flocked to her performances, every one of them sold out, would surely like this to change. But Holender's last offer was Lehár's operetta *The Merry Widow*, which, not surprisingly, Bartoli found perplexing. "I mean, I've never even been married; why would I want to sing a widow, merry or sad?" she once told me. "Besides, it's really written for soprano." It's also in German.

The cheerful skinflint was in his plush office giving an interview to a writer from *Gala*, an Austrian *People*-type magazine, which was doing a day-in-the-life-of story on the general manager. Now I was part of the story, which Holender, a craggily handsome, toothily charming sixty-two-year-old with a ski tan and alpine blue eyes, was basically scripting himself, with a conversational flow that slowed only when he answered his telephone, lit a cigarette, or stared at the television monitor, which was showing a dress rehearsal of *Idomeneo*, an early Mozart opera in the opera seria style, meaning it is long on formality and recitatives and short on drama. Assistants were scurrying over the stage making last-minute fixes and adjusting Plácido Domingo's regal robe. The tenor was singing the title role of a Cretan king who nearly sacrifices his son, Idamante, to fulfill a promise to Neptune, the stormy god of the seas. Kirchschlager was singing Idamante, a role Bartoli had recorded with Domingo for DG but had yet to sing on stage. That recording had finally been released, after a complicated gestation that included the replacement of Kathy Battle and Cheryl Studer after their relationships with the set's conductor, James Levine, had soured.

Domingo was here to celebrate the thirtieth anniversary of his Staatsoper debut. The company's light rehearsal schedule made Mr. D an ideal visitor, even if he isn't the greatest Mozart singer. On the recording, his voice squeezed out Mozart's delicate notes only with the greatest effort, but over the speakers he sounded like he was managing quite well.

Staring at the monitor, the *Gala* journalist made the mistake of thinking the stage set hadn't arrived yet. "Is this a scene change?" she asked, looking at a woebegone assortment of broken columns threatened by a cantilevered slab of concrete. "Naaa. That's what the set looks like. A cultural conflict," Holender explained, laughing at his own ugly production, which would open the next day to mediocre reviews.

He took a phone call and leaned back in his chair to ponder his beautiful high ceilings.

Holender is said to love the ladies, but these days women are giving him trouble. A local paper reported that he has a feud going with the newly appointed female director of the Vienna Boys Choir. Now he was saying something disparaging about American feminists. So what have they done? "They," he said, getting off the phone, "have threatened to boycott the next tour of the Vienna Philharmonic because of the orchestra's medieval men-only tradition." He made a face. Holender was caught up in the festering controversy because the Philharmonic also plays for the opera house (though not everyone in the opera-house orchestra is a member of the Philharmonic). So far, the Philharmonic had been able to maintain its comic ways because it is a private organization. But the orchestra gets a small government subsidy and the opera house gets a huge one, and pressure for change was mounting. Ronald Wilford of CAMI, which tours the orchestra, had just told him he was finding it increasingly embarrassing to book an all-male orchestra in the United States.

"When do you think Vienna will make it into this century?" I asked him.

"Probably by next week," he snarfed. "It's inevitable." Holender wasn't kidding. A week later, he effectively if unwillingly undermined the boys-only policy of the Philharmonic by announcing that as far as the opera was concerned, women would henceforth be allowed to audition.

He changed the subject to one he liked more: his novel casting approach. Holender preferred to sign artists to yearly contracts instead of paying them per performance, an ensemble approach that was more common decades ago. Holender loved it because he saved money and stiffed his old agent colleagues in the bargain. He was once a manager before this cushy job fell into his lap.

"Zurich and Stuttgart are doing this too, but my approach has been less influential than I would have thought," he said, shaking his head in amazement. He lit another cigarette. "Think about it. German companies are crying poverty at the same time that they are paying fifteen to twenty thousand marks a night for what is often just a slightly above-average singer. For that I can have them a whole month. I pay up to thirty thousand marks a month. It's good for singers too. They still get paid if they are sick. There are risks. For instance, in *Idomeneo* we don't have, say, Barbara Bonney or Anne Sofie von Otter, but Angelika Kirchschlager."

"You also don't get Frau Bartoli," I pointed out.

He laughed. "Her agent, what's his name, is coming here next week to discuss just that." He paused a moment to look into his calendar. "Ha! I don't want to say anything nasty. But through a concert career, you don't have an opera career. *Cenerentola* I don't do in this theater. Paah. Frau Bartoli is a very musical person. But if she doesn't sing opera, she won't grow. Take a singer from the past, Elisabeth Schwarzkopf. She also sang many recitals, but it was not the basis of her career. Or Pavarotti. He's still stopping by here just to prove he can still sing opera. At age sixty-one, it's still important to him.

"Consider a younger singer who is or was also expensive, Dmitri Hvorostovsky. Years ago I wanted him. He was too expensive. Now I get a call saying 'Can we speak about it?' and now I say, I wouldn't take him at half the fee. He's a good singer, not more, not less."

"There are plenty of new singers," Holender continued. "You just need to take a chance and book them early, and we do that here." His long list included Andrea Rost, Vesselina Kasarova, Terfel, Alagna, and Ramón Vargas.

"People say I'm anti–old singers. That's not true. But there's not space for everybody."

"I've heard you're also anti–fat singers."

Holender snorted. "I can't hire Americans like Alessandra Marc or Sharon Sweet. The Viennese public would laugh."

"What about Jane Eaglen?"

He shrugged. "When she first sang for me, I forget quite when, she was, well, what should I say, *wohlgenährt*—well-nourished. 'Now don't you get fat on me,' I said. The next time I saw her, there was already a big change." He looked annoyed. Her eating habits seem to have torpedoed a project of his, the first production here in decades of Verdi's *I vespri siciliani*.

"I mean, even I know enough about *Regietheater* to know I can't do that show with her in it." In *Regietheater*, meaning "director's theater," there's usually a conceptual underpinning that requires singers to attempt acting.

Herr Holender was running out of time. He invited his visitors to tag along to the rehearsal. Domingo was standing in the auditorium facing a camera and a microphone, having managed to fit a TV interview into a short break, which would now not be wasted. The *Gala* woman taped the taping.

He was smiling, so I had to assume no one was asking him what his wife of thirty-seven years, Marta Domingo, thought about the twenty-one-year-old Romanian nymph he had been squiring around Vienna, where she studied voice. Was he giving her private tutorials? Over the years, the tenor had demonstrated a shrewd talent for soprano spotting, promoting the most talented to productions of *La traviata* he was conducting.

The *Gala* girl finished her interview; the rehearsal continued. Kirchschlager stepped out, a petite woman dressed in the pantaloons of Idamante. Her voice sounded much lighter and more silvery than Bartoli's. But like Cecilia, she sang with a smile.

"People who don't know much about opera, they see Frau Kirchschlager and they say: 'Who is that?' " Holender whispered, sitting down for a few minutes. The show ground to a halt as an assistant director rushed to the stage to push the cast into a slightly different formation underneath the threatening concrete cantilever.

Holender waved to a tall, sulky girl with a lot of hair, who sauntered over to his seat and knelt next to him in the aisle.

"Tell me, what do you want to sing next May?" he said to her. "Echo or—what's her name again?—Gerhilde, Grünhilde, something. Do you know both roles?"

She stared sleepily at him. "Ummm. Who? I don't know any Wagner," she yawned. "Echo I sort of know, maybe." Her German was halting, but she hadn't been spending her days stuffing herself with cream tarts and chocolate layer cake at the Hotel Sacher and so her future seemed bright, especially given the general manager's deep interest in her well-being.

"What's the matter? Are you sleepy? Didn't you sleep well last night?"

He played with her hair and stroked her face. She rolled her eyes. I tried to imagine Joe Volpe casting an opera with his fingers in a singer's hair. It was a stretch.

Holender began singing a trio from *Ariadne auf Naxos* all by himself.

"I think Echo is a nice role. You'll sing Echo in May."

He wrapped her hair around a finger.

"That okay?"

"Mmmmmmmm."

A FEW DAYS LATER, Luciano Pavarotti offered a song recital at the Metropolitan accompanied by Leone Magiera, the first husband of Mirella Freni, and a mouselike presence at the piano. Mr. P's last appearance in New York had not gone well—a Verdi Requiem at Carnegie Hall during which he briefly lost his way in a piece he had sung many times. Would he use the Met recital to reveal new interpretive depths and concentration? Schubert's *Winterreise* perhaps? But Mr. P was still firmly looking backward, seeking to recapture his past, and he arrived onstage with his talismanic handkerchief, music stand, and that sheaf of dog-eared notes. I don't know what disturbed me more—hearing him stumble during "Ave Maria," a hymn a child could manage, or watching him. "Do you still love me?" he seemed to plead, opening his arms wide and grinning automatically and inappropriately after some sacred, soupy songs. It seemed as hard for us to say no as for him to let go; and a few weeks later, some of us were back for what was not *La forza del destino*.

Mr. P had not been able to learn the music of Alvaro, the Inca prince who accidentally shoots the father of the woman he is eloping with one night in Spain. But he had come up with an offer that the Met could not really refuse. He had offered to sub himself as the king of Sweden in Verdi's *Un ballo in maschera*. Same tenor, same composer, different costume, same soprano (Deborah Voigt). Never in the history of the Met had the company changed the entire run of an opera during the season, but what was the ill-prepared company going to do? Who would want to buy a ticket to a hideous production with Pavarotti's understudy, Kristján Jóhannsson, a hearty lump from Iceland? You had to wonder about the Met's planning capacities, since it was obvious that neither Mr. P nor Domingo could go on for much longer. At some point someone there would have to go out and find another tenor.

And so Mr. P took a painkiller for his hurting joints, draped himself in Gustavo's flowing white jabot and satin cape, and sat down on his throne. "My friends . . . soldiers," he gestured, addressing the deputies, nobles, and officers awaiting, just like us, the king's first words. And as he began to sing of the radiant Amelia, his voice took on some of its fabled sheen and glistened like the silvery embroidery on his vest. He sipped water when the need arose and seemed a man much refreshed.

I WAS MISSING the Love Couple. Spring would return Gheorghiu to New York for *Carmen*, but that was a long time to wait. A friend filled me in long-distance from London. Gheorghiu, she said, was about to make a recording in London called *Czardas*, after the Hungarian dance that sometimes energizes productions of Johann Strauss's *Die Fledermaus*. Solti would conduct, the venerable conductor of her career-boosting *La traviata* recording. This *Czardas* sounded like a good idea—light tunes of charm and melody sung by a singer whose metier might in another time have been the operetta stage.

Incredibly, the disc turned into yet another Verdi sampler, even though Gheorghiu is not anybody's idea of a Verdi singer: hers is a slender voice incapable of dramatic dynamic contrasts and passionate cries. But that didn't seem to bother the folks at Decca, who apparently figured a sound engineer could provide whatever volume and experience the soprano lacked. So one afternoon, Sir Georg set aside some time to coach the young singer in the music room of his handsome house in St. John's Wood. Now in his mid-eighties, Solti had studied with Arturo Toscanini, who started life as a cellist and was in the orchestra sawing away at the world premiere of *Otello*. Solti was history incarnate, and most singers would thank their lucky stars to absorb the maestro's wisdom.

Gheorghiu arrived forty minutes late, trailing Alagna. They didn't seem to have an excuse, but Solti was gracious, and they got to work on Desdemona's "Willow Song" from the last act of *Otello*. Filled with disturbing thoughts, haunted by a song she heard in her youth, the doomed Desdemona interweaves her own sadness with that of the song's abandoned girl. "Salce, salce!" she cries. "The weeping willow shall be my garland."

A poetic singer will lean into "Salce" (willow) with that tiny expressive scoop called a portamento.

"*What was that?!*" Solti cried in disbelief, stopping the pianist, as she sang the phrase without a portamento. "No, you must not sing it like that! Angela, you should sing it portamento."

She looked at him in a puzzled way. "Maestro," she said. "I do not sing the portamento unless the composer wrote it."

"But Angela," he replied, astonished. "I tell you it is correct. Believe me."

"It's not written in my score," she insisted. Alagna got up to say he too did not feel Verdi had wished for a portamento on "Salce."

Solti somehow controlled his famous Hungarian temper as others in the room gaped in disbelief at the cheeky couple. He stood up and walked to a bookcase and creaked up a ladder to pull down his old score.

"Look at my score. Here it is—a portamento. This is the way Toscanini conducted it. Believe me, it is right to use a portamento here. The marking is his. Here, look," Solti pleaded.

But Gheorghiu, graduate of the Bucharest Conservatory, would not be persuaded. She just couldn't see her way to singing it his way. She considered singing portamento old-fashioned and sentimental, just as her husband did. Solti became so agitated he told them both to get out and find another conductor. The evening's recording session was cancelled.

The next day, he wearily relented. But the absurd album was not finished by the time of his death in the fall.

It made me think of the *Don Giovanni* album Bartoli had been looking forward to that rainy day in Amsterdam. She should have been getting set to record it right now at the end of January with Claudio Abbado. Well, DG was recording it all right, but not with her. Not long before the sessions started in Milan, Bartoli discovered that while Abbado had *wished* to record with her, this did not mean he *was* recording with her. DG had signed another Zerlina, Patrizia Pace— not exactly a name to help move a three-CD set out the doors, but perhaps someone who would show up for the recording sessions. Was he punishing Bartoli for failing to sing that esoteric Debussy piece back in December? Whatever the reason, she was now free to sing in András Schiff's Schubert gala at Wigmore Hall. But Bartoli chose to stay home while DG made another recording of *Don Giovanni* very few people wanted.

CHAPTER TWENTY

Where's the Maid?

B̶AD NEWS AT THE MET is always posted just past the ticket takers by the left loop of the grand staircase. Regulars know to cast a brief glance of dread in that direction to see who's cancelled now. But the gold-framed message on a Saturday afternoon in March 1997 was unusually cryptic and attracted puzzled attention.

It said: "In this afternoon's performance of *Così fan tutte* the roles of Ferrando and Guglielmo will be sung by Richard Croft and Nathan Gunn, respectively, replacing Stanford Olsen and Mark Oswald, who are ill. In addition, the role of Despina will be sung by Marie McLaughlin, replacing Cecilia Bartoli."

Now what did that mean? Where could she be if she wasn't sick, like the two gents and also conductor James Levine? Trapped in a bank vault? Engrossed in a Maria Callas biography?

Matinee performances, once the season is in full swing, are regularly broadcast live by the Texaco–Metropolitan Opera Radio Network to stations all over the world. Managers usually fight to get their artists on the air, especially if they have records to sell. It's a major negotiating point in a contract. Singers who don't win the first night (with hopefully career-advancing reviews) pant for the Saturday broadcast, when millions tune in.

There was no question Bartoli was back in New York, for the revival of the same production of *Così* in which she had made her debut last season. Her contract called for her to sing two performances and then join the Met on its upcoming tour to Japan. I hadn't been to the first performance, on Wednesday, but had seen her at the opening the following night of a new production of *Eugene Onegin*, Tchaikovsky's opera about a Russian bookworm and letter writer who gets the humiliation of her life when she opens her soul to a dashing dandy, but regroups and marries spectacularly, masking her broken heart behind a facade of regal dignity.

Robert Carsen, a chicly minimalist European favorite, was making his Met directing debut along with the conductor Antonio Pappano— he of the wonderful *Don Carlos* in Paris last spring. But imaginative newcomers are often ground to bits by the Met's bureaucratic machine, and this was not a great night. Pappano sometimes lost the chorus, which had been positioned backstage by the director, who did not wish them to clutter up his pristine set—a white box filled with autumnal leaves suggestive of remembrance and despair. What would have been a perfect concept for one of the smaller houses in avant-garde Germany—say, Wiesbaden—came off too minimal and understated for the Met's hugeness, and there was little to distract us from the extreme vocal and physical discomfort of Galina Gorchakova and her Onegin, Vladimir Chernov, both of them old-fashioned singers who require garden benches to sit on and birches to embrace. For some time now, neither had resisted the lure of big fees for the wrong roles—mostly in the Italian repertoire—and they both had worn down their vocal capital in the process.

Pressing up the congested aisle during the intermission, I ran into a glum couple—Bartoli and Osele. But the cause, as it turned out, wasn't the *Onegin* production. She liked it, actually. What she didn't like was her own *Così* last night, and as we trudged into the lobby she listed some of the problems:

(1) Levine had cancelled, for starters. The usually robust maestro

had taken ill while in Miami for the Three Tenors and been told by his doctor not to travel. (2) His replacement was Martin Isepp, a skilled harpsichordist and a treasured fixture at Glyndebourne but not a big-time conductor. Apparently the stage-pit coordination had not been totally smooth. (3) The singers cast as Ferrando and Guglielmo had cancelled and been replaced by young artists.

"And then," she added, "the set got stuck during the show."

I could see she was upset, though these things happen often enough on opera stages full up with fancy sets and frail singers. In my wallet I keep a cast notice once slipped into a Met program:

"In this performance of *Don Giovanni* the role of Donna Anna will be sung by Carol Vaness, replacing Sharon Sweet, who is ill. Miss Vaness was originally scheduled to sing the role of Donna Elvira in this evening's performance and the Metropolitan Opera is deeply grateful to her for agreeing to sing Donna Anna on extremely short notice. Patricia Schuman will sing the role of Donna Elvira. The role of Don Ottavio will be sung by Stanford Olsen, replacing Jerry Hadley, who is also ill. Bryn Terfel has injured his back and is also unable to sing in this evening's performance. The role of Leporello will be sung by Herbert Perry."

The unexpected—the trembling nobody who triumphs, the indisposed artist who delivers the performance of her life, the collapsing set—opera memories are made of such things.

But just because Bartoli is a quick study doesn't mean she likes surprises. *Così*'s massive cast-and-conductor change had clearly disturbed her equilibrium. By the time Gorchakova had blasted her goodbyes to the frail baritone, Bartoli had decided she really couldn't sing the matinee show of *Così* and instructed her manager, Mastroianni—who was backstage in the throes of diva dienst with his client Gorchakova—to inform the Met. So in the middle of the night, Billinghurst and Friend started the weary business of getting another Despina. Bartoli had an understudy, Clare Gormley, a promising light soprano from the Met's Young Artist Development Program. But could the company expose her to an international broadcast? Gormley had apparently not rehearsed onstage. What if she came down with the shakes? The only other Despina who knew the production was sturdy Marie McLaughlin, inconveniently domiciled in Kent (as in England, not Connecticut). Her manager was called to put McLaughlin on alert, meaning she should carry passport and cell phone at all times.

By Friday, the Met had made a decision. Tracked down in the early afternoon at her voice teacher's that day, McLaughlin drove straight to the airport, cajoled her way onto the fully booked Concorde, and arrived Friday evening.

Volpe, not happy and monitoring the situation from his Florida vacation home, let it be known that even if Bartoli changed her mind, McLaughlin would go on. And that furthermore Bartoli would not be announced as indisposed.

Thus the carefully phrased posting in the lobby of the Met that greeted us as we arrived for the matinee.

General managers can never figure out exactly what they want: polite technicians who always show up and sing the notes, or festive monsters of egotism who drive them nuts but create a buzz at the box office. As Maria Callas understood: "A little scandal is good for business." But the divinity never sang, let alone cancelled, Despina, the maid. She sang major roles like Tosca and Norma. Blowing off the Met and slighting internationally respected colleagues like Carol Vaness and Susan Graham—who were singing the two sisters— seemed just possibly an ill-considered example of overreaching.

Matters became surreal when Bartoli asked whether the Met would consider broadcasting the tape of last year's *Così* matinee if she went onstage to sing this year's. Clearly she worried about being heard on an international broadcast that could be taped by anybody and saved for posterity. An obsessively fastidious singer groomed in the hothouse atmosphere of the recording studio, where she could do take after take until each note sounded just the way she wanted, was bound to find that prospect unappealing. Somebody had to remind her this wasn't a recital. There were others in the cast who might actually wish to be heard live.

Vaness and Graham were still rolling their eyes by the time the curtain finally rose on the matinee performance. It went without a hitch. McLaughlin was lively in her apron, and the young gents,

Nathan Gunn and Dwayne Croft's tenor brother, Richard, fleet of voice and nice to look at. Gunn, especially, just in his late twenties, made a big impression. Handsome and charming, with an eye for the audience and a gracious attitude toward his colleagues, the amber-voiced baritone exuded the charismatic confidence that comes naturally and can rarely be acquired.

Graham added to the week's entertainment by stepping in for a sick colleague next door at Avery Fisher Hall, singing a Berlioz song cycle in the evening, Dorabella during the day, and talking to the *New York Times* in whatever time she had left over. Graham seemed to be picking up speed every month. While she lacked Bartoli's extravagant recital personality, Graham in a costume, male or female, was so incandescent she could make junk sparkle. I am remembering Massenet's twilight soufflé *Chérubin* (Mozart's page, a little older). Graham had sung it to huge acclaim at Covent Garden in the winter in a staging that also featured the coloratura Elizabeth Futral, another American with a growing European career. The two of them had made it sound like *Rosenkavalier*.

Meanwhile, Bartoli appeared at Tower Records a few steps away from the Met the day after the cancellation. She claimed a bad back had kept her from the matinee.

"This doesn't look so good," I suggested to her manager.

"What did you want me to do? Put a gun to her head?" Mastroianni asked. "Two things I learned from my CAMI days with Ronald Wilford. One: Do not expect singers to be logical. Two: Do not force anyone to sing something they do not want to. It will backfire. Something will go wrong. I laid out the options and warned her as calmly as possible that all actions have consequences. Opera houses look on artists as business partners and will eventually favor the reliable ones."

Pausing for a minute, he added: "The music is perfect. It is, after all, by Mozart. But the world in which we live is not. I remember when June Anderson was my client, that fact was a constant depressant. She is not alone."

Perhaps Bartoli was no longer as needy of his advice, now that she shared so much of her time with her hard-to-please live-in career counselor, Claudio Osele, whose preference for Italy seemed to fit perfectly with Bartoli's fondness for Europe and its excellent train network. Though invitations were hardly lacking, she had no plans to concertize in North America and had not accepted any Met engagements beyond the new *Figaro* in the fall of 1998. Osele was more around than ever, his typical silence hovering like a question mark in the background. When Bartoli had given a short, private concert at the Villa Medici in Rome in the early spring, he'd preceded her with studiously conceived introductions that he read from the stage as guests stared at their shoes. The small family vineyard hardly required his full-time attention, and I wondered whether with no career of his own, but a serious interest in baroque music, he might not make himself available to manage hers and save her a few pennies.

Meanwhile, attention was drifting to the next engagement and possible drama. Bartoli had song recitals with Levine in the coming week in Princeton and New York, yet here she had just informed the Met—whose artistic director he was, after all—that the *Così* hadn't been perfect enough for her to be in it. Would Levine feel a little offended? Might he feel the need to recuperate a little while longer in Florida and stick her with another, less accomplished accompanist?

Naaa. What did he care? After all, *he* didn't have to deal with the problem or pay for the Concorde, and may even have found the whole incident rather amusing. He played both concerts, looking tan and cheerful at Tully Hall where she began with "Vaga luna" and instantly cast the kind of spell emanating from Bellini's silvery moon. There's nothing complicated about this song thematically or technically; every student next door at the Juilliard School could do it. But Bartoli's seamless line and subtle suggestiveness lifted the song from the étude books into a higher realm. It was a surprising bit of alchemy that also transformed the Donizetti candy, Viardot's mini-melodramas, and the otherwise laughable "Enigme éternelle" by Ravel in his exotic tourist mode. The way the audience listened rapturously and intently to her song about a butterfly made you wonder what effect she might have entering the somewhat more complicated emotional worlds of Brahms or Mahler. Maybe someday Levine would lead her there. In the meanwhile, he scampered cheerfully over the keyboard when not blowing her kisses between sets, or placing his hand over his heart in a manner that could make a strong man heave into a bucket.

Even a guy like Joe Volpe, though he kept his composure as he headed backstage, trailing Sarah Billinghurst, whose teeth had to be hurting from all the smiling she was doing. He parked himself outside the dressing room of his sometime Despina. He knocked. No answer. He knocked again. Finally, the door opened and he stepped inside.

"Cute little pieces. Nice evening. Heh heh," he grinned, emerging five minutes later to push through a bunch of Decca hand-holders and hangers-on who were taking care of the autographing and the bouquet transport.

Afterwards, I stopped by a dinner at Duomo, the small Italian restaurant behind Lincoln Center. Sitting down across from her other favorite pianist, Jean-Yves Thibaudet, Bartoli needed little prompting to launch into the highlights of the last few days. "Why this fuss about one performance? This hysteria?" she asks. "Isn't this out of proportion? It was just one performance. I sang every single one last year."

Thibaudet just laughed into his boldly heraldic Versace tie. "Look, you're a story."

"That's what my father said," she said. "Even the Italian papers printed something, and he told me: 'Cecilia. How amazing. You get as much coverage for not singing as for singing!'"

I couldn't help wondering what her mother thought—a singer forced by circumstance into a home life mixed with chorus work. What did she think about her daughter passing up an opportunity to be heard by millions? But Silvana, always reticent, was an ocean away, caring for her sick father and probably worrying about her son, Gabriele. He lit up the restaurant as he arrived smiling and waving, his arm around Antonella, but I'd heard he had recently been back in the hospital. The Delfici ensemble was in town to join Cecilia for a few concerts.

The next day, they all began the drive to Chicago, Bartoli heading up the caravan in her fancy new coach—a $186,000 Silver Spur placed at her disposal by the Rolls-Royce company. It came with a driver and such diva-friendly frills as a video system and ankle-deep lambskin carpets—quite a lot of car for a frugal Fiat driver, but I guess a saint might find such a perk hard to resist. Barely inside the Loop, the Silver Spur suddenly lost its power steering, and in a reverse bit of magic, a humble rental had to be pressed into service.

You can't look around corners.

That week, I picked up the February 1997 issue of *Classic CD*, a British magazine with a cover feature on the thirty-one-year-old Bulgarian Vesselina Kasarova—"the Mezzo for the Millennium." Unknown when she replaced Marilyn Horne on short notice in *Tancredi* in Salzburg a few years ago, Kasarova seized the moment and now was singing the bel canto repertoire all over Europe, including the trouser roles Bartoli avoided onstage. Along the way, Kasarova had acquired an exclusive contract with RCA Red Seal and a blow drier. The latest release showed off a mezzo with a brilliant high range and a chic new hairdo.

Talent and good fortune beyond the dreams of most mortals brings rewards and burdens. I think of Dame Kiri Te Kanawa, who floated up from New Zealand to the top of the world. In 1990, she opened a window into the psyche of the celebrity singer in an unusually frank video portrait by the director Nigel Wattis. With wonder she described how in 1944 a social worker from an orphanage brought her to a European-Maori couple, who wished to adopt a boy. They rejected the little bundle, who was also half-Maori. Months later, the same person returned with a now larger bundle and asked if they had possibly changed their minds. The couple was fated to take her, and they did. They loved her, recognized her talent, instilled her with ambition, and finally sent her off to London. If Te Kanawa did not marry the prince, she did sing at his wedding. Millions tuned in to hear Kiri Te Kanawa sing Handel's "Let the bright seraphim" at St. Paul's Cathedral in 1981 when Prince Charles married Diana. She was suddenly the most famous opera singer in the world. Not long thereafter, the fear of not living up to her fame provoked, she said, a complete collapse of her health and professional confidence.

"I was becoming very well-known, being wanted all over," she recalled, a hint of self-mockery and amazement flitting across her beautiful face. Often, she required sleeping pills to quiet the demons of the night, and constantly asked herself, How can I please? How can I get through all the jobs? Te Kanawa forced herself to perform because she sensed that otherwise she might never return to the stage.

"Just getting out the dress to iron was painful," she said, before changing the subject and leaving us with the nearly unabsorbable vision of Dame Kiri hovering tensely over an ironing board.

CHAPTER TWENTY-ONE

Clean Plate Club

O NE NIGHT I WAS WATCHING *The X-Files* and encountered a fat-sucking vampire with very dry skin who befriended large women he met through on-line chat rooms. I thought of Jane Eaglen.

The famous web potato had not been signing on much lately. Where was she? Had someone blown the Kathy Kent cover?

I'd last seen her as Norma in the fall of 1996 at the Los Angeles Opera, a performance she sang forcefully even after falling in her dressing room and wrenching her shoulder. "When someone like me falls, it is problematic," she admitted to the people propping her back up. Attention shifted to the tenor singing the ingeniously self-serving Roman soldier who beds down two Druid virgins. José Cura, a long-limbed tenor from Argentina, was starting to make the rounds after a big success in Covent Garden's summer Verdi festival. His voice sounded special—baritonal in flavoring but with a free, ringing top—and he had the intensity and commanding presence of a leading man.

With a magical voice, even the largest singer becomes beauty incarnate. But in the spring of 1997, Eaglen seemed ever more perplexing and hard to camouflage. Breathing problems afflicted her recording for Sony of Bellini and Wagner arias. And her May debut with the New York Philharmonic came off oddly. Looking a trifle rumpled and not very cheerful, she offered a securely pumped-out but tonally thin Liebestod from Wagner's *Tristan und Isolde* and then after an ardent reception puttered off for dinner at Shun Lee across from Lincoln Center. Maybe a spare rib went down the wrong way. She cancelled the next day's performance.

I called up Speight Jenkins, a skinny ex–music critic turned general manager who has put the Seattle Opera on the map with his adventurous productions, among them a thrilling *Ring* cycle and an offbeat *Norma* that introduced Eaglen to America. I knew he had an opinion on singers of size, because he once lost a wager at an editors' lunch at the *Wall Street Journal.* Jenkins bet that the immense but very promising Brünnhilde he'd recently signed for a future *Ring* cycle would lose weight because he had made it clear she would otherwise not sing in the show. We bet the stress would make her eat more. We won. She did not sing and eventually disappeared from the opera stage.

Jenkins would be reunited with Eaglen for a new *Tristan und Isolde* in the summer of 1998 with Ben Heppner and Michelle DeYoung, neither of them small but both fleet of foot and powerful of voice. DeYoung, a beautiful, statuesque blonde not yet thirty years old with a voice that reminded many of a young Jessye Norman, had a good chance of turning into a major singer. The clarion-voiced, Canadian-born Heppner was slowly emerging as the Wagner hope of the millennium, a heldentenor who might finally release us from the worn ramblings of the ubiquitous Siegfried Jerusalem.

Was Jenkins worried about his Isolde?

No, he was not. "Now, I do believe that we are in a theatrical business, and I think that people who are hugely overweight simply are not credible to audiences if they are playing romantic roles. We are, after all, in the fantasy business," he said. "To be an exception, a person has got to be unique vocally and have the capacity to convey a character dramatically." Jenkins thought Eaglen remained an exception.

"I'm not only talking visually," he added. "Certain operatic characters must be able to run or at least to move very quickly, to climb, to fall down and get up quickly. These are not inconsequential problems." He mentioned Andrea Gruber, a mite by Eaglen standards but a Forgotten Woman shopper in real life even so. When she sang Aida in Seattle, Gruber worked with a personal trainer so she was sure to rise quickly after her father, Amonasro, threw her to the floor as the libretto demands. Jenkins thought that, God willing, Eaglen might be persuaded to see her way to the treadmill.

The general manager loved this topic and he had more to say. "Weight will usually create vocal problems as the singer grows older. They have to breathe much more just to make the heart work through all that fat. All that gulping for air can harm the vocal line." He felt obligated, he said, to tell size-plus singers who audition for him that their weight would hold them back. Most opera-house managers would probably invent some other excuse not to hire the weight-challenged thanks to the Americans with Disabilities Act, which protects the clinically obese, though I've yet to hear of a company being sued for size discrimination.

Had he studied the eating habits of the extra-large? I asked Jenkins. When he took them out, did they order double portions and slather butter on their bread loaves?

They did not. They seemed to be furtive eaters. Jenkins blamed room service. "It's a lonely business. They go back to their hotels after rehearsals, feeling depressed, and order up bacon cheeseburgers with extra fries and a pint of vanilla ice cream to feel good."

Cows have a lot to answer for. Singers love ice cream. They love the way it feels sliding down their gullets, cooling their excitable cords and calming their nerves. Even Callas. Her friend and biographer, the Dallas critic John Ardoin, once described to me his visits to her suite in the Plaza Hotel in New York when she was giving her master classes at Juilliard in 1971–72. Never mind her affection for American hot dogs, Callas retained the fashion-plate looks she had achieved with great determination in the 1950s. (When dining out, she had a clever habit of having other people order what she wished to eat, then picking off their plates.) But after an evening of television—*I Love Lucy* was a favorite—the diva would send him down to procure vanilla ice cream from a special stand in the lobby. "It was something like three dollars a scoop," he recalled, still horrified.

Vanilla is a favorite. In the 1970s, my alto-singing friend Sheila Nadler, Mrs. Klinghoffer in the John Adams opera *The Death of Klinghoffer*, often went down to coach with Rosa Ponselle, who resided in a grand mansion outside of Baltimore with a lot of furniture and pets. She kept squirrels in a special cage, and Nadler would hear her singing to them as she came up the road. "Squeegee!" Ponselle would trill, and feed her bushy-tailed favorites whatever special treats she'd not consumed herself. Fittingly, she was born in 1897 in Meriden, Connecticut, the birthplace of the mythic steamed cheeseburger. At first a music-hall entertainer, she was only twenty-one when she sang with Enrico Caruso in the Met premiere of *La forza del destino* and not quite forty when she retired. She still had a voice—one of the most evenly beautiful, judging by her records and admirers—but her nerves had started to fray, leaving her with a fear of high C. She had also lost a repertory fight with another one of those egomaniacs the Met often attracts as general manager. She wished to sing *Adriana Lecouvreur*; he did not wish to hear it. Ponselle adorns a thirty-two-cent postage stamp; he is forgotten.

Ponselle loved to eat as much as she loved to teach. After a long session spent singing Aida to Nadler's Amneris and dispensing useful advice—"Always add a sob, Sheila, if you're running out of breath!"—it was time to pack the cones. "Pack it in all the way to the bottom!" Ponselle would shout from the spacious living room to Nadler in the kitchen. Tiring of vanilla, Nadler finally introduced her to butter pecan.

"The greatest thing about retirement," Régine Crespin, one of the sexiest singers of the more recent past, said to me one day as we were enjoying a cappuccino with a slice of carrot cake (each), "is that I no longer think about what I eat. And I smoke and drink with pleasure." She shocked everyone in a café in Manhattan by lighting up with impunity. "But before, I thought I owed it to my fans to be, well, magnificent."

Magnificent hasn't always been easy to achieve, especially for Americans, who eat more junk food than their European rivals and then find themselves stuck in foreign lands that do not spend a large percentage of the GNP on running shoes, diet products, and health clubs. But Europe is slowly catching up, and you no longer need to sprint through Paris, Munich, Milan, or Rome looking for a health club. Worried about germs, Bartoli finds them unappealing. Her preferred exercise is walking, and she does a lot of it, though a Decca executive—who requested anonymity—recently wondered how she might be encouraged to undertake even longer hikes. "The time is coming when her press photos and public presence could be reconciled only by wishful thinking," he worried. Her public expects a sparklingly vivacious gamine. "Hey, Decca! Drop dead!" she might as well be saying in the funny portrait photo that appears in the May 1997 issue of *Bon Appetit*. She put uncooked pasta in her hair, strung baby tomatoes around her neck, and fashioned earrings out of garlic and onions. She held up kitchen spoons. Silvana helped her with the arrangement.

George Lang of the Café des Artistes, the legendary eatery near Lincoln Center, told me he hopes to create a special layer cake for her someday, continuing a tradition harking back to such hearty eaters as Luisa Tetrazzini, the fabled coloratura and opera queen of the early twentieth century, who fueled her engine in the morning with a plate of spaghetti. The Palace Hotel in San Francisco concocted Chicken Tetrazzini in her honor in 1911. She was happy to eat it. "I would not diet. If I diet, my face sag," she pointed out.

A rotund woman draped in many strings of pearls and the proudly twinkling owner of several diadems and many diamonds, Tetrazzini is the kind of singer people have in mind when they say, "The show isn't over until . . ." Still, judging by Golden Age opera books, the Fat Lady was actually outnumbered by sylphs and glamorous sirens, though I've heard the theory that girdles helped and pictures were often retouched. Even so, Geraldine Farrar was so beautiful she got to make a silent (!) film of *Carmen*. And even in her seventies, Maria Jeritza exuded chic confidence sweeping into the Met in high regalia and obstructing some cowering subscriber's view with the broad-rimmed black hats she never removed.

When singers aren't worrying that they will not get to sing Zerlina because they are the size of Sieglinde, they are worrying that losing weight will hurt their cords and bring them disaster. A little extra out in front functions like a protective buffer as they face some three thousand talentless and probably overweight strangers, who may soon boo them.

The bigger they get, the more singers think of Callas, who supposedly lost her voice when she went on a diet or ingested a tapeworm, or whatever it is she may or may not have done to try to look like Audrey Hepburn. In fact, Callas made some of her great recordings when she was thin. Even so, if you lose weight incorrectly and don't wait for your muscles to catch up to your fat loss, you can do damage to your vocal support. A lot of opera singers I know spend their lives singing, eating, worrying, dieting, eating.

The typical diva diet was recently anonymously posted on the Internet. It's easy to follow:

BREAKFAST

½ grapefruit
1 slice of whole wheat toast
8 oz. low-fat or skim milk

LUNCH

4 oz. lean broiled chicken breast
1 cup steamed spinach
1 cup herbal tea
1 Oreo cookie

MID-AFTERNOON SNACK

Rest of Oreos in pack
2 pints Haägen Dazs ice cream, preferably vanilla
1 jar hot fudge sauce with nuts, cherries, whipped cream

DINNER

2 loaves garlic bread with cheese
Large cheese pizza

4 cans or 1 large pitcher of beer

3 Milky Way candy bars

LATE-EVENING NEWS

Entire frozen Sara Lee cheesecake eaten directly from the freezer

AND KEEP IN MIND:

1. Movie-related foods do not have additional calories, because they are part of the entire entertainment package and are not part of one's personal intake.

2. Cookie pieces contain no calories. The process of breaking causes caloric leakage.

3. Foods that have the same color have the same number of calories. Examples include spinach and pistachio ice cream, cauliflower and whipped cream.

4. If you fatten up the people around you, you will look thinner.

I had been thinking about this hugely important subject because I was about to visit cyberspace with Deborah Voigt and see how her diet was going. Last year, there was a joke floating around that the Met was planning a big concert tour starring Voigt, Eaglen, and Sharon Sweet. They were going to call it the Three Tonners. "Pound for pound, more sound!" the ads would say.

Sweet once surprised the backstage crew at the Met by absent-mindedly devouring the prop chicken that Don Giovanni had hoped to enjoy in the opera's banquet scene. Donna Anna has a lot of down time, and Sweet, bored out of her wits waiting in the wings to sing her last aria, started picking at the platter. "It was just staring up at me," she explained when the Met's prop department inquired about its condition. Stage left was known as the chicken wing for a while.

Waiting for Voigt, I thought back to April 1992, when she made her first big splash in the opera world. The show was Richard Strauss's *Elektra*. You could relive it by drilling a hole in your head, but it was best to be there. With its night-piercing shrieks, anxious whispers, psychotic characters, and churning score, *Elektra* usually makes for a satisfying night at the opera. But that evening rated particularly high thanks to Hildegard Behrens in the title role of the woebegone daughter of Agamemnon and Klytemnestra. When the opera starts, Elektra is a bundle of mental and physical problems, but singing isn't meant to be among them. Behrens muttered and moaned through the first part of Elektra's monologue, swooped up to high B-flat, and then tried out an earsplitting high C that had even hard-of-hearing subscribers gasping in their seats. Undeterred, she soldiered on with a personal improvisation based only glancingly on the score and avoiding all other high notes.

Once onstage, Elektra never leaves. Pressing out one painful note at a time, Behrens entered opera annals with one of the most bizarre performances by a major artist in living memory.

Thankfully, Elektra has a sister, Chrysothemis. Deborah Voigt had the part, and while most of us had never heard of her before, we did then as she sang loud enough for two people. She just stood there calmly and became sound incarnate. The audience went wild. Not since the prime of the glamorous Viennese dreadnought Leonie Rysanek had anyone cut through the outsized orchestra with such ease and with plenty remaining for those power surges that make Strauss with the right singers so exciting.

Soon Voigt was sharing Sieglinde's dinner bowl with Plácido Domingo. It is Siegmund who brings hope to the unloved Sieglinde—his twin sister, as it turns out. "Du bist der Lenz" ("You are the spring") is Sieglinde's big moment, and Voigt delivered it with a gale-force power no winter could withstand. Nowadays, when opera houses the world over require a dramatic soprano, thirty-six-year-old Voigt leads the list.

It didn't hurt that Voigt lost eighty pounds in the last two years so she could seriously consider Tosca, a diva part.

Voigt appeared at my door after a morning on her treadmill looking sporty in a chic denim shirt with a velvet collar and a black skirt. With her bright blue eyes, smooth, pretty face, and blond, slightly waved hair, she now resembled Katia Ricciarelli in her weight-shifting heyday when she filmed *Otello* with Domingo and Justino Díaz. Ricciarelli's contract specified that she had to lose about thirty pounds before the production commenced. Ricciarelli didn't make the deadline, but since the movie suffered several delays, her diet struggles were saved for posterity. Desdemona is thin in some scenes and pinkly plump in others.

Voigt asked for club soda and sat down bookended by Emma and Sugar (the latter once employed as a food sniffer by the Beagle Brigade at JFK Airport and still a terror around the dining table) to describe the famous *Elektra*.

"I remember sitting behind the palace doors waiting to go on with cold hands—my version of stage fright—and suddenly catching my breath when I heard her crack. I mean, I felt sorry for her, but then I thought, Well, okay . . . they are going to need something now. *Let's sing some high notes!* I don't mean to seem insensitive, but you have to seize these moments." Voigt laughed.

Once reluctant to discuss the weight issue, Voigt could barely be contained. I asked her if there was one moment that had made the difference, and she said yes, you bet: an embarrassing encounter with Solti. They were meeting to discuss several recording projects, including *Tristan und Isolde*, and as she was leaving the baton-shaped maestro suddenly took her by the shoulders. He looked deeply into her beautiful eyes and asked: "Why are you so fat?" PC talk had yet to come to Europe. "You are not meant to be fat," he continued, blithely oblivious to her discomfort. "I can tell by looking at you."

"That did it," Voigt remembered. "My eyes were welling up, to my annoyance. I was just tired of the whole issue. It pushed me over the edge."

Voigt said she knew her weight was keeping her out of certain houses and gluing her to a few roles in which size seemed not to matter, mostly Wagner, and Strauss's Ariadne. She figured she had maybe fifteen great years left on her cords. So she got herself a treadmill, a diet plan from her doctor, and therapeutic comfort. Many of us eat because we feel deprived in some larger sense. Further deprivation is often unbearable without a long stint on the couch. "There is usually some truth to pop psychology," she admitted. Already as a teenager she'd found solace in the refrigerator. Her well-meaning but tough parents restricted her so much her outlets were church music and eating.

Recently, the new Voigt also found herself in a city so ugly she stayed inside a lot, exercising at her hotel. Stuck in Dresden, a town incinerated by Allied bombers and rebuilt by Communist planners, Voigt dropped quite a few pounds while rehearsing Strauss's *Die Frau ohne Schatten*. News of the new Voigt spread quickly through the cyber-friendly opera world.

"Here we go," Voigt said. Sitting down with my Toshiba laptop, she called up www.artsinfo.com/deborah_voigt and hooted as her home page appeared. Flip the album pages and you could see the chins disappearing. More clicks brought up her schedule (she's booking into the year 2002) and photos of Ballo, her cat, now exiled to California with her grandmother. You can also download sound bites from several recordings, or send her e-mail. CAMI, her management, set the site up as a promotional experiment. The response has been overwhelming.

We clicked into the mail slot. Very polite correspondents. No jokes like: "Yo, Deb! What's the difference beween a Wagnerian soprano and the average American football offensive lineman? . . . Stage makeup!"

Or "Miss Voigt: What's the difference between a soprano and a terrorist? . . . You can negotiate with a terrorist!"

"I wish I had a dollar for every time someone asks what's it like to sing with Pavarotti or Domingo," she said. One of the two amigos, she won't say which one, could use a little Binaca now and then. "But mostly, I hear from young singers who want encouragement to persevere, or they need a voice teacher." She responds to all queries, updating the site every two weeks.

After a Tel Aviv concert with Zubin Mehta, Voigt's site recorded five thousand hits. That's big for a singer, a whole new world. (The Met's Web site records one million hits a month, though some of course are just browsers.) Soon visitors will be able to order up CD titles, ask her advice, and plan holidays around her performances. "Who would have thought it! Here I am, Deborah Voigt, the full-service cyberdiva!" she chuckled.

Suddenly the Buddy Box stirred to life, signalling that a friend of mine was also on-line. It was Thierry Fouquet, the general manager of the opera in Bordeaux, who was sitting in the company lighting box keeping up with his e-mail as the sounds of *La traviata* filled his eighteenth-century auditorium. "Who's singing?" I asked.

"Leontina Vaduva," he typed back. "Her first Violetta. The tenor's good too, a young Mexican, Alfredo Portilla. Very stylish. What's happening over there?"

I told him I was having coffee with Deborah Voigt.

"Deborah Voigt! *Fantastique!*" Fouquet wrote. "Can you please ask her if she is free for a *Flying Dutchman* in the spring of 1998?"

She reached across me and typed in: "Sorry! Busy at the Met with *Lohengrin*."

A few days later, Voigt was back at the Met singing Sieglinde in *Walküre* with Hildegard Behrens as Brünnhilde when Jonathan Friend wearily stepped to the stage for an announcement, some of which was hard to hear. "Ms. Behrens . . . blah blah blah . . . not fully recovered . . . blah blah blah . . . indulgence." I guess Behrens had finally worn out her welcome among a few long-suffering fans. Someone shouted "All the time!" Others laughed and booed.

Voigt had a triumph.

CHAPTER TWENTY-TWO

Monumental Concert

"THIS IS THE STORY of my brilliant career:

"1. 'Who is Patricia Racette?'

"2. 'So-and-so isn't available? Well, get me that younger version of so-and-so. What's her name? . . . Who? Oh, right, Patricia Racette.'

"3. 'Get me Pat Racette! I must have her!'

"4. 'Get me a cheaper, younger version of Pat Racette.'

"5. 'Who is Patricia Racette?' "

Such are the stages in a singer's life as described by, in fact, Pat Racette, who heard it from a big-cheese agent (not hers).

I'd been at a photographer's studio all morning in downtown New York, watching her spend five thousand dollars on a portfolio of photographs showing her in different outfits and poses. She'd just taken off the slinky gown of a sultry sex goddess and was pulling on a leather biker's jacket to appeal to another segment of the opera crowd. "Got to cover all the bases," she said, pouting.

"You doing anything in Germany?" the photographer asked.

"Not that I'm aware," Racette answered, puzzled.

"I'd try and scare up a fluffy white kitten for a bedroom shot," he said, helpfully. "They love a little kitsch."

Emmeline had been a great success for an opera that wasn't written by a dead person, and she had come out of it with a bunch of great reviews. Orbiting ever higher, she was leaving the Mimì-and-Musetta business to others for a few years, she announced. "Now is the time to flaunt my high E-flat," she declared, unzipping her jacket a little.

Her calendar was crowding up, with Violetta in *La traviata* for Santa Fe and the Bastille. In between came Mathilde of the long aria about a dark forest in Rossini's grandest opera, *William Tell*, for the San Francisco Opera.

Maybe not a good choice, I worried. "You might skip stage three. Way too heavy a role in a house that size and a big orchestra."

"You're wrong," she said.

"Hmmm. Okay."

I guess it wouldn't matter much in the long run. There's always someone waiting in the wings. A month ago, I'd never heard of Christine Goerke, a young dramatic soprano just out of the Met's Young Artist Development Program. She would spend the summer season at the Glimmerglass Opera in Cooperstown, New York, for her first important role, in Gluck's *Iphigénie en Tauride*. Judging by an early rehearsal, hers was a voice of exciting magnitude.

Some wait longer. The little-known Albert Dohmen had just had a success suddenly replacing Bryn Terfel in a *Wozzeck* production at the 1997 Salzburg Easter Festival, because the overbooked star had failed to set aside enough time for study. Dohmen was nearly forty when his moment came.

Every frog has his day, Mastroianni was saying one night. He was home keeping company with a large parrot he sometimes borrowed from a neighbor when he was feeling lonely. They were watching their favorite cartoon, *One Froggy Evening*.

Its story is brief: A crane operator discovers a strange box in the cornerstone of an old building he's knocking down. Inside is a little frog, spiffy in tails and top hat. "Hello my baby, hello my girl," the frog croons. A singing frog! My fortune is made, the guy thinks, and runs to a talent agency. Gesturing excitedly, he opens the box. The frog just belches. The impresario throws them out.

Trudging home, the ex–crane operator sees a sign: "Theater for Rent. Hippodrome." Hopeful, he puts up a banner: "Singing Frog." The dress rehearsal is superb, and soon the audience arrives for opening night. The frog just sits there. The frog will only sing when he wishes to sing. Later that night, on a park bench, with no one watching, the frog pops out for a full-throated rendition of Figaro's aria from *The Barber of Seville*; a policeman checks both into a nuthouse for disturbing the peace. In a flash forward to 2056, a spaceman finds the boxed frog and flies off, dollar signs flashing above his helmet.

"That's what it's all about, the singing business, more or less," Mastroianni said.

He was not going to Rome. The "Bartoli for Italy" campaign, which he had started planning exactly one year ago, right after the Levine gala in May of 1996, had undergone some wrenching, last-minute changes that left him morose and out of pocket. If everything had gone according to his plans, his video company would now be festooning the Palazzo Farnese and the Teatro Valle with electric cable and flowers. Bartoli would be warming up for two concerts at the Valle, both to be spliced into a single recital and augmented with "beauty shots" of the mezzo showing off her hometown and attending a gala dinner at the Farnese on behalf of the World Monuments Fund. The proceeds from the concerts and the dinner, which were linked for the most expensive tickets, would go toward the conservation of an ancient Roman temple on the Tiber. But the cost for renting the Teatro Valle came in at an astounding $125,000, once the flowers, stagehands, piano rental, and other extras had been added up. Even with Bartoli and Thibaudet donating their services, the expenses were too high for a benefit, and the WMF had been forced to withdraw from the video, leaving Mastroianni and his client with a public-relations nightmare.

Here was a concert she really wanted to sing—her first recital, after all, in her hometown. But even Rome had heard about her *Così* cancellation.

I left him to his misery and flew to Rome to experience the face-saving solution: Bartoli singing at a gala dinner concert for the WMF at the Palazzo Farnese, the French embassy generally closed to the public.

By five o'clock, contessas, baronessas, ministers, ambassadors, fashionistas, and local goddesses of Cinecittà began streaming across the huge piazza in front of the Farnese. They passed underneath the stupendous cornice designed by Michelangelo and into a somber courtyard which led into a perfectly manicured garden sloping toward the Tiber. The concert was on the first floor, the *piano nobile*. Stands of clustered apples and golden bows decorated the double staircase to a landing lit with torchères and Renaissance sculptures. Liveried servants were just opening the doors to the high-ceilinged, rectangular Hercules Room, named after the strongman whose statue towered over rows of delicate, gilt-edged chairs facing the concert grand at the other end. Two muscular goddesses from a Farnese tomb framed the piano.

It was a perfect evening. As twilight brushed the room in golden tints, the sound of water splashing in the fountains below drifted through the tall, open windows. A more atmospheric setting was hard to imagine. Finally, a set of giant doors opened and Bartoli walked onstage in one of her best dresses, voluminously green and off the shoulder, trailing the red-socked Jean-Yves Thibaudet.

The recital, brief but elegant, extended gracefully from a Bellini base onwards to a French group by Viardot and Ravel, before returning to homeland arias, every one of them gratefully applauded. Italian audiences have never really warmed to song literature in languages not their own, and this one was, except for the serious jewelry, no different. But when she concluded with a smiling eruption of Rossini fireworks, the audience, which had probably come more for dinner with the fashionable French ambassador, responded rapturously and was rewarded with two encores.

The door opened in the back and she disappeared. After some speeches, the champagne reception started. No sign of Bartoli. "Is there a secret torture room?" a guest asked the ambassador. "Of course!" he exclaimed. "But it is a state secret." Finally I spotted her standing alone, inexplicably changed into a pants suit and unrecognizable to the swirling crowds who clustered around the glittering Thibaudet in another reception room. We hadn't communicated in some time. Getting Bartoli to put paper in her fax machine is like pitching pennies into the ocean to open a bank account. I've been busy, she explained, preparing for a recital at Vienna's prestigious Musikverein with Thibaudet. Then she had a big trip coming up, to Japan, where the Met was bringing *Così*.

Why anyone who hated the sight of a plane would fly across half the planet to sing Despina was hard to figure. But she also had a two-week recital tour, and Decca had sweetened the pot by arranging for a recording session with Mr. P, who was also planning to go to Japan. Remarkably, they had met only once—several years ago, when he was recording Puccini's *Manon Lescaut* with Mirella Freni and Bartoli sang the tiny role of the musician. Decca was planning to release a two-CD set of the tenor's greatest hits freshened up with a new track of Mr. P with Bartoli. The present and the past: it sounded appealing, and I found myself thinking of perhaps buying a last plane ticket—I had run out of vacation time—even if it meant a long haul across so many time zones I wondered which of us would be dreading it more.

I left the dinner once the parfait dessert arrived, hoping to catch some of the live telecast of *Otello* with José Cura from the Turin opera house. Cura's voice at full throttle was several sizes larger than Alagna's lyrical instrument, and much had been made of the event in the Italian press—finally a successor to Plácido Domingo? The senior tenor was tiring of the part and seemed eager to leave his cape to the thirty-four-year-old Argentinian, whom he was also conducting in an aria recital for Erato. As I turned on the TV, Cura was just starting to strangle Barbara Frittoli, showing off a muscular torso. All that remained was Otello's song of suicide, "Niun mi tema," which he sang with a burnished, tragic tone.

Bartoli must have had trouble getting a taxi. It had started to rain as the dinner ended, and cabs were few. Newspaper reports two days later were enthusiastic about both Cura in Turin and Bartoli in Rome, but the *Corriere della Sera* also included a mini-interview with an aggrieved star. Though she had seemed pleased with the evening, she was, in fact, not pleased. "No one showed me in. No one brought me flowers at the end of the concert; no one got me a cab. I was waiting in rain for twenty minutes," she complained, adding that it was her first concert for WMF and just maybe her . . . She let the thought drift. The WMF, never having staged a concert before, had delivered flowers to her dressing room instead of presenting them formally at the concert's end. And while she had been offered a limo, the organizers had not realized that in divaspeak "No, thank you" translates into "Must you ask? But of course!" and had failed to send one.

Just two years ago, *60 Minutes* had broadcast a charming profile of Bartoli singing with her mother, having fun at a birthday party, and generally behaving, in the words of the broadcast, like "a most uncommon diva." The first scene showed her setting off briskly by foot to catch a tram to her premiere of *Cenerentola* in Zurich. Those days were gone, I guess.

It looked like "Bartoli for Italy" was probably going to be a short-lived campaign—and indeed, the monuments of the world were soon looking for another voice to hymn their plight.

The Met was equally bereft a few weeks later. Days before leaving for Japan, Bartoli fell off a curb, twisting her neck so badly she required a neck brace, and couldn't go anywhere even in a train. In Tokyo, Joe Volpe was observed skulking around his hotel waiting for daily health reports, but by the time she felt well enough to fly, Clare Gormley had already been stitched into Despina's outfit, and she was told not to bother.

Angela Gheorghiu usefully provided enough amusement to deflect some attention from the absent Bartoli. The Met was also presenting *Carmen*, and Gheorghiu was singing the dress rehearsal when Volpe noticed she wasn't wearing Micaëla's blond wig, which she had never liked. Head-toppers often become a major issue for singers—invariably a substitute for some other problem eating away at their gut—but the beloved ones are usually allowed their sartorial diversions. Many seasons ago, Franco Corelli so hated his hat in *Werther* he would only carry it in under his arm. But he was the fabulous Franco, and he could have strolled into Charlotte's humble homestead wearing a sun visor.

Volpe insisted that Gheorghiu wear the wig, although the sight of Gheorghiu carrying in the unloved wig would have done much to lighten up Micaëla's dreary scene in those Pyrenees. "That wig is going on with or without you," he said, writing his epitaph.

It wasn't particularly rational—the wig's ugliness was indisputable. Gheorghiu must have thought he was kidding, and left the rest of the rehearsal to Ainhoa Arteta. Then she reappeared to sing the opening night.

"What are you doing here?" Volpe gaped. "I fired you. You don't sing the dress, you don't sing the opening."

Gheorghiu had just learned there are a lot of Micaëlas in this world and only one Met general manager. The wig's next appearance included Gheorghiu.

Had the time come to worry about the Love Couple's trajectory through opera history? Would they pass from the scene like the comet Hale-Bopp? The twosome had also stunned Covent Garden by withdrawing from a new *Faust* production planned for them the next season. Then they complained bitterly to a London paper that nobody loved them anymore. The article was entitled "The Bonnie and Clyde of Opera."

Defending his wife and himself from criticism he found unfair, the excitable Alagna with his uncertain English only alienated even more people. "Those women who said I was not good. They were prostitutes," he yelped. "From the street. Hah! And that man who said I didn't hit the top C, I know he is a homosexual. It's outrageous, outrageous." Not the sharpest tool in the shed, poor Alagna obviously meant no harm, and soon apologized.

I hoped they weren't slipping to slot number four in the career path outlined by Patricia Racette. It was hard not to notice that the Met at least was giving a lot of roles to Marcello Giordani, another good-looking Sicilian tenor, but a few inches taller and less goofy. He had made his debut the same season as Alagna and in the same role, but nobody had paid much attention until the 1996 New Year's Eve gala performance of *Bohème* with Racette as Mimì. Not only did his appealingly husky voice rise easily to high C, Giordani had a pleasant (nonsinging) wife and an equally well-behaved dachshund.

ONCE RELEASED from the neck brace and travel obligations, Bartoli became a model of diligence. The score of Paisiello's 1789 opera *Nina* migrated from the boot of her car to her mother's piano in preparation for a new production staged with her in mind in the spring of 1998 at the Zurich Opera. Perhaps she would create a boomlet for the once famous Neapolitan who spent years in Russia as the favorite composer of Russia's Catherine the Great, a woman admirable in many ways, but most importantly for the ukase she issued addressing the intolerable length of operatic productions. Operas may be only two hours long! the empress decreed. Paisiello was happy to oblige. It was for St. Petersburg that he composed his once popular two-act *Barber of Seville*—just one of his hundred-plus operas, which at the Bartoli rate of two opera productions a year might be a lifetime occupation.

Then in July she journeyed north to Milan, where Mr. P was waiting to record the duet from Mascagni's *L'amico Fritz*. More importantly, she was reunited with the conductor Riccardo Chailly for the recording of Rossini's *Giovanna d'Arco*, which had been delayed by her brother's illness, and the more cheerful *Il turco in Italia*, which Maria Callas had restored to favor in a sparkling La Scala show forty years ago. It was Chailly who had conducted Bartoli's *Cenerentola* at the Teatro Comunale in Bologna, but they had had a falling out during the recording sessions in 1992: the ornaments Chailly wished to use in the recording hadn't been the ones Bartoli wanted to sing. But such matters were now forgotten.

The Met's production of *Cenerentola* in early October was her next major engagement. She arrived on time, thank heavens—the excitable Volpe would probably have climbed onboard the Concorde with a gun—and started rehearsals just as Pavarotti and Eaglen confronted their first joint appearance in one of the most enormous and expensive productions in the history of modern stagecraft, Zeffirelli's *Turandot*. Outfitted with so many supernumeraries fluttering so many fans they could ventilate China, it marked the epitome of the director-designer's contribution to the Met: a cast-proof production. It didn't really matter who was wearing the costumes; you were happy just to see the sets.

CHAPTER TWENTY-THREE

Midnight

"WHY DOES HE DO IT? He seems in pain," I asked Herbert Breslin, who was prowling around the bar in the tomblike lower depths of the Met during the second intermission of *Turandot*.

Breslin rolled his eyes. "Are you deaf?" he asked. "Listen to the applause. He enjoys it. He sings. That's what he does. What would you have him do?"

Nearly two years had passed since Breslin and I had been in this house wondering how Mr. P would survive *Fille du Régiment*. Here we were again, watching the tenor drifting through his solipsistic universe, keeping company with his former self and revisiting favorite tunes.

He had expressed the desire to reprise "Nessun dorma"—the megahit from his first Three Tenors Concert. And the Met had obliged, even though it meant he would also have to sing the opera that went with it. Nobody had learned anything from the *Fille* debacle, and now in late September 1997 we were once again stuck in the middle of another dubious adventure in which the only winner was the Met's box office. Mr. P sounded frail, his legs hurt, and he required extras to guide him around the stage. Unable to walk up the few steps leading to the gong that must be rung by all suitors of the vengeful virgin, he delegated the task to a retainer. Then he forgot a bit of music in the second act and smiled strangely at the singing sphere standing next to him. Jane Eaglen, making her first appearance at the Met in a role once owned by the galactic Birgit Nilsson, sang the notes dead on, but without pinning our ears back.

Would she really have the stamina for Isolde, a very long-winded lovebird, in Seattle next summer? Concern over Eaglen's health was mounting. I'd heard that Sharon Sweet, fresh from triumphs as Turandot in Paris, had put aside the knitting projects she liked to undertake in her spare time to see if she could get through Isolde without an oxygen tank.

Mr. P got his fix of applause after briefly touching the aria's high B—a half-tone down from the dreaded C of *Fille* and still too high even so—but it wasn't like the thrilling receptions of the past that now imprisoned him. He could still rely on the rising tide of affection to bring him safely to shore, but for how much longer? He would sing a few more times, and in the winter put on the faded suit of Nemorino, but there was no elixir for what ailed him. I hoped he knew that the love for opera he had inspired in so many of us would be repaid in the fond memories we would have for the rest of our lives, even as a stream of new singers passed through Lincoln Center.

I'd just heard Alfredo Portilla—the tenor who was singing in the Bordeaux *Traviata* when I went cybersurfing with Debbie Voigt—in a *Macbeth* at the New York City Opera starring Mark Delavan and Lauren Flanigan, riveting in a buzz cut and wild red dress. Portilla's burnished tenor took me back two decades to a *Lucia* when a surprising young guy with a voice of velvet named José Carreras sang with Beverly Sills.

Standing in front of the Met where the posters are displayed, I saw newcomers mixed in with familiar names. Kirchschlager would soon make her debut as Annio in *La clemenza di Tito*. Voigt was singing Ariadne, and while the removal of the phen-fen diet pills from the market had resulted in a slight inflation, no one who heard her would have minded washing up on the abandoned princess's desert isle. Fleming, having triumphed as Manon at the Bastille, now rouged herself up for the Met with Giordani as her cavalier. And Racette was scheduled for Ellen Orford in a revival of *Peter Grimes* that showcased, at one of the later performances, a young dramatic tenor named Anthony Dean Griffey.

A Sold Out sign decorated the poster for *Cenerentola*, which was now in rehearsal for the first time at the Met. Fittingly, the company was using a new edition just off the presses. Overseen by Philip Gossett of the Rossini Foundation in Pesaro, it removed the distortions and mistakes that had come to blight the score since the premiere. Gone, for instance, was a rum-ti-tum percussion section added by hacks who wished to make Rossini sound more conventionally important.

Maybe *Cenerentola*'s happy music cheered its conductor, James Levine, up a little during a stressful autumn. His power had just been pricked with the appointment of Valery Gergiev to the new post of principal guest conductor. It wasn't much of a surprise—the charismatic Gergiev had been cultivated by Billinghurst and Volpe for some time—but it came just when Levine's own attempt to head the Munich Philharmonic Orchestra took an embarrassing turn. Levine's extravagant pay package, cobbled together by CAMI's Ronald Wilford ($1.14 million for twenty-four concerts a season, plus the occasional benefit performance), his age, and finally his sex life all became part of a widely reported and drawn-out debate in Munich's city council. Levine must have the skin of a Naugahyde suitcase. Finally he was cleared to conduct Munich's third-ranking orchestra. He was not, of course, giving up his artistic directorship of the Met; neither did Gergiev think of reducing his tasks at the Kirov. In the supposedly not-for-profit music world, a conductor can have as many jobs at inflated salaries as his manager extracts and jet travel permits.

Meanwhile, Cesare Lievi, the director, who had been such a picture of quiet modesty at our meeting in Brescia, turned out to have shaky nerves and a temper under pressure. He screamed a lot during rehearsals when things didn't go the way he had imagined them and then would go hide in the men's room to recover. He hadn't learned

English as he had hoped to and spoke a weird mixture of Italian and German to the cast and through a translator to the chorus. "You must obey me!" he shouted at one assistant who hadn't scurried quickly enough to execute yet another muddled order. "I make the art; you do the work" was another observation that had people giggling into their scores (and e-mailing like mad). He kept either changing his mind or forgetting his ideas. Pointing to Michele Pertusi, who was playing Alidoro—the prince's angel-like tutor, who takes Cenerentola to the ball—Lievi asked him to sprinkle gold dust on the furniture he touched when he entered the baron's ramshackle house looking for a crust of bread and a possible bride for his employer. A kind of fairy dust that would transform Cinderella when she touched it. It would be the magic bond between Cenerentola and Alidoro. That was the concept. But when the scene was rehearsed again a week or so later, the Italian bass forgot to sprinkle the glittering dust. When one of Lievi's many assistants pointed this out, the director looked puzzled. "What fairy dust?" he asked.

"The fairy dust! You know, *the magic element?*"

"What are you talking about?" he wondered.

Even Bartoli, not a notably difficult artist once she's shown up, lost patience with Lievi's thumbsucking. One afternoon, he called an extra meeting to discuss his concept with the cast. Bartoli failed to appear, and after waiting for ten minutes, he hurried to her dressing room and knocked on the door. She was clearly inside—friends could hear her accompanying herself on the piano. As if delivering a textbook example of passive-aggressive behavior, she kept singing away sweetly, ignoring his knocking. He finally gave up and returned to his meeting, which proceeded without her. By the dress rehearsal, Lievi still hadn't gotten through the entire piece.

I ran into him a few days before the opening. He looked like a white bunny rabbit with his pale face and bloodshot eyes.

"So big, the place," he gasped. "I had no idea."

"ARE YOU SURE?" I asked Bartoli over lunch just before the opening night on October 16. She had just told me the rehearsals were moving along okay in a typical goodhearted attempt to put a nice spin on a situation and a fellow artist. Bartoli was possibly the least gossipy person it had been my luck to encounter.

I gave her my thoughts on *Turandot* and asked if she was planning to sing Cenerentola when she was sixty years old.

She laughed a little. "Women go through menopause; you know that," she added. "Let's go a little slowly here. What's that old saying? Make haste slowly. I like that. This last year, it was not good."

Her brother's health had worsened. Gabriele had come to New York for the concert she sang with the Delfici at Carnegie Hall in early September. But he had been too frail and feverish to walk to the stage and played from a wheelchair. The evening raised $1.5 million for brain-tumor research at the Columbia-Presbyterian Medical Center. She started to say something about the unpredictability of fate but let the thought drift and picked at her pizza. The cancer had returned, I gathered, and the family was hoping for a miracle.

A few old ladies walking out of the restaurant recognized her and stopped to ask her to sign their napkins. They were very loud. But she smiled immediately and thanked them profusely for their flattering words.

Were there any new thoughts on the small house the Met had once hoped to open to showcase more intimate pieces with her in them? I asked. But Volpe had mentioned nothing, she said, and had not yet stopped by the rehearsals to say hello. It upset her, that I could tell, but not enough to make her feel contrite about the *Così* broadcast cancellation.

"What is the point of singing if the conditions are not right?" she asked me. "And disappoint people who have the right to hear you at your best?"

"But couldn't one argue that not singing at all would be the greater disappointment in an imperfect world?"

I was not convincing.

We talked of the future instead. She was looking forward to singing Ravel's *L'Heure espagnole* with Pierre Boulez in April 1999, and she was also contemplating Bellini's *La sonnambula*, perhaps for the

Met. While the opera's sleepwalker usually sings soprano, there was a version written for Maria Malibran that might be an appealing challenge. In the meanwhile, the only offer she had accepted at the Met was the *Nozze* next fall, which Jonathan Miller would direct. At the start of her career, Bartoli had often sung Cherubino, the love-addled teenage page. Now she would sing Susanna, another maid role, but twice as long as Despina and usually cast with a lyric soprano. While Bartoli's voice soared easily into the soprano register, it was unusual for her to be contemplating a long soprano role outside the recording studio. It struck me as a surprising undertaking.

But she was full of new ideas about what to sing and where and how much not to sing (working half a year struck her about right). Mélisande was also on the horizon. Debussy's doomed child bride who flutters ethereally through a medieval forest muttering mysteriously in singsongy French was so utterly remote from the earthiness of Despina or Cenerentola it seemed a nearly inconceivable act of self-reinvention. Though Frederica von Stade was once a rapturous Mélisande, this part, too, is usually sung by a soprano. Was she changing voice categories? She shook her head. She viewed the outing, planned for the 1999 Maggio Musicale in Florence—the annual May Festival—as part of a strategic return to her European roots. More Vivaldi and Haydn was likely, and Handel too, eighteenth-century composers who suited her voice and style more than the blockbuster repertoire she would continue to avoid. Ideally, she wanted to spend more time close to home, though Bartoli hardly needed me to point out that her largest record-buying public was in fact on another continent: More than half her record sales were right here in the United States. Yet she had not signed up for any new recital tours.

"But I am European," was her explanation.

What about the vineyard and the vintner?

"You mean marriage? I don't know yet," she said, shrugging. As we left, she mentioned she was thinking of trying to do a straight play. I'm sure she'd be good. She has a wonderful way with words. But what a nutty idea! I thought of June Anderson, who at the height of her career, when opera directors were begging her on bended knee to sing Norma, was hoping someone would cast her in a musical so she could dance like Ginger Rogers.

But I guess the absence of struggle can weigh one down in a way most ordinary mortals will never fully understand. When everything is offered, choice can become a paralyzing proposition. Bartoli could conceivably downscale herself to the point of disappearing altogether from public view. Given her frugal ways, by the fall of 1997, I figured she probably had socked away close to ten million dollars and could live happily ever after.

Angela Gheorghiu cheered me up as I sat at my desk wondering where the Bartoli career was going. Paris was on the line—not Vampira herself, but a vassal in her domain.

The soprano had recently shown up at the Bastille for some discussions concerning her future engagements, including the late-fall production of *La traviata*—the show Jonathan Miller had been so dreading when we met in New York two years earlier. After a pleasant meeting with one of Gall's assistants, she was asked if she would like to see the model.

Bien sûr! She would be delighted.

So he showed it to her.

"And this, this, Madame Gheorghiu, is the set for the last act," he said. In one of the most heartbreaking death scenes ever written, Violetta, hallucinating, impoverished, and mortally ill with TB, awaits the feckless Alfredo. In a desolate bedroom stripped of all the gilt-edged memorabilia of her former life, she lies in bed reading a remorseful letter she has received from Alfredo's father, announcing his return. "Teneste la promessa"—"You have kept your promise"—she whispers in an anguished voice, falling back into her pillows from the effort.

Gheorghiu stared. She stared some more.

"Hey. Who are those other beds for?" she finally asked.

Armed with his knowledge of medicine, Dr. Miller had placed Violetta's deathbed in the dreary hospital in which so many courtesans and lonely women down on their luck had died in the nineteenth century.

The hapless assistant explained the concept.

It fell on deaf ears.

"Impossible!" she cried. "I die alone!"

For a while, they were taking bets backstage at the Bastille whether Madame would withdraw as she threatened. But after complaining got her nowhere, she showed up for rehearsals and even the opening night. Perhaps she chuckled into Violetta's pillows when Miller's reviews, unlike hers, turned out to be pretty bad.

Had the wig incident in Japan let enough air out of the Love Couple's balloon to return them to Planet Earth? Alagna, too, showed up at La Scala in the late fall to sing the one-aria tenor role in *Macbeth* and flew gamely to Manchester and London to replace Pavarotti in two concerts. Not only had Mr. P come down with a cold, but he had received an annoying bill from the Italian tax authorities for ten billion lire, which he disputed since he was a resident of Monte Carlo.

What could I have been thinking? By April 1998, things were back to normal. Joe Volpe fired the Love Couple from a new production of Verdi's *La traviata* planned for the next season. The news made the front page of the *New York Times*. He found them annoyingly laggard in signing their contracts and overly eager to push an aesthetic agenda that conflicted with that of the production's designer and director, Franco Zeffirelli. Alagna apparently had a designer brother who wished to offer his suggestions. I guess her wig problems had turned them against the director of the animal-infested *Carmen* they once professed to love. The rest of us were left to wonder how many more millions the Met was going to give Zeffirelli, who had already designed the Met's most recent, hugely unattractive production of *Traviata*. I was hoping that the duo's next loud duet would be in front of the snoozy board of the Metropolitan Opera, but a few days later, Gheorghiu and Alagna were deflected to an old production of *L'elisir d'amore* in another season. And who got the job of singing Violetta? The soprano who should have gotten it in the first place, Renée Fleming. A little-known tenor named Marcelo Alvarez was told to brush up on Alfredo. There's always someone in the wings.

• • •

PERHAPS IT COULD HAVE used a bit more fairy dust, but *Cenerentola* puttered along smoothly and cheerfully when it finally opened on October 16, 1997. Lievi may have been a space cadet in the rehearsals, but together with his designers, Maurizio Balò (sets and costumes) and Gigi Saccomandi (lights), he had succeeded in creating a strangely tilted world in which reality coexisted uneasily with dreams and fantasies. The show was both charming and at times disturbingly dark. Cenerentola's dysfunctional family resided in a large room dominated by an orange sofa missing a leg and an outsized fireplace that underscored the weariness of her cinder-sweeping existence.

"Una volta c'era un re," Bartoli sang again, shining shoes as the opera opened. When Alidoro knocked on the door, she hastened past her two hissing sisters, stopping to adjust her cap and make sure she looked as good as possible. It was a nice touch. You never know who might come calling, so look your best! I thought of how she pushed the dreadful pianist from his bench and accompanied herself when she auditioned for Mastroianni in Pesaro years ago.

Walls suddenly ruptured to admit the prince's retinue. Plucked from the surrealistic world of René Magritte, they all wore the dark suits and bowler hats of look-alike bureaucrats. Lievi had Simone Alaimo play the stepfather, Don Magnifico, not as a buffoon but as a cruel maniac, and when he not only refused to permit Cenerentola to go to the ball but claimed to his visitors that his stepdaughter was dead, his ravings and her protests gave the work a chilling edge. Alidoro pulling a little cord to open a set of tiny golden wings restored the sense of whimsy as he arranged for her transport to the princely palace, where a tilting pile of clocks dominated the background, frozen at five to midnight. The prince who lived there was a dapper charmer, splendidly sung by Ramón Vargas, a tenor with high notes and a nice sense of comic timing.

Even so, the pasta-flinging banquet that once had amused Zurich fell flat in New York—clearly a scene Lievi hadn't gotten round to staging, though Levine saved the moment with his lively, crisp conducting of a difficult ensemble. Finally, a stage-filling wedding cake pulled into view, topped off by Cenerentola and her prince.

"I was born to sorrow and tears," Bartoli sang, climbing down for the most glittering music of the evening. "I suffered with a silent heart. But by some sweet enchantment, in the flower of my youth, swift as a flash of lightning, my fortune changed."

She paused a minute to forgive her shuffling stepfather and stepsisters, cheerfully forking wedding cake into their low-slung jaws. Then, as everyone sang, "You are a goddess worthy of the throne," she rewarded them for their thoughts with a perfectly launched rocket of glistening coloratura. The delighted audience went crazy and hurled flowers at her feet.

"Hmmmm," said CAMI's Matthew Epstein, standing in the back of the orchestra. "I guess she proved it. She can sing a big role in a big house. Good for her." The kinglet of CAMI had himself advanced to a larger palace: he was leaving to become artistic director of the Lyric Opera of Chicago. I looked forward to the day when he would be negotiating her fees with his old nemesis, Jack Mastroianni.

In the Dress Circle, Gabriele Bartoli applauded his sister from his wheelchair as she took her curtain calls and fielded her bouquets. Two days later, he returned to Rome, where he died in late December.

NOT LONG AFTER THE OPENING, I was walking along Central Park West with my two dogs when I saw a familiar trench coat flapping in the wind, two stuffed tote bags for ballast.

The four of us trotted over to Mastroianni's office. It was nine in the morning. He wished to give me a press package on his new client, a fourteen-year-old German nymph who played the violin. Julia Fischer was one of the artists newly adorning his roster. Ana Maria Martínez, a young Puerto Rican soprano, had also joined J. F. Mastroianni Associates, and Galina Gorchakova had departed. I gathered she was another singer with a difficult-to-please mate, a husband who wished her to reach her full box-office potential with greater speed. As for Bartoli, it seemed that the conflicts that had surfaced during the spring had been smoothed out, at least for now. He mentioned that he had just negotiated her new five-year contract with Decca, though he had to assume that the company found her diminishing U.S. presence extremely worrisome.

Mastroianni lifted Emma onto his lap and saw the remains of his fried-egg sandwich disappear from his desk.

Bartoli, he said, was off doing a good deed, just like in the opera.

"She got up at seven this morning," he started to say, and then laughed as I nearly choked. That, of course, was beyond good. It was a miracle.

A chauffeur was driving her and Claudio to Montreal to sing a gala for the financially strapped Montreal Symphony and Charles Dutoit, the conductor who'd taken a chance on her in 1990. She was contributing her fee.

The phone rang.

"What?!" he said, turning the color of death. "Wait, don't do anything. Just let me think. I'll call you back. Where are you?"

It was Bartoli calling from her cell phone. The chauffeur, who had driven down from Montreal during the night, was so sleepy, he was weaving along the highway. She'd forced him to pull over. They were on the New York State Thruway near Albany.

There goes that concert, I thought. This girl really has trouble with transportation. Scary planes, snowbound trains, the nonexistent stagecoach in Houston, the Rolls-Royce in Chicago with the steering problem. Now a beached limo.

"What do we do now?" Mastroianni wondered out loud. "She's meant to rehearse today. If she doesn't rehearse, she won't sing. If she doesn't sing, Montreal doesn't have a gala. If we send a new driver, she'll get there too late. If they send a driver, same thing."

The phone rang again. Bartoli was back on her portable.

"You're going to drive the limo? Are you crazy?" he asked.

He listened for a few minutes.

"Are you sure? Wait, stay there."

Mastroianni started calling Montreal. He put the phone down. They called back. He called her. "You can't drive the limo," he told her. "You need to have a chauffeur's license and insurance.

"Is there an airport near Albany? Yes, what about it? You want to fly?" He sounded incredulous.

No, she didn't want to fly. They were going to wake the driver, make him find the airport, and leave him there to sleep while they rented a car.

"Okay, sounds . . . well, sounds good. Do you know where Montreal is?"

No, they didn't. Somewhere north and to the right.

Three hours later, the phone finally rang.

"We're near the border. We're on our way!" she shouted.

Acknowledgments

I'm indebted to Cecilia Bartoli, Sonny Mehta, Robin Desser, Daniel Henninger, Robert Bartley, Matthew Gurewitsch, Glen Hartley, and Lynn Chu, without whose cooperation and support this book would not exist.

I'd also like to thank the following for their time or inspiration: Yves Abel, Roberto Alagna, Thomas Allen, June Anderson, John Ardoin, Karen Ashley, Klaus Bachler, Gregory Barbero, Silvana Bartoli, Chais Baumiere, Sarah Billinghurst, Steven Blier, Herbert Breslin, Victor Callegari, Joseph Clark, Peter Clark, Beth Clayton, James Conlon, Kevin Copps, Bruce Crawford, Dwayne Croft, Charles Darwin, Ken DeWitt, Michelle DeYoung, Plácido Domingo, Bruce Donnell, Jane Eaglen, Stuart Emmrich, Matthew Epstein, Richard Estelita, Mary Lou Falcone, Patrick Farrell, György Fischer, Lauren Flanigan, Judy Flannery, Renée Fleming, David Foster, Jonathan Friend, Neil Funkhouser, Elizabeth Futral, Hugues Gall, Angela Gheorghiu, Rodney Gilfry, Ginger, François Giuliani, Jane Glover, John Goberman, Philip Gossett, Susan Graham, Paul Griffiths, Henry Gronnier, Andrea Gruber, Thomas Hampson, Theodora Hanslowe, Peter Hemmings, Ioan Holender, Albert Innaurato, Speight Jenkins, Mary Jane Johnson, Peter Jonas, Peter Jones, Peter Mario Katona, Peter Kazaras, Lesley Koenig, Allan Kozinn, Brian Large, Jennifer Larmore, Jay Lazarus, Dan Lerner, James Levine, Bruce Levy, Lottie Lindberg, Lisa Lustgarten, Marlene Malas, Lotfi Mansouri, Jack Mastroianni, Trish McCaffrey, Susanne Mentzer, Randy Michaelson, Jonathan Miller, Ray Minshull, Evans

Mirageas, Pål Christian Moe, Maria Montas, Guus Mostart, Danny Newman, Leo Nucci, Opera-Listers, Anne Marie Owens, Cindy Oxberry, Ann Panagulias, Luciano Pavarotti, Nicholas Payne, Jennifer Perciballi, Walter Price, Alison Pybus, Patricia Racette, Christopher Raeburn, Robert Rattray, Joe Reese, Patricia Reller, David Resnicow, William Riley, Chris Roberts, Lisa Rossi, Craig Rutenberg, San Domenico, Gene Scheer, Christina Scheppelmann, Irene Schneider, Charles Sheek, Beverly Sills, Patrick J. Smith, Steven Swartz, Jean-Yves Thibaudet, Jonathan Tichler, Alec Treuhaft, Carol Vaness, Edgar Vincent, Walter Vladarski, Deborah Voigt, Joseph Volpe, Herbert Weinstock, Susan Woelzl, Caroline Woodfield, Liz Yeh, Jean Sincere Zambello, Diane Zola.

And especially to: Francesca Zambello, Marilyn Perry, Sheila Nadler, Olga Christine Hoelterhoff, Heinz Hoelterhoff, Sugar, Emma, Fuzzers, Genghis, and my beloved Frieda, who did not live to eat this book.

❦